*Marxism and class theory:*
*A bourgeois critique*

# Marxism and class theory:
# A bourgeois critique

### Frank Parkin

*Lecturer in Politics and*
*Fellow of Magdalen College, Oxford*

TAVISTOCK PUBLICATIONS

First published in Great Britain in 1979
by Tavistock Publications Limited
11 New Fetter Lane, London EC4P 4EE

Phototypeset in V.I.P. Palatino by
Western Printing Services Ltd, Bristol
Printed in Great Britain at
the University Press, Cambridge

**British Library Cataloguing in Publication Data**

Parkin, Frank
    Marxism and class theory.
    1. Social classes
    2. Communism and society
    I. Title
    301.44′01        HT609

    ISBN 0–422–76790–5

*To Rosa*

# Contents

# Acknowledgments

The author and publishers are grateful to the following who have given permission for material to be reproduced:

*Figure 1* page 79, first appeared in G. D. Newbould and J. R. Sparkes, 'Managers' Pay', *New Society* February 17, 1977, p. 337.

*Table 1* page 80, is reproduced with the permission of the Controller of Her Majesty's Stationery Office, from *Royal Commission on the Distribution of Income and Wealth*, Report No. 3, (1976), *Table 25*, p. 55.

# Preface

Lenin's wry comments on the efflorescence of Marxism in Russia at the turn of the century seem quite pertinent to our own time and place:

> 'Marxist books were published one after another, Marxist journals and newspapers were founded, nearly everyone became a Marxist, Marxists were flattered, Marxists were courted and the book publishers rejoiced at the extraordinary, ready sale of Marxist literature.'

Lenin was not too enthusiastic about a species of Marxism that appeared to be more congenial to the literati than to the class that really mattered. On these grounds alone, it is unlikely that he would have felt very differently about the Marxist products that have been manufactured and marketed in western universities over the past decade or so. Contemporary western Marxism, unlike its classical predecessor, is wholly the creation of academic social theorists – more specifically, the creation of the new professoriate that rose up on the wave of university expansion in the 1960s. The natural constituency of this Marxism is not of course the working class, but the massed ranks of undergraduates and postgraduate students in the social sciences; its content and design mark it out exclusively for use in the lecture theatre, the seminar room, and the doctoral dissertation. Hence the strange and fascinating spectacle to be witnessed in social science faculties throughout western Europe and beyond of diligent bands of research students and their mentors busily combing through the pages of *Theories of Surplus Value* in search of social reality.

## Preface

As if to make secure its newly-won respectability, professorial Marxism has, in the manner of all exclusive bodies, carried out its discourse through the medium of an arcane language not readily accessible to the uninstructed. Certainly no-one could possibly accuse the Marxist professoriate of spreading the kind of ideas likely to cause a stampede to the barricades or the picket lines. Indeed, the uncomplicated theory that has traditionally inspired that sort of extra-mural activity is now rather loftily dismissed as 'vulgar' Marxism – literally, the Marxism of the 'common people'. This is not necessarily to suggest that the new breed of Marxists are less dedicated than the old to the revolutionary transformation of society; their presence at the gates of the Winter Palace is perfectly conceivable, provided that satisfactory arrangements could be made for sabbatical leave.

Classical Marxism, including the applied or vulgar version espoused by the working-class movement, counterposed itself sharply to bourgeois social theory, the intellectual construct of its class opponents. Professorial Marxism, on the other hand, is less fitted to adopt such a stance, rooted as it is in that most bourgeois of all western institutions. This is illustrated by the fact, to be dwelt upon later, that many of the recent contributions to Marxist class analysis bear the unmistakable imprint of bourgeois sociology – in particular that version of it associated with the writings of Max Weber. Nevertheless, there is perhaps something to be said, if only on grounds of courtesy, for respecting the standard Marxist classification of all non-Marxist concepts and theories as bourgeois. As the subtitle of this book indicates, I have willingly agreed to have this label pinned on to my own work. Given what now passes for Marxist theory, almost any imaginable bourgeois alternative seems preferable.

This preference is made particularly clear in Part One, 'Rethinking Class Analysis', in which the Weberian concept of social closure is used as the basis for an alternative model of class to that recommended by Marxism. No-one will fail to notice that the same moral and intellectual prejudices are present throughout the discussion in Parts Two and Three.

The division of the book into three parts is meant to signal the fact that each of the broad issues treated could be read as more or less separate essays. The parts are connected more by their relation to a common general theme than by an unbroken narrative thread. Those who prefer that dramatic format in which all expository strands are neatly tied together in the final act will have good cause for complaint. The reader is also entitled to advance warning that what follows is not intended to be an exhaustive review of the Marxist literature on class and social theory. This does not call for much in the way of apology since a great deal of that literature is intrinsically forgettable. Even in being selective· I run the risk of being charged with paying undue respect to certain arguments to which the only appropriate response is incredulous laughter. It is for the reader to judge whether my own attempts at solemnity have been entirely successful.

I should like to express my gratitude to Steven Lukes for his sharp and constructive comments on a preliminary draft of Part One. My colleague, R. W. Johnson, took time off from more important things to read the entire manuscript and to produce in response a kind of monograph of his own which forced me to make extensive revisions to the original draft. My debt to him is especially great.

*Oxford*
*November 1978*                                                F.P.

PART ONE
# Rethinking class analysis

# 1
# Introduction

One of the objects of class theory has been to identify the principal line of social cleavage within a given system – the structural 'fault' running through society to which the most serious disturbances on the political landscape are thought to be ultimately traceable. The geological metaphor of stratification, with its attendant imagery of surfaces and substructures, has been employed freely in the service of both Marxism and sociology as part of the theoretical discourse on class. Such imagery would seem, however, particularly congenial to Marxism, given its fondness for the contrast between the outward appearances of social reality and the underlying structures that supposedly contain the essence of things. One of Marxism's various claims to higher understanding is that it enjoys privileged access to these subterranean levels of meaning closed off to the humdrum bourgeois mind. Thus, one of the routine indictments of sociological and, above all, Weberian analyses of class is that they are pitched at what is solemnly called the wrong level of reality. That is to say, attention is directed to the manifest forms of social inequality as revealed in the distributive system, instead of upon the concealed forces of the productive system that are believed to govern the pattern of distribution and much else besides.[1]

Seen through Weberian lenses social classes do appear to take shape by way of the aggregation of groups that share a common set of life-chances and circumstances, as measured by the conventional indices of distribution. For Marxism, by contrast, classes are defined in terms of systemic properties, independently of the social make-up of constituent groups. The inbuilt antagonism between capital and labour imposes its own intractable class reality, however much this may be overlaid by the complexities of distribution. The human raw material of class analysis that Weberian usage designates as 'actors', thereby singling out the role of conscious agency and volition, is transformed by Marxist usage into the status of 'embodiments' or repositories of systemic forces.

In this respect, if no other, the Marxist position has some rough affinity with those bourgeois models of class that demarcate social boundaries by reference to the arrangement of positions in the division of labour. Dahrendorf's view that 'class membership is derived from the incumbency of a social role',[2] and the functionalist credo that stratification theory relates first and foremost to 'the system of positions, not to the individuals occupying those positions',[3] thus share with Marxism an explicit downgrading of those aspects of class and collective action that are attributable to the social characteristics of those who occupy the slots in the formal model. The leading assumption in each case is that such solid realities as property relations, bureaucratic authority, or the division of labour impose their own stern discipline upon the social actions of incumbents, such that if one set of incumbents was entirely replaced by another the system would continue as before, propelled by its own interior logic. The motives, values, and expectations of actors cannot therefore be treated as primary driving forces.

The awkwardness of this theoretical stance becomes evident whenever social groups act in blatant nonconformity with their assigned place in the formal scheme of things. Marxism in particular has been greatly exercised by the need to account for the well-known tendency for the embodiments of labour to act politically in ways not altogether consistent with the stated opposition towards capital and its representatives. Behavioural irregularities of this kind are usually put down to ideological disturbances whose effects, though real enough, are not expected to be permanent; as the social order becomes subject to increasing strain, the correspondence between class alignments and the basic cleavage at the heart of the system is thought to become ever closer.

The most damaging weakness in any model of class that relegates social collectivities to the status of mere incumbents of positions, or embodiments of systemic forces, is that it cannot account properly for those complexities that arise when racial, religious, ethnic, and sexual divisions run at a tangent to formal class divisions. Societies marked by conflict between religious or racial communities do not exhibit the same type of class structure as societies lacking such conflict, notwithstanding similarities in their occupational systems and property relations. White South African workers and Ulster Protestant workers are organized in social and political formations that differ profoundly from those of their counterparts in England or Scandinavia. The fact that each of the former two sets of workers is identified politically and morally far more closely with its own bourgeoisie than with its co-workers in the subordinate ethnic group suggests that the collective social attributes of those who embody labour are of decisive importance in analysing class formation. In many cases it actually seems to matter whether incumbents and embodiments are black or white, Catholic or Protestant.

The Marxist preoccupation with the realm of production, increasingly held up as its mark of theoretical rigour, obscures from view any recognition of the possibility that some line of cleavage other than that between capital and labour could constitute the *primary* source of political and social antagonism. To accept that social inequalities and injustices stemming from racial, religious, linguistic, and sexual divisions could have a reality *sui generis*, not reducible to causes buried deep in the capitalist mode of production, would look suspiciously like a Weberian approach with all its peculiar fascination for distributive patterns and outcomes. It would, in short, be to fall into the old bourgeois error of confusing the appearance of reality for its very essence.

## II

The strength of the Marxist case in this respect depends very much upon the validity of the explanatory claims made on behalf of the master concept 'mode of production'. It is upon this concept that so many of the theoretical pretensions of latter-day Marxism are based, demarcating as it allegedly does the place where idealist thought ends and the science of historical materialism begins. It must however be reported that its explanatory performance so far cannot truly be said to have lived up to its star billing. Part of the trouble arises from serious ambiguities in its definition and usage; there is, in particular, some uncertainty as to whether the mode of production is to be understood as a conceptually distinct element of the social system, or as a kind of shorthand expression for the entire institutional structure.

On the first reading, productive relations are treated as conceptually separable from other social relations and institutions, the character of which they are held to shape, influence, or determine, according to taste. On the second reading, productive relations are defined in a far more catholic sense to encompass most of the key institutions of society, so rendering any distinction between a set of independent and dependent variables largely inappropriate.

The tendency among contemporary Marxist writers to hover uncertainly between these two positions is understandable enough. Outright endorsement of the first position is felt to be no longer feasible, given its kinship to the now discredited Marxism of Second International vintage. This is the interpretation that draws very heavily on those aspects of Marx's theory that set up a metaphorical distinction between base and superstructure, the former having a more or less determinate relationship to the latter. In this uncomplicated schema the institutions of production are located firmly in the base, and are, indeed, almost coterminous with it; changes in this level ultimately give rise to corresponding changes in political, legal, and other institutions. 'The hand mill gives you a society with the feudal lord, the steam mill a society with the industrial capitalist.' The main doctrinal support for this case is of course provided by the terse, magisterial statement in the Preface to the *Critique of Political Economy*, a formulation in which 'forces' and 'relations' of production are clearly distinguished from one another and marked out on their eventual collision course. The mode of production in this schema is thus quite narrowly and sharply defined, and singled out as the motor force underlying system change.

The rejection by contemporary Marxists of this apparently embarrassing legacy bequeathed them by theorists of the Second International is largely on the grounds that the base-superstructure model promotes an oversimplified view of the role and character of productive relations. Productive relations cannot be located within a narrowly conceived material base for the reason that any such relations automatically impinge upon legal and political institutions that surround the rights of property and their enforcement. Legal and political forms are not separate entities determined by the relations of production, they already *are* part and parcel of the relations of production.

By the same token, suspicion is also cast upon the classical distinction between forces and relations of production, since this is to suggest that some elements of production fall outside the orbit of social relations, thereby opening the way for an unwarranted emphasis on the role of technology, and more maddening talk about steam mills. Consequently, the modern Marxist tendency is to dissolve the distinction between forces and relations of production into the inclusive category 'mode of production'.

'Relations of production and forces of production cannot be defined independently of the concept of their combination and any attempt to identify the forces of production or the relations of production in a given society in the absence of an elaborated concept of mode of production must be doomed to empiricism.'[4]

It is not only empiricism that is put to flight by this new formulation but also the notion of the productive system as a causal agency. Since all major institutions are directly implicated in the mode of production, and are indeed part of its very definition, there is no separate, external realm of social life upon which it could make its impress. It is indistinguishable from the social system as a whole. Thus, in pre-capitalist social formations, according to Anderson,

'The "superstructures" of kinship, religion, law or the state necessarily enter into the constitutive structure of the mode of production . . . In consequence, pre-capitalist modes of production cannot be defined *except* via their political, legal and ideological superstructures, since these are what determine the type of extra-economic coercion that specifies them.'[5]

The spectre of vulgar determinism has been here exorcised by the simple theoretical expedient of ensuring that no important areas of the social remain to be determined. As a consequence, the mode of production can hardly serve as an explanatory variable of any significance, let alone of surpassing importance. Major transformations in social structure cannot be accounted for by reference back to prior changes in the mode of production when this itself is defined by the very institutions being transformed.

The model of the social system favoured by contemporary western Marxism is one in which all elements are intricately related, so that the meaning and significance of any one element derive from its place in the total configuration – rather in the way that any one dot in a *pointilliste* painting only 'makes sense' in relation to all the other dots that make up the complete picture. The mode of production is no longer one important element among others; it has become the total *gestalt*. Thus Poulantzas:

'By *mode of production* we shall designate not what is generally marked out as the economic (i.e. relations of production in the strict sense), but a specific combination of various structures and practices . . . A mode of production, as Engels stated schematically, is composed of different levels or instances, the economic, political, ideological and theoretical . . .'[6]

In this intricate scheme of things nothing can be known or

explained until all is known, parts cannot be analysed until the totality is analysed. Everything reacts to and feeds back upon everything else, so bringing about the unification of those two domains once known as base and superstructure. In the process, Marxism's key explanatory concept turns into nothing more than a synonym for the social structure itself, occasionally masquerading as one of its principal parts.

# III

Even when the mode of production is defined in its narrower and useful sense it does not capture within its explanatory embrace the complexities of social formation revealed by the distributive system. That is, the contours of the stratification order cannot be read off from the fact that a given society has a capitalist mode of production – understood as a system rooted in private property and market relations. Societies that fall under this general classification exhibit a variety of distributive patterns and social cleavages, as exemplified in the contrast already touched upon between capitalist societies in which racial, confessional, or ethnic divisions figure as the focal point of political antagonism, and those in which class divisions are paramount. If the capitalist mode of production, understood in the narrow and useful sense, can co-exist with a variety of social and class formations, including bourgeois, racial, fascist, etc., its causal ties to these different social formations must be tenuous in the extreme.

The claim that different social arrangements can in some strange way be accounted for by the selfsame constant factor is not an altogether novel one; it is implicit also in the conservative doctrine that all social flux and variety derive ultimately from the same fixed and unchanging human nature. The capitalist mode of production and human nature would thus seem to be handy formulae for those attracted to the intriguing enterprise of tracing social differences back to a single primary source. In neither case, of course, is there very much doubt that the presumed connection will elude discovery.

The recommendation to think of the distributive system as a kind of secondary outcrop of the mode of production is made even more resistible by the fact that broadly similar patterns of social stratification and inequality are found among societies with very different property rights and economic institutions. Western Marxists have themselves frequently bemoaned the fact that the condition of the proletariat in Soviet society is not so remarkably different from that of workers under welfare capitalism. Access to property and the distribution of its fruits under the socialist mode of production appears to bear more than a passing resemblance to the rules of allocation enshrined in the capitalist productive system. If two such contrasting modes of production can give rise to apparently similar distributive outcomes – at least in respect of the class that really counts – the Marxist case for the displacement of one mode by the other is not exactly given a boost. It is therefore not wholly surprising to learn that the economic system of the developed socialist states is best regarded as a variant of the capitalist mode of production and does 'not constitute a fundamentally different societal type' after all.[7] Since the capitalist mode of production reigns everywhere supreme it naturally follows that the theory of the classless society remains unscathed by history. Of such stuff is Marxist science made.

# IV

All this seems to reinforce the point that distributive arrangements and social formations should not be regarded as side effects of a particular productive system, such that the latter is granted some sort of theoretical primacy over the former. And this remains so however much the proposition is hedged about with qualifications concerning the labyrinthine movements and delayed-action effects of a mysterious 'final instance'. Structured inequalities arising from communal or sexual divisions do not require any specific type of productive system in which to flourish. The historical and comparative record would suggest that they are able to adapt themselves remarkably well to all known variations in the division of labour and property rights.

In an earlier period it might have been argued that these divisions and conflicts between communal groups were peripheral to the overwhelming reality of class antagonism, and could justifiably be relegated to the theoretical sidelines. But now that racial, ethnic, and religious conflicts have moved towards the centre of the political stage in many industrial societies, any general model of class or stratification that does not fully incorporate this fact must forfeit all credibility. This is a theme that recurs throughout the chapters in Part One, and which lies behind the proclamation that some rethinking of class analysis is overdue.

## Notes

1 For a recent restatement of this position see Crompton and Gubbay 1977.
2 Dahrendorf 1959:149.
3 Davis and Moore 1945:242.
4 Hindess and Hirst 1975:69.
5 Anderson 1974:403–4.
6 Poulantzas 1973:13.
7 Crompton and Gubbay 1977:19.

# 2

# The 'boundary problem' in Marxism and sociology

The persistent attractions of Marxist class theory have almost certainly been boosted by the less than inspiring alternative offered by academic sociology. In so far as there is any sort of tacitly agreed upon model of class among western social theorists it takes the form of the familiar distinction between manual and non-manual labour. No other criterion for identifying the class boundary seems to enjoy such widespread acceptance among those who conduct investigations into family structure, political attitudes, social imagery, life-styles, educational attainment, and similar enquiries that keep the wheels of empirical sociology endlessly turning. Paradoxically, however, although the manual/non-manual model is felt to be highly serviceable for research purposes, it is not commonly represented as a model of class cleavage and conflict. That is to say, the two main social categories distinguished by sociology for purposes of class analysis are not invested with antagonistic properties comparable to those accorded to proletariat and bourgeoisie in Marxist theory. This would be less cause for comment if proponents of the manual/non-manual model normally construed the social order as a harmonious and integrated whole; but to construe it instead in terms of conflict, dichotomy, and cleavage, as most of these writers now appear to do, seems to reveal an awkward contrast between the empirical model of class and the general conception of capitalist society.

The strongest case that could be made out for identifying the line between manual and non-manual labour as the focal point of class conflict would be one that treated capitalist society as the industrial

*mental/man
real
class
div
in society*

firm write large. It is only within the framework of 'factory despotism' that the blue-collar/white-collar divide closely corresponds to the line of social confrontation over the distribution of spoils and the prerogatives of command. And this is particularly the case in those industrial settings where even the lowest grades of white-collar staff are cast in the role of managerial subalterns physically and emotionally removed from the shop-floor workers. Within the microcosm of capitalism represented by the typical industrial firm, the sociological model of class has something to recommend it as an alternative to one constructed around the rights of property.

The drawback is, however, that social relations within the capitalist *firm* are a less accurate guide to class relations within capitalist *society* than they might once have been. The reason for this is that the post-war expansion of the public sector has given rise to an ever-increasing assortment of non-manual groups in local government and welfare services that cannot in any real sense be thought of as the tail-end of a broad managerial stratum aligned against a manual workforce. Frequently, in fact there is no manual workforce to confront in the occupational settings within which these white-collar groups are employed.[1] And even where teachers, social workers, nurses, local government clerks, lower civil servants, and the like do form part of an organization that includes janitors, orderlies, cleaners, and other workers by hand, they do not usually stand in the same quasi-managerial relationship to them as does the staff employee to the industrial worker in the capitalist firm.

The usual rationale for treating intermediate and lower white-collar groups as a constituent element of a dominant class is that these groups traditionally have identified themselves with the interests of capital and management rather than with the interests of organized labour. But for various reasons this identification is easier to accomplish in the sphere of private industry and commerce than in the public sector. In the latter, as already pointed out, not only is there usually no subordinate manual group physically present to inspire a sense of white-collar status elevation, but also the charms of management are likely to seem less alluring when the chain of command stretches ever upwards and out of sight into the amorphous and unlovely body of the state. Moreover, public sector employees do not have the same opportunities as those in the commercial sector for transferring their special skills and services to different and competing employers; all improvements in pay and conditions must be negotiated with a monopoly employer, and one who is under close budgetary scrutiny. All this makes for a relationship of some tension between white-collar employees and the state *qua* employer, a condition more akin to that found between manual labour and management than between white-collar employees and management in the private sector. Thus, the validity of the manual/non-manual model as a representation of class conflict relies more heavily upon a view of the commercial employee as the prototypical case of the white-collar worker than really is justified, given the enormous growth of public-sector employment.

What this suggests is that manual and non-manual groups can use-fully be thought of as entities socially differentiated from each other in terms of life-chances and opportunities, but not as groups standing in a relationship of exploiter and exploited, of dominance and subordi-nation, in the manner presumably required of a genuine conflict model. Expressed differently, the current sociological model does not fulfil even the minimal Weberian claim that the relations between classes are to be understood as 'aspects of the distribution of power'. Instead of a theoretical framework organized around the central ideas of mutual antagonism and the incompatibility of interests we find one organized around the recorded facts of mere social differentia-tion.

Even the case for social differentiation is weaker than it was for-merly, though it is by no means in complete disarray. The original argument rested on the claim that the lower white-collar groups enjoyed a protected economic and social status by virtue of their proximity to managerial elites. The prerogatives of the latter filtered down to the lower echelons in the form of incremental salary scales, security of employment, career prospects, and various other hidden perquisites, all of which more than compensated for the apparent similarities in the actual earnings of lower white-collar and manual workers, and so put the status pretensions of the former on a sound material foundation.[2]

It would be premature to suggest that this foundation has been eroded to the point where office and shop-floor conditions are virtu-ally indistinguishable, as claimed by certain of the headier predictions of white-collar proletarianization. After all, the proletarianization thesis has an ancestry almost as long as the social stratum whose demise it so confidently predicts. The pertinent question is not so much whether the lower white-collar groups continue to enjoy vari-ous symbolic and non-pecuniary advantages over manual workers, since it is a fairly safe bet that they do; rather, it is whether under conditions of chronic inflation these benefits can be thought to weigh heavily in the balance against the benefits of immediate income. The attractions of lower white-collar life associated with security of tenure, promotion opportunities, pension rights, and the like, are bound to count for far more under stable economic conditions than during an era of mounting inflation when the major preoccupation is with the present size of the pay packet, as against future, long-term benefits.

The attempt to control inflation by tightening the purse strings of the state tends of course to make itself especially felt among public-sector employees. It is not simply that bargaining over salaries takes place within a stricter set of controls and limits, but also that the conditions of work and career prospects deteriorate as educational, welfare, medical, and social services fall under the axe of government spending cuts. Under these conditions, it is hardly surprising that almost all the outbursts of white-collar militancy over the past decade have occurred within the public sector. Inflation and its consequences would thus seem to sharpen the distinction between private- and public-sector employment, whereas the manual/non-manual model assumes a rough homogeneity of condition among all lower white-collar groups.

Sociological models are almost bound to take on something of the imprint of the age in which they are put together; and the model of class recommended in a period of general affluence and economic growth is likely to look a strange and awkward thing in a period haunted by the anxieties of inflation, recession, and economic stagnation. But however real and persistent the fine distinctions between blue-collar and white-collar groups might prove to be, following the possible onset of new golden age of capitalism, the fact remains that a model of class based upon such distinctions would still be theoretically deficient on the grounds already set out. Perhaps the ultimate source of this deficiency lies in the fact that the probing spotlight of class analysis is directed almost exclusively on inequalities stemming from the division of labour, so that the role of private property is relegated to a theoretical limbo. This has come about partly as a result of sociology's reaction to classical Marxist categories, and in particular the rejection of an all-inclusive category of 'propertyless labour'. Such a blanket term patently failed to capture the variety of market conditions of those who sold their services, glossing over crucial differences between the industrial proletariat and the newly-emergent salaried middle class.

Sociology's response was to focus directly on the division of labour itself, treating this as the main arena in which the observable realities of class played themselves out. The manual/non-manual model is simply the most formalized expression of this theoretical stance. Thus, originating as an attempt to break down the portmanteau concept of labour, the sociological model of class has succeeded, unwittingly or otherwise, in defining out of existence the sister concept of capital. The powers and privileges emanating from the ownership of productive property are of a very different order of things from

14

those resulting from the division of labour. A model of class relations that addresses itself exclusively to inequalities surrounding the occupational order is therefore bound to be defective.

Although it is usually acknowledged that property ownership does set up certain class interests, the silent assumption appears to be that these interests are broadly in line with the interests of the non-manual class, or at least its upper stratum. But the fact that this may indeed be the case does not dispense with the need to explain the association theoretically. The apparent unison between capital and important elements of labour is an intriguing feature of the system, and one that calls for explanation. It is difficult to see how the issue could even be posed, let alone resolved, within the confines of a model from which property has been thought away.

In the light of all this it is unsurprising that the sociological model of class should seem to have few friends and that many social theorists should turn to that alternative tradition that places property at the very centre of its analysis, and which treats class relations as manifestations of power. The resurgence of interest in Marxism has no doubt also been encouraged by the various recent efforts to refurbish classical doctrines as a response both to changes in the class structure of contemporary capitalism, and to the well-rehearsed objections to the orthodox thesis. It is therefore of more than passing interest to consider how far the neo-Marxist analysis of class succeeds in meeting the criticisms of bourgeois sociology while retaining faith with the original enterprise.

## II

One of the difficulties encountered by the Marxist theory of class is that of translating the conceptual abstractions of capital and labour into the concrete social categories of bourgeoisie and proletariat. These difficulties have arisen in part because the tendency of the bourgeoisie under advanced capitalism to overflow the boundaries set by property has been accompanied by the tendency of the proletariat to contract to a point where it is considerably less than the sum of labour. This has resulted in a need to account for the theoretical status of those intermediate groups that cannot be given an unequivocal class location on one side or other of the decisive boundary. In the classical formulation of the problem, the social space between the two great classes was deemed to become progressively less habitable as the centrifugal forces of class struggle and crisis flung all *dritte Personen* to one camp or the other. The characters singled out for liquidation in this historical drama were those upon whom capitalism itself had already passed sentence: the small traders, artisans, shop-keepers, and peasants. Their fate was sealed by the fact that they were marginal to a productive system that was rapidly encroaching upon every sector of society.

The vulnerability of the petty bourgeoisie to the pressures of big capital was sufficiently demonstrated by the passage of events to give at least qualified support to the polarization thesis. However, awkward questions were raised by the discovery that the social territory vacated by the old petty bourgeoisie was found to be occupied by a newcomer in the guise of the 'new middle class'. The problem posed by this new intermediate stratum arose from the fact that, unlike its predecessor, it was in no sense external to the capitalist productive system but an essential feature of it. Since it was not historically doomed it needed to be incorporated into the general class model.

Contemporary Marxism has approached this task partly with the aim of rebutting those interpretations that equate the rise of a new middle class with the virtual dissolution of class boundaries and class conflict. The standard formulation of this view suggests that the expansion of the tertiary sector results in a shift from a pyramid-shaped class system with a heavy proletarian base, to a diamond-shaped system with a prominent 'middle mass' and ever-diminishing working class. On this construction, the proletariat is scheduled to follow the historical destiny of the old petty bourgeoisie rather than that of an ascendant class.

Marxism's own account of these developments is designed not simply to reassert the political status and potential of the modern proletariat and the reality of class divisions; it is addressed at the same time to the resolution of what Poulantzas has referred to as the 'boundary problem' – that is, the location of the politically relevant line of cleavage under conditions of monopoly capitalism.[3] This is not regarded as a purely academic exercise, of course, but a necessary prelude to the conduct of political strategy. Marxists need to be clear about where the frontier between the proletariat and the new salaried bourgeoisie is to be drawn if the revolutionary tasks of the former are to be correctly formulated. Failure to identify the social composition and contours of the working class is felt to be an invitation to revisionism and the political defeats associated with it.

It would not be exaggerating unduly to suggest that the problem of the new petty bourgeoisie or middle class exercises the minds of latter-day western Marxists to the same degree as did the problem of the peasantry among an earlier generation. It hardly needs to be added that the range of solutions proposed for the former problem concede little in the way of ingenuity and variety to those that were offered for the latter. In considering these, it is convenient to classify them into three broad categories, according to the degree of inclusiveness by which the proletariat is defined in relation to other classes. First, what might be called the *minimal* definition refers to those Marxist theories that apply extremely rigorous and restrictive criteria in the classification of proletarian status; second, the *maximal* definition, which refers to those theories at the other extreme that adopt fairly inclusive, catholic criteria; and, third, those theories that adopt an *intermediate* position somewhere between these poles.

The most systematic exposition of the minimal definition is that offered by Poulantzas as part of a more general enterprise which ranks perhaps as the most ambitious and sustained attempt to construct a Marxist theory of class applicable to modern capitalism. Poulantzas' starting point is the rejection of that line of thought that equates the category of wage labour with membership of the working class – an equation that would seem to bear an uncomfortably close affinity to the familiar conservative claim that 'today we are *all* working class'. Many groups are exploited by capital, but few it seems qualify for proletarian status. Poulantzas' strategy is to introduce two separate classificatory devices, each culled from Marx's own work, which have the effect of paring down the large and unwieldy bloc of exploited wage labour to reveal the lean shape of the proletariat proper. The first of these is the distinction between productive and unproductive labour – a distinction it should be recalled that bears not upon the actual nature of the work performed but on the social context of its performance. Very simply, productive labour is that which yields surplus value, unproductive labour is that which does not. Expressed more formally, productive labour is that which is exchanged against capital to produce surplus, whereas unproductive labour is merely a charge against revenue. Thus, the barber who trims Marx's beard is performing unproductive labour if he is working on his own account, since the service provided is essentially no different from that given by a household servant. Each entails a direct charge against revenue and makes no direct contribution to capital accumulation. If, on the other hand, Marx's barber is a paid employee he is performing productive labour by creating surplus value for the barbershop owner. On a somewhat more elevated plane, the unproductive category comprises not only those who perform services directly against revenue but also those employed by the state whose incomes are met from taxation. Taxes are siphoned off from the wages of productive workers or from surplus value, so that in effect the labour of 'state servants' is similar to that of household servants in being an exchange against revenue.

The crucial point of all this is that only those workers whose labour is productive in this special sense are to be defined as a constituent part of the proletariat. Unproductive wage labourers are consigned to the ranks of the new petty bourgeoisie. In other words, the status of *exploited* labour is theoretically downgraded, as it were, by comparison with its unproductive status; it is the latter that now settles the issue of class location. The effect of this is that the line of class demarcation is drawn at a considerably lower point in the stratification hierarchy than it would be in the orthodox Marxist model. Furthermore, this invisible line is pushed down still further by the addition of Poulantzas' second distinction, that between mental and manual labour. Mental labour is conceptual shorthand for those occupations that include elements of a supervisory or disciplinary nature (occasionally referred to by Marx as the 'labour of superintendence') as well as professional occupations that enjoy special privileges by virtue of their claim to the 'monopoly and secrecy of knowledge'.[4]

The supervisory component of mental labour is especially prominent in occupations within the technical sphere of production, where the need for direct surveillance of the workforce is essential to the exploitation process. Now those who perform supervisory functions are not only wage workers but productive labourers to boot, in so far as they are just as instrumental in creating surplus value as the workers whose activities they oversee. However, the activity of mental labour is, in Poulantzas' schema, automatic grounds for exclusion from the proletariat and inclusion within the new petty bourgeoisie. Technicians, foremen, engineers, and the like, far from occupying the vanguard role assigned to them by some French theorists of the May events, 'do not as a group belong to the working class . . . because in their place within the social division of labour they maintain political and ideological relations of subordination of the working class to capital . . . and because this aspect of their class determination is the dominant one'.[5]

Direct surveillance and control of the industrial workforce is not the only form that the labour of superintendence assumes. The modern state has more subtle ways of ensuring social discipline and conformity – a task entrusted to the welfare professions in their capacity as moral entrepreneurs. The mental labourers of the welfare services therefore take their place alongside the supervisory and managerial wing of the new petty bourgeoisie. Combining Poulantzas' two sets of variables we thus arrive at four distinct types of wage labour: productive mental; productive manual; unproductive mental; and unproductive manual. Only the productive manual category counts as working class; it is the only form of wage labour that contributes to surplus value without at the same time being implicated in the apparatus of supervision and control. All the remaining categories comprise different elements of the new petty bourgeoisie, and are thus politically suspect.

One of the theoretical effects of this schema is to posit a concealed conflict of interests between productive and unproductive workers on the grounds that the latter are in some sense parasitic upon those who create value. This is similar to a position advanced some time ago by Sweezy, who suggested that those whose wages were met from surplus value had 'an objective bond linking their fortunes with those of the ruling class'.[6] Here too it would seem that the opposition between workers who create value and those who are a drain upon it overrides all unity arising on the basis of a shared exploitation. If, as appears to be the case, the ratio of unproductive to productive workers is continually increasing, the implication of this analysis for the future of the labour movement is somewhat startling. As one of Poulantzas' sympathetic critics plaintively declares, the strict application of his criteria reduces the western working class to pygmy proportions.[7] It is somewhat ironic that a theory intended, among other things, as a critique of a bourgeois model of class that seemed to extinguish the proletariat, should itself propose a set of definitions pointing to a similar conclusion. It will be necessary to return briefly to Poulantzas' schema after considering the two other main varieties of Marxist class analysis.

## III

The *maximal* definition of class is one in which the significant boundary is drawn at a point towards the top of the stratification system, so that the problem becomes that of deciding which residual groups fail to qualify for inclusion in a proletariat construed as the 'universal class'. The starting point here is that strand in Marx's work that equates the exploited class with the people, and the triumph of the revolution as the victory of the vast majority over the privileged few. The frontiers of class are here determined by expressly political criteria, in that the fundamental distinction is between those social groups whose functions are specific to capitalism and those whose services would also be required in a socialist alternative. Landlords, *rentiers*, property speculators, stockbrokers, and the like are unmistakably part of the bourgeoisie by virtue of the fact that their activities would not be transferable to the new society, thereby giving them a vested interest in the survival of capitalism. All those groups that, by contrast, have a future under socialism, including the new middle class, are by this fact alone part of a heterogeneous political class objectively opposed to the bourgeoisie. This is not to say that all the various elements having a vested interest in socialism are expected to arrive at the same understanding of their class position; but the long-run expectation is that, as the crisis of bourgeois society intensifies, the schism between those who have no alternative future and those who do will make itself felt at the conscious level.

In the maximal definition of class, the distinction between productive and unproductive labour takes on an entirely different meaning. Baran, for example, defines unproductive labour as that 'resulting in the output of goods and services the demand for which is attributable to the specific conditions and relationships of the capitalist system, and which would be absent in a rationally ordered society'.[8] Even though it is acknowledged that various sections of the new petty bourgeoisie do 'live off the economic surplus', this is politically negated by the more important fact that they perform functions 'which in a rationally ordered society, far from disappearing would become multiplied and intensified to an unprecedented degree'.[9]

This moral classification of the 'universal class' is one that normally underlies the political programme of western Marxist parties seeking power through the ballot box. The transition from *Klasspartei* to *Volkspartei* is commonly justified on the grounds of a changing ratio of white-collar to industrial workers, and the affirmation that the former are no less than the latter subject to the degradations and injustices of capitalism. Socialism carries the promise of their common emancipation in the formula that workers 'by hand and by brain' should enjoy the full fruits of their labour. The strategy of the mass Marxist party is thus to emphasize the minority character of bourgeois opposition and to present itself as the natural political home of all who sell their labour, whatever the colour of their collar.

The doctrinal argument for the political incorporation of the new middle class is taken a stage further in the writings of certain east European Marxists, in which the scientific and cultural achievements of socialism are held to be directly dependent upon the leadership and quality of white-collar cadres, rather than upon the creative capacities of the proletariat.[10] The guiding role and achievements of the professional groups under socialism are felt to contrast vividly with their diminished standing under capitalism, a message earlier hinted at in the *Communist Manifesto*:

'The bourgeoisie has stripped of its halo every occupation hitherto honoured and looked up to with reverent awe. It has converted the physician, the lawyer, the priest, the poet, the man of science, into its paid wage-labourers.'[11]

Under socialism, the implication seems to be, the halo would be restored to its rightful owners, if only as the refracted light emanating from all emancipated labour. There is certainly no indication here of any incompatibility of interests between the purveyors of unproductive mental labour, even in its most distilled form, and the human beasts of burden. Marxists who seek a maximal definition of the modern working class need not fear any dearth of textual support from the most impeccable of sources.

# IV

The minimalist theory of class could be said to concentrate its efforts on the identification of the boundary between proletariat and new petty bourgeoisie, whereas the maximalist theory emphasizes the boundary between the latter and the bourgeoisie proper. A third Marxist version locates the primary basis of cleavage not above or below the new petty bourgeoisie, but within it. The contrasting forms and attributes found within the realm of non-manual labour itself contain the key to the entire class system. According to Becker, for example, the really crucial line of class demarcation under monopoly capitalism is that between 'administrative labour', broadly understood as white-collar professions, and the managerial class. 'The middle class is only an appearance; its reality is a cleavage between administrative labour and the managers.'[12]

'The split between the managers and administrative labour divides the ranks of white collar labour and marks an ineradicable schism within the middle class of modern society . . .

'It is above all the fact that administrative labour is technically useful for the work of social co-ordination . . . that distinguishes it from the "labour" of managers. The latter's function derives exclusively from the circulatory needs of capital.'[13]

Whereas the tasks performed by technical and professional groups are thought to qualify as socially necessary labour, managers in any shape or form merely 'weigh upon the producers parasitically'.[14] This cleavage running through the very core of the middle class is expected to erupt onto the political surface as capitalism enters its final phase.

One feature that this type of analysis shares in common with others so far considered is that class boundaries are conceived of as lines of separation between certain occupational groups. Whatever the moral or technical criteria employed, the classificatory scheme entails the demarcation of some units from others in the division of labour. An altogether different approach is that which defines the schism within the new middle class as one grounded not so much upon occupational differences as upon the contradictory relationships that are believed to permeate this class as a whole. That is, the entire class is seen as internally divided against itself. On the one hand it receives its 'petty share in the prerogatives and rewards of capital', while on the other it 'bears the mark of the proletarian condition'.[15] Braverman's suggestion that the new middle class is a mixture of elements derived from both the major classes is elaborated upon in some detail by Carchedi.[16] In Carchedi's formulation, the opposition between classes turns upon the performance of two mutually conflicting activities: those associated with the 'global functions of capital' and those of the 'collective worker'. To perform the global functions of capital is to undertake the tasks of technical supervision and control essential to the exploitation process; to perform the function of the collective worker is to play that part in the complex division of labour that contributes to surplus value, the hallmark of an exploited condition.

The novel point here is that a hard and fast distinction between the two functions cannot be made along conventional occupational lines, because all components of the new middle class assume *both* functions to varying degrees. Hence this class is simultaneously 'both the exploiter and the exploited'.[17] This results in an incipient polarization within the white-collar class between those whose activities are geared disproportionately to the global functions of capital and those who approximate more closely to the condition of the collective worker. The latter are potential candidates for the label of white-collar proletariat, since they gradually become stripped of those residual supervisory functions that face them in the direction of the bourgeoisie, and take on instead the subordinate status of exploited wage labour. The new middle class under monopoly capitalism thus occupies what Wright, in a broadly similar analysis, refers to as a 'contradictory class location'.[18] Inhabitants of the Marxist no-man's-land between bourgeoisie and proletariat, they crystallize within themselves all the tensions and contradictions with which the system is riddled.

## V

As the foregoing discussion indicates, the variety of interpretations on offer make it more than usually difficult to speak of 'the' Marxist theory of class. In some respects the range of differences within this camp has tended to blur the simple contrast between Marxist and bourgeois theories; and this is particularly so given the tendency for Marxists to adopt familiar sociological categories under substitute names. The most striking example of this is the tacit acknowledgment of the role of *authority* in the determination of bourgeois status. This arises from the need to find some theoretical principle by which the managerial stratum, in particular, can be assigned to the same class as the owners of capital. Although allusions may occasionally be made to the fact that managers are sometimes shareholders in the companies that employ them, it is clear that this is a contingent feature of managerial status and could not be regarded as theoretically decisive. Managers with and without private company shares do not appear to be different political and ideological animals.

The exercise of discipline over the workforce, on the other hand, is a necessary feature of the managerial role, not a contingent one; and as such it recommends itself as a major criterion of bourgeois class membership. Indeed, for some Marxists managerial authority has in certain respects superseded property ownership as *the* defining attribute of a capitalist class. According to Carchedi, 'the manager, rather than the capitalist rentier, is the central figure, he, rather than the capitalist rentier, is the non-labourer, the non-producer, the exploiter. He, rather than the capitalist rentier, is capital personified.'[19]

Interestingly, by proclaiming that the supervision and control of subordinates is the new hallmark of bourgeois status, Marxist theorists have come surprisingly close to endorsing Dahrendorf's view of the determinate role of authority in establishing the class boundary. Their strict avoidance of this term in favour of some synonym or circumlocution ('mental labour', 'global function of capital', 'labour of superintendence') is perhaps a tacit admission of this embarrassing affinity with Dahrendorf's position. Although none of these writers would accept Dahrendorf's proposition that authority is a general phenomenon that encompasses property, it is nevertheless the case that their treatment of authority relations, however phrased, takes up far more of their analysis than the discussion of property relations.

To make property the centrepiece of class analysis would bring with it the duty of explaining precisely why the apparatus of managerial authority and control was thought to grow out of the institution of private ownership. Presumably it has come to the attention of western Marxists that societies that have done away with property in its private forms nevertheless have their own interesting little ways of seeing to the 'superintendence of labour'. The view that class and authority relations under capitalism are a unique product of private ownership must rest on a belief that these things are ordered in a very different way under the socialist mode of production. The fact that this mode of production figures not at all in any of the class analyses referred to suggests that Marxists are none too happy about drawing the very comparisons that are so essential to their case. After all, supposing it was discovered that factory despotism, the coercive uses of knowledge, and the privileges of mental labour were present not only in societies where the manager was 'capital personified', but also in societies where he was the party personified? Marxists would then be faced with the unwelcome choice of either having to expand the definition of capitalism to embrace socialist society, or of disowning the cherished concepts of private property and surplus extraction upon which their class theory is grounded. The obvious reluctance to engage in the comparative analysis of class under the two ostensibly different modes of production is therefore understandable enough. As for the credibility of Marxist class theory, it would seem that the advent of socialist society is about the worst thing that could have happened to it.

A further difficulty encountered by this theory is the attempt to arrive at some general principles by which to demarcate the established professions from routine white-collar employees, a distinction required by the evident self-identification of the former with the general interests of the bourgeoisie. In place of any general principles, however, resort is had to an eclectic assortment of descriptive indices demonstrating that 'higher' white-collar groups are in various ways simply better off than 'lower' white-collar groups. Braverman, for example, lists advantages such as higher pay, security of employment, and the privileged market position of the professions.[20] In similar vein, Westergaard and Resler suggest drawing a line of class demarcation beneath professional and managerial groups on the grounds that 'they are not dependent on the markets in which they sell their labour in anything like the way that other earners are'.[21] Their incomes 'are determined by market rules and mechanisms over which, in effect, they themselves have considerable influence in their own corners of the market'.[22]

The one notable thing about this kind of analysis is that despite its avowedly Marxist provenance it is indistinguishable from the approach of modern bourgeois social theory. It is, after all, Weber rather than Marx who provides the intellectual framework for understanding class in terms of market opportunities, life-chances, and symbolic rewards. The focus upon income differences and other market factors is difficult to reconcile with the standard Marxist objection to bourgeois sociology that it mistakenly operates on the level of distribution instead of on the level of productive relations. It might also be said that it is from Weber rather than Marx that the postulated link between class position and bureaucratic authority most clearly derives. The fact that these normally alien concepts of authority relations, life-chances, and market rewards have now been comfortably absorbed by contemporary Marxist theory is a handsome, if unacknowledged, tribute to the virtues of bourgeois sociology. Inside every neo-Marxist there seems to be a Weberian struggling to get out.

Parkin accuses Pof bengal...an

# VI

These recent contributions to class theory also raise anew the perennial problem for Marxism of how to account for the awkward discrepancies between classes defined as embodiments of productive relations and classes as active political agencies. Although on the face of it these definitions would seem to depend not at all upon normative elements, however broadly conceived, the introduction of political and ideological criteria is felt, by some writers at least, to be indispensable to the exercise. To his own question, 'What are social classes in Marxist theory?', Poulantzas replies:

'They are groupings of social agents, defined principally but not exclusively by their place in the production process, i.e. in the economic sphere. The economic place of the social agents has a principal role in determining social classes. But from that we cannot conclude that this economic place is sufficient to determine social classes. Marxism states that the economic does indeed have the determinant role in a mode of production or a social formation; but the political and the ideological (the superstructure) also have a very important role.'[23]

Carchedi also declares that the identification of classes at the productive level must be supplemented by an analysis that takes full account of the symbolic and behavioural determinants of class. This is because no matter with what scientific rigour and precision the taxonomic categories of class are set out it seems that prominent social groups continue to act in flagrant disregard of such categories. It appears, for example, that 'certain strata of the working class which, from the point of view of production relations belong to [the] proletariat . . . become part of the petty bourgeoisie on political and ideological grounds.'[24] Purely normative and cultural factors must therefore be invited to take their proper place in the general explanatory model.

The insistence on this point is a recurring refrain in contemporary Marxism and arises from the desire of its practitioners to distance themselves as far as possible from the Marxism of the Second International and from anything smacking of economic determinism. A clear distinction is thus drawn between the 'structural determination of classes' in the economic sphere and 'class position' in the sphere of political action. Whereas 'vulgar' Marxism assumes that the latter is a straightforward function of the former, neo-Marxism inserts a series of qualifications that greatly reduces this dependency relationship and accords considerable leeway to the separate effects of politics and ideology. Indeed, for Poulantzas, political and ideological relations are accorded virtual parity with economic relationships in the full definition of class, notwithstanding all prior assurances of the primacy of the economic. So much so, that he feels it necessary to warn his readers not to commit the reverse error to that of vulgar Marxism by reducing the structural determination of class to political and ideological features.[25]

The fact that the two aspects of class are now said to operate to a large degree independently of each other implies that discrepancies between the two levels should be regarded as natural occurrences. The discredited version of Marxism assumed that disjunctions between the economic and political realms would be overcome by the accelerating pace of crisis in which real interests translated themselves into manifest interests. Although neo-Marxism tends to shy away from any such bald assertions, it is difficult to see what alternative position could recommend itself 'in the final analysis'. Certainly Poulantzas' own remarks concerning the capacity of classes to break through the barriers of ideology and reveal themselves in their true state are very much in line with the traditional view:

> '. . . to say that there is a working class in economic relations necessarily implies a specific place for this class in ideological and political relations, even if in certain countries and certain historical periods this class does not have its own 'class consciousness' or an autonomous political organisation. This means that in such cases, even if it is heavily contaminated by bourgeois ideology, its economic existence is still expressed in certain specific material politico-ideological practices which burst through its bourgeois "discourse".'[26]

Neo-Marxist writing on this whole question indicates in fact a considerable degree of uncertainty and vacillation as to how to restate the celebrated *an sich-für sich* formula. The dilemma is that in rejecting the uncomplicated view of a one-way determinism, greater allowance has to be made for the independent influence of non-material factors. But whereas conceptual categories relating to the role of production can be framed in terms of general principles applicable to capitalism as a system wherever it is found, no comparable principles are available for the analysis of politics and ideology. The latter, it seems, are only to be understood as 'the always unique historic individuality of a social formation, in other words the concrete situation of the class struggle'.[27] There is no 'pure model' of ideological and political relations to complement the pure model of the capitalist mode of production. Consequently, the greater the penetration of ideological and political factors into the analysis, the greater will be the shift away from general theory to particularistic accounts set within the framework of this or that society, or this or that epoch.

In addition, of course, such a strategy throws into serious doubt the explanatory value of the carefully elaborated categories employed in the treatment of the boundary problem. The introduction of political and ideological criteria do not have the effect of rounding out the preceding analysis so much as displacing it altogether. Since classes in the full Marxist sense are collectivities forged in the heat of political struggle, and since the contours of this struggle never correspond to the boundaries of the class model, the effort expended in constructing such a model seems to fall squarely within the commonsense meaning of unproductive labour.

## Notes

1 The hospital setting provides, perhaps, the most important exception. Industrial conflicts between medical staff and the manual workers' unions over issues such as 'pay beds' are unusual in having clear-cut ideological, rather than bread-and-butter, causes.
2 The *locus classicus* of this argument is Goldthorpe and Lockwood 1963. It also occupied a central place in my *Class Inequality and Political Order* (1971).
3 Poulantzas 1975.
4 Poulantzas 1975:270.
5 Poulantzas 1975:242.
6 Sweezy 1946:284.
7 Wright 1976:23. Wright refers specifically to the American working class, though his objection presumably has general applicability. Poulantzas'

reply to this objection is that the American working class must be defined in an 'imperial context'; all workers employed by American capital, in whatever country, are proxy members of the American proletariat. At one conceptual stroke this class is thus transformed from the smallest to the largest proletariat in the capitalist sphere. Poulantzas 1977:119.

8  Baran 1957:32.
9  Baran 1957:33.
10  Richta *et al.* 1967.
11  Marx and Engels 1969:111.
12  Becker 1973:276.
13  Becker 1973:437 and 442.
14  Becker 1973:444.
15  Braverman 1974:407.
16  Carchedi 1975.
17  Carchedi 1975:53.
18  Wright 1976:26.
19  Carchedi 1975:48. For Braverman, too, managers and executives are 'part of the class that personifies capital . . .' (1974:405).
20  Braverman 1974: Chapter 18.
21  Westergaard and Resler 1975:92.
22  Westergaard and Resler 1975:346.
23  Poulantzas 1975:14.
24  Carchedi 1975:70.
25  Poulantzas 1975:15–16.
26  Poulantzas 1975:16.
27  Poulantzas 1975:14.

# 3

# Internal class cleavages and the ethnic factor

Any solution proposed to the boundary problem raises in turn the troublesome issue of internal class cleavages, or, more properly, the relationship between the two. Although in Marxism and sociology alike the relations within classes are normally understood to be a partial function of the relations between classes, the connection is not usually made explicit. For the most part, inter-class relations are viewed as an expression of certain generic features of property rights, authority relations, or the division of labour. Divisions within classes on the other hand are not usually construed in terms of similar systemic principles, and least of all are such divisions represented as an extension of the same principles that govern inter-class relationships. The internal class distinctions commonly employed appear to take shape under the imprint of purely national conditions and so lack those universal properties that characterize the relationship between class and class. Thus, in the sociology of the working class, the terminology of affluent and traditional, old and new, rough and respectable, secular and deferential, and so forth, sets up distinctions that appear to derive more from the peculiarities of British society than from the universal, systemic features of capitalism.[1]

This capitalism-in-one-country approach serves perhaps as a more acceptable framework for the analysis of internal class relations than of the relations between classes because of the striking contrast in what is taken to be sociologically problematic in the two cases. Inter-class relations are usually conceived of as inherently antagonistic, a condition only to be comprehended through the idiom of dichotomy and conflict. At the intra-class level, however, the emphasis upon

29

competitive struggle gives way to a rather more bland concern with the niceties of social differentiation. The subject of investigation here becomes (among the working class) variations in life-style, attitudes, and social consciousness, or (among the middle class) variations in the social composition and recruitment of elites. Sociological ingenuity is directed to mapping out the social contours of a territory in which a truce has been declared in the *omnium bellum contra omnes*. Social differentiation within a given class, moreover, is analysed by reference to conceptual categories that generally do not correspond to existentially based groups with the capacity for mobilization; even less could they be said to constitute social collectivities engaged in mutual competition for scarce resources.

Marxism has always displayed a greater sensitivity to this issue than has sociology. Marx himself proposed a number of subclassifications within both major classes, such as the distinction between finance capital and industrial capital within the bourgeoisie, or that between the lumpen-proletariat and the working class proper. Lenin's writings, too, are peppered with references to labour aristocracies, cadres, and vanguards – all constituent elements in what might be thought of as the moral stratification of the working class.

These internal distinctions, unlike those commonly employed in sociology, are designed to single out groups that have the capacity for collective social action. Indeed, the entire point of the exercise is to evaluate the extent to which the activity of such groups contributes to, or detracts from, unified class conduct. Even so, however fully acknowledged internal class divisions may be in Marxist theory, these divisions are not deemed to have the same irreconcilable character as exploitative class relations. In drawing attention to the 'objective economic stratifications within the proletariat', Lukacs felt bound to insist that they were not even 'remotely similar to those which determine the division into classes'.[2] To put inter-class relations on the same footing as the relations between what Stalin dubbed 'non-antagonistic strata' seemed to lead to a theoretical position that dissolved the political cohesion of the working class:

> 'For, since Bernstein, the opportunists have striven constantly to portray the objective economic stratifications in the proletariat as going so deep and to lay such emphasis on the similarity in the "life situations" of the various proletarian, semi-proletarian and petty-bourgeois strata that *in consequence the unity and the autonomy of the class was lost.*'[3]

Thus, notwithstanding a greater readiness to identify politically relevant intra-class divisions, Marxism has shared with sociology a general reluctance to put them on the same theoretical plane as inter-class divisions. The common preference has been to treat them as related but essentially different phenomena requiring separate levels of analysis.

## II

One of the reasons for all this has been the tendency to analyse class relations within the context of an assumed cultural and ethnic homogeneity. As a result, there has been little if any attempt to incorporate within the framework of analysis those forms of internal cleavage that arise on the basis of religious, linguistic, racial, and cultural differentiation. Clearly, once intra-class divisions are examined from the vantage point of these ethnic formations, then the absence of a vocabulary of conflict and mutual antagonism seems positively bizarre. Part of the reason for this state of affairs is that earlier generations of social theorists tended to regard ethnicity as a spent force. It was widely felt that the homogenizing influence of the modern industrial state would be too powerful to allow the survivial of those traditionalistic and narrower 'tribal' loyalties that flourished under agrarian systems. This is one of the assumptions that bourgeois social theory shared in common with Marxism. Marx's portrayal of capitalism's 'civilizing mission' emphasized precisely those elements that acted as a corrosive force upon status group attachments, and their replacement by the wholly impersonal and instrumental relations of the marketplace. Indeed, in his schema the final showdown between the two great contending classes could not take place until this historically prior clearing operation had been accomplished, the reason being that the survival of primordial or tribalistic group identities would inhibit that ultimate condition in which class membership alone defined the contours of the moral order.

Ethnic or cultural enclaves still surviving in the corners of the capitalist nation-state were looked upon by Marx as historical remnants harbouring the seeds of political reaction.

> 'These remains of nationalities, mercilessly trampled on by history – as Hegel says – these national left-overs will all become and will remain until their final extermination . . . fanatic partisans of the counter-revolution, since their entire existence is in general a protest against the great historical revolution.'[4]

Seen from this perspective, a future socialist order, however much scope for human diversity it might foster in other spheres, seemed unlikely to offer itself as a promised land for the cultivation of ethnic identities. Kautsky looked forward to the new epoch when the proletariat would be familiar with one of the universal languages, thereby paving the way for the 'gradual withdrawal and ultimately the complete disappearance of the languages of the smaller nations, and for the union of all civilized humanity into one language and one nationality . . .'.[5]

Weber, too, for all his sensitivity to the place of 'ethnic honour' in human affairs, nevertheless regarded it as one more example of irrationality. Communal consciousness and ethnic identity flourished only in the absence of 'rationally regulated action'.[6] He contrasted the 'ethnic fictions' of the Greek city state, which were due to the 'low degree of rationalization of Greek political life', with the absence of such fictions in Rome – a place where rational organization was allegedly more widespread.[7] Wherever else it might linger on, ethnicity could hardly be expected to survive the great tidal wave of bureaucratic rationality sweeping over the western world.

The fact that Marxism and bourgeois social theory from their very beginnings failed to take ethnic divisions seriously was not due to the absence of conflict across communal lines, of the kind with which we are increasingly familiar. It was much more to do with the adoption of a certain methodology. As Lockwood has pointed out, the classical theorists tended to focus upon the universal and necessary properties of the social system and to treat other factors as purely contingent.[8] In defining the chief characteristics of capitalist society they selectively emphasized those features such as the schism between labour and capital that were common to *all* capitalist societies, irrespective of their cultural and historical differences. Whereas class could be presented as a universal and inherent attribute of capitalism, the same could not be said of ethnic divisions; the split between religious, racial, or linguistic sections of the population appeared to owe more to the peculiarities of history than to the logic of any productive system. The proper theoretical strategy was, therefore, to treat ethnic factors as 'complicating features' that simply disturbed the pure class model, rather than as integral elements of the system.

Thus, one of the less welcome legacies bequeathed by the classical writers to contemporary social theory has been to render it theoretically unprepared to deal with the renaissance of ethnic identity and conflict in the very heartlands of western capitalism. Societies within this orbit that are wholly free of political troubles between communal groups are rapidly approaching the status of deviant cases. Ethnic conflict would now appear to be as normal a feature of advanced industrial societies as class conflict, even though its theoretical treatment is still at a relatively primitive stage.

The emergence of these 'archaic' forms of cleavage and antagonism in western Europe is partly the result of the migration of workers from the poorer lands of the southern perimeter into the heavily industrialized countries of the north, as well as the flow of labour from the old colonial territories into the former imperial motherlands. In addition, however, the picture has been complicated by the eruption of political antagonisms between religious and language groups that have been part of a single nation-state for centuries. Marxism and sociology have thus been faced with two interlocking problems: first, how to account for the synchronization, as it were, of obviously disconnected communal conflicts, especially in societies where such conflicts have been fairly dormant over a long period; and, second, to consider the nature of the connection, if any, between ethnic or communal relations on the one hand and the more familiar pattern of class inequality on the other. Because ethnic divisions typically cut across class divisions, this would seem to call for some reconsideration of what constitutes the 'boundary problem'.

# III

A general approach to the problem which makes the cleanest break with classical tradition is advocated by those theorists who see the new ethnicity not as a factor to be explained within some larger class context, but rather as one that has virtually displaced class as the major form of social cleavage and political identity. According to Glazer and Moynihan, until quite recently in the west 'the preoccupation with property relations obscured ethnic ones', but now 'it is *property* that begins to seem derivative, and ethnicity that seems to become a more fundamental source of stratification'.[9] Not the least of the reasons adduced in support of this view is that the nature of collective action mounted by ethnic groups has undergone a significant change in recent times. Originally dedicated to fighting rearguard actions of cultural preservation, they have now adopted more combative forms of activity expressly designed to alter the distribution of rewards in their members' favour. It is not simply that ethnic groups have assumed political functions comparable to those of a subordinate class; they have in important respects become more effective than social classes in mobilizing their forces in pursuit of collective ends.

The reason for this is suggested by Bell, as an extension of his thesis on the character of the post-industrial society.[10] In this type of society the increasingly white-collar composition of the working class leads to its gradual 'demoralization', in the sense of a weakened ability to mount forms of activity that combine both instrumental and affective appeals. The new working class of the modern industrial state has been severed from the history, ideology, and symbolism of the old labour movement, leaving it with only the most narrowly defined economic goals as a motive for action. It is into this moral vacuum that ethnic groups are drawn. They *can* provide the badge of moral identification and the yearning for collective dignity that fuel the engines of political action among the dispossessed. If the period of quiet calm following the end of ideology has now abruptly expired, it appears to be succeeded by one in which entirely new political banners are raised aloft and inscribed with insignia quite unrecognizable to any surviving warriors of the class struggle.

The theoretical grounding for this type of analysis is to be found in Weber's well-known thesis concerning the periodic oscillations between class politics and status-group politics. In Weber's capsule statement of the matter, classes are more likely to be the primary or politically significant social formations under conditions of general economic dislocation or crisis, whereas status groups flourish during periods of relative stability and social peace. Since ethnic groups are, in Weber's own writings, virtually the paradigm case of status organizations, their period of ascendancy would naturally be expected to coincide more or less with the relative decline in the salience of class. Thus, as if with Weber's schema in mind, Bell adds a cautious rider to his analysis, suggesting that class organization and conflict could again come to the fore in the event of a worsening in the economic climate.

The assumption quietly at work here is that the sense of identity with, or membership of, a class or ethnic group is essentially an either/or affair, such that a moral commitment to one precludes involvement in the other.[11] It is a conception of political and social identity that yields little to those notions of situational choice and context that, as Marx might have put it, allow a man to think of himself as an industrial worker in the morning, a black in the afternoon, and an American in the evening, without ever thinking of himself wholly as a worker, a black, or an American. In so far as class and ethnic identities can be held *simultaneously* and activated, as it were, according to situational exigencies, then the less persuasive are those models of Weberian origin that emphasize instead their periodic alternations as determined by the severity of the economic climate. It would in any case tax all Weber's ingenuity to convince a modern audience that the new wave of ethnic consciousness and communal disturbance has occurred under conditions of economic tranquillity and peaceful co-existence between the classes.

Theories that proclaim that ethnic stratification has now displaced class stratification as the central fact of inequality under advanced capitalism would seem to fall squarely outside the Marxist pale. However, the powers of innovation within this camp are again amply demonstrated by the attempt to harness the notion of ethnic primacy to a theory of political conflict that owes as much to Marx as to Weber, in its moral overtones at least. This is the analysis of communal minorities as 'internal colonies' within the body politic of the nation-state. Viewed from this angle, ethnic minorities are to be understood as embryonic nations that are exposed to similar forms of material and cultural exploitation as those experienced by subject nations under imperial rule. Ethnic minorities are in effect Third World contingents in the heartlands of the First World. In Hechter's presentation of the thesis, the transition from backwardness to modernity occurs as a series of uneven waves moving across state territory and conferring special benefits on the core regions first affected, and corresponding deficits on the peripheral areas.[12] This pattern of uneven development takes on special significance where spatial units correspond to distinct cultural units and where, in particular, the people of the core are ethnically distinguishable from those of the periphery. The outcome is a 'cultural division of labour' based on an unequal exchange relationship that has all the hallmarks of a colonial situation.

Although the model of internal colonialism would appear to be applicable largely to conditions of ethnic conflict in which a clear territorial component is present, its earliest formulations arose, paradoxically, as an account of racial cleavages in the United States, where the prospect of 'colonial liberation' for the black minority must have seemed especially bleak. As Blauner points out, the model of the internal colony was suggested by black activists as an alternative to the race relations approach of academic sociology, which tended to locate the problem of racism in the defective attitudes of individuals, rather than in a formal system of power and dominance.[13] It has thus been the American rather than the European experience that has inspired a fundamental restatement of the relationship between class and ethnicity by use of the colonial analogy, even though on the face of it the analogy seems more applicable to the European setting.

Now once the dominant ethnic group has been defined as a kind of occupying power, there is very little theoretical temptation to point up differences and conflicts within this power, along the lines of class.

35

For all practical intents and purposes the white working class can safely be assumed to be an integral part of the exploiting racial group, politically indistinct from the white bourgeoisie. Indeed, in some versions of the argument the white working class is identified as the principal beneficiary of the system, so furnishing the 'bulk of the counter-revolutionary force against the Negro revolt'.[14]

The exploitative nature of the 'white proletariat', or its ethnic counterpart under different systems, is a recurring theme in radical interpretations of communal conflict. Hechter, for example, suggests that the working-class movement in Britain served to strengthen the grip of the English ruling class upon the Celtic minorities by furthering the 'negative integration' of the latter into the United Kingdom.[15] The clear implication is that by organizing itself along the lines of pure class action the labour movement succeeded in diverting attention away from those injustices and inequalities that are directly attributable to the subordination of the Scots, Welsh, and Irish minorities, and from which English workers have indirectly benefited. The central moral strand in this entire thesis is that exploitation and its accompanying degradations arising on the basis of ethnic differences have a *prior* claim to remedial action over the large and small injustices of class. Seen from this angle, any argument to the effect that class exploitation is the foundation of all other forms, including ethnic, and that therefore the political unity of the proletariat is the first item on the agenda, can easily be made to appear as a subtle defence of the racial and cultural *status quo*: Marxism becomes the Englishman's best friend. Thus, if stratification theory in its beginnings is marked by a reluctance to treat ethnicity as little more than a ripple across the surface of the class structure, there are now indications from several quite different quarters of a complete theoretical reversal; it is now class that is just as likely to be treated as a complicating feature of a social system moulded largely by the realities of ethnic forces.

It might perhaps have been anticipated that some resistance to this tendency would have been registered on the part of those theorists for whom the notion of an exploitative proletariat would be a hopeless contradiction in terms. Yet orthodox western Marxism has been noticeably unproductive in this entire sphere. There has in fact been very little advance beyond that line of approach that presents ethnic conflict either as a joint product of bourgeois cunning and proletarian gullibility (the *impera et divide* thesis) or as a 'displacement' of social antagonisms whose origins are to be found in the multiple contradictions of the capitalist mode of production. On current evidence it would be quite forgivable to conclude that the preferred Marxist response to the fact of racial or communal strife is to ignore it. Not one of the various incursions into class theory examined in the previous chapter makes any serious attempt to consider how the division between blacks and whites, Catholics and Protestants, Flemings and Walloons, Francophones and Anglophones, or between indigenous and immigrant workers might bear upon the boundary problem.

Westergaard and Resler do at least concede the existence of such divisions in capitalist society, but only in order to stress their secondary or derivative importance in relation to class. They go so far as to assert, against all the dramatic evidence to the contrary, that racial and similar inequalities do not have 'the force, the sweeping repercussions of class inequality'. Nor, apparently, do they even give rise to the 'communality of condition which marks class position in the economic order'.[16] Clearly, the inhabitants of Harlem and the Bogside have not been informed of this.

Considerations of ethnicity could, of course, have no possible place in Poulantzas' formal class schema; more remarkably, however, his lengthy analysis of the nature and origins of German fascism succeeds in avoiding any discussion of racial ideology or the Jews.[17] An account of Nazism that identifies the contradictions of monopoly capital as the source of the malaise could hardly allow much significance to Auschwitz and the final solution of the ethnic problem, other than as one of those complicating, secondary features.

It is, in any case, difficult to see what kind of explanation could be expected from those formulations that draw heavily upon the conceptual storehouse of political economy. Notions such as the mode of production make their claims to explanatory power precisely on the grounds of their indifference to the nature of the human material whose activities are structurally determined. As earlier pointed out, to introduce questions such as the ethnic composition of the workforce is to clutter up the analysis by laying stress upon the qualities of social actors, a conception diametrically opposed to the notion of human agents as *träger* or embodiments of systemic forces. Presumably, for Marxists operating within this schema the existence of communal divisions within a class need be thought of as no more a hindrance to the theory than the equally important divisions along, say, the lines of skill; the expectation being that the growing tension between capital and labour serves to reduce the importance of purely internal class differences. In this respect, ethnic cleavages could be expected to undergo the same healing process as that which gradually mended the breach between the labour aristocracy and the labouring poor – the more so, of course, as capitalism enters (once again) its final phase.

Some such background assumption is clearly at work in Boserup's analysis of communal conflict in Northern Ireland. In this account, the political antagonisms between Protestants and Catholics are found to be rooted in the contradictions set up between two competing forms of capital – an indigenous 'clientalist' form expressing local particularisms, and monopoly capital enshrining metropolitan and global interests. The tensions generated by these opposing types of capital are said to be of an intensity that distorts the normal line of cleavage between bourgeoisie and proletariat. The fact that communal conflict so heavily overlays class conflict is thus to be understood as a 'manifestation at the political level of the transition from one variant of a capitalist social formation to another'.[18] An end to sectarian violence and the calming of those historic passions associated with the border question must therefore await upon the eventual displacement of archaic capital by its more rational monopoly forms. At that point, class politics will supplant tribal politics. Western Marxists, it appears, number themselves among that shrinking band whose faith in capitalism's civilizing mission remains unshaken.

Finally, and improbable as it may seem, Marxist class theory has also been pressed into service in the analysis of *apartheid*. To seek to impose class categories upon such a palpably racial system would seem to be somewhat akin to adopting a Parsonian integrationist model in the analysis of, say, the modern Lebanon. In the face of a fairly unambiguous political alliance between white South African workers and the white capitalist class, Marxism is at pains to portray a more intricate and complex state of affairs. Beneath this surface appearance, the phantom forces of the capitalist mode of production are silently burrowing away at the foundations of the racial order by exacerbating class tensions within the dominant ethnic group, thereby threatening the political cohesion of white supremacy.

Although scrupulous care is usually taken to avoid any straightforward assertion that black and white sectors of the proletariat must, of necessity, be drawn together in a class alliance against the bourgeoisie, some such long-term expectation is more or less implicit in the conceptual framework adopted. What would be the point of the forced march across the wastelands of political economy if at the end of it all the ultimate and decisive role of class forces was denied? Such a denial would merely leave the way open for that type of approach that treated racial conflict as an irreducible political phenomenon, and which conceptualized racial groups as social actors rather than as *träger*. As Wolpe complains:

> 'The consequence of this acceptance of the "actor's" definition of the situation coupled with the salience given to race . . . is that the ideological and political are given a predominance such as either to obliterate differences in relations of production or to give the appearance that the political and ideological define new

relations of exploitation. In either event the economic level is deprived of any autonomy whatsoever and the result is that differential economic relations of different classes are all but eliminated. This may have important political repercussions, since it insists *ab initio*, that since *class relations of production* are politically and ideologically defined, therefore, whatever the nature of the contradictions and conflicts which may occur in the development of South African capitalism, there is no *possibility* of the white working class or any fraction of it ever entering into an alliance with African workers in a struggle to overthrow the capitalist state.'[19]

If the non-Marxist approach does indeed lead to such a conclusion, this would seem to illustrate its soundness rather than its deficiency.


# IV

One additional reason why communal conflicts might be thought not to merit the same degree of theoretical attention as class conflict is that the former, however socially disruptive, are believed to lack the capacity for transforming the social system. Rosa Luxemburg was prepared to concede that opposition to class exploitation was usually of lesser intensity and violence than the resistance to communal forms of oppression.[20] Nevertheless, exploited classes alone possessed the political will and leverage to translate opposition into outright social revolution. Communal actions could not go beyond violence and protest to the creative act of political renewal. Communal conflict, in Lockwood's words,

'is not first and foremost directed at an alteration in the structure of power and deference but rather at the usurpation of power and deference by one section of the community to the disadvantage of the other. Ethnic and racial conflict has this orientation primarily because it is in the nature of the experience of the relationships of the majority and minority groups that the salient "cause" of disaffection inheres in the given and unalterable properties of individual actors and not in the contingent properties of social systems. Because of this, racial and ethnic conflict is more akin to rebellion in ethnically and racially homogenous societies in which the social order is likewise regarded as ineluctable. Thus revolutionary goals are unlikely to emerge from the antagonisms of groups in plural societies unless ethnic and racial divisions happen to coincide with lines of economic and other power relationships.'[21]

To the extent, then, that communal conflicts are seen to have more in common with rituals of rebellion than with revolutionary politics, it would seem that Marxists at least could be excused duties in this field, abandoning it perhaps to social anthropology or the sociology of religion. Such a position implies, of course, not only that classes under advanced capitalism still retain their explosive potential but that they are also a greater threat to the survival of the state than the forces unleashed by communal disturbances and grievances.

However, it should be said that whereas the modern proletariat appears to have a purely theoretical capacity to reconstitute the social order in its own image, ethnic groups have frequently displayed a more than abstract commitment to dissolving the boundaries of the nation-state and redrawing them anew. Given the aura of sanctity and omnipotence surrounding the state in current Marxist theory it should surely follow that any threat to its sovereignty from within would qualify as a supremely political act. The fact that the breakaway state might continue to be a version of capitalism does not make its activities any less political. Leviathan does not take more kindly to the prospect of its own dismemberment simply because the reconstituted part may share a natural affinity to the parent body.

There is any case no guarantee of such affinity. Separatist movements not uncommonly link national aspirations with proposals for a radically new social order. Marxism's traditional coolness towards such movements stems from the belief that they are vehicles for nothing more politically imaginative than petty-bourgeois ambition. However high-sounding their proclamations, the likelihood of separatist movements producing anything more than miniature reproductions of the capitalist original is rated very low, given their adulteration of class politics by national sentiments. A reconciliation between Marxism and nationalism, in the context of the modern capitalist state, would thus seem to be feasible only if a direct programmatic link could be established between separatist demands and the wider class struggle.

Such a link has, in fact, recently been discovered by Nairn. On his reckoning, nationalist movements in Britain, far from being politically retrograde, actually represent 'a detour on the way to revolution'.[22] The separatist revolt, in bringing about the disintegration of the central state power, leads to the enfeeblement of those ancient institutions and practices that have always been a stumbling block to socialist progress. Once the pillars of the old order have crumbled, opportunities present themselves for radical social reconstruction in the core region no less than in the periphery. In freeing themselves, the colonial subjects emancipate their imperial masters. The nationalist way thus opens up one more route on the well-signposted road to socialism.

Whatever credence may be allowed to this argument, it does at least serve to illustrate the point that ethnic or communal conflict often seems to call for explanation by reference to the concept of nationalism as much as by the conventional categories of stratification theory. At any rate, wherever a strong territorial component is present, it is unlikely that an account of communal conflict couched wholly in terms of distributive injustice will capture the special significance of those actions and sentiments by which a given group seeks to claim for itself the status of a separate people.

The affinities between ethnic groups and nations were discussed by Weber at some length. Although he regarded ethnic communities as a species of status group, they were also of particular significance by virtue of the fact that, unlike other status groups, and unlike social classes, they could undergo metamorphosis from being part of a state to becoming full nation-states in their own right. Partly because of this, ethnic honour was to be understood as a 'specific honour of the masses', in so far as it was a source of positive self-esteem available equally to all members of the group, irrespective of their social standing by other criteria.[23] Ethnic honour was therefore to be distinguished from other forms of status honour, which typically rested upon hierarchy.

The view of ethnic communities as embryonic nations is somewhat at odds with the recent assertion by Glazer and Moynihan to the effect that ethnic identity has become an *alternative* to national identity. According to these writers, the resurgence of ethnic pride displaces not merely class affiliation but also the sense of national belonging.[24] This might well hold true for those many ethnic communities in the United States that have no historic association with a territorial homeland within the boundaries of the wider state; but it would come as surprising news to Basques, French Canadians, Scots, and Welsh – to name a few of the groups for whom ethnic identity and national identity are virtually interchangeable terms. Perhaps it was because of these complications raised by the territorial aspect that Weber felt 'the collective term "ethnic" would be abandoned' in the long run because it was 'unsuitable for a really rigorous analysis'.[25] However this may be, the term shows no more sign of going away than the type of social collectivity it describes.

Even allowing for the territorial complications, a case can still be made for treating ethnic cleavages within the general framework of a stratification model. And this is particularly so in regard to those common ethnic situations marked by the systematic use of formal and informal discriminatory practices that bespeak the subordination of one communal group by another. Moreover, because divisions along communal lines almost always cut across class divisions, to ignore the effects of ethnicity is to impoverish class analysis. It becomes increasingly less possible to operate with models of class based predominantly on categories drawn from the division of labour, property ownership, or the productive system, when the political character of collective action is conditioned by the social and cultural make-up of the groups involved. This suggests not only that ethnicity and communal conflict should be taken at least as seriously as class and class conflict, but that the two sets of phenomena should be closely integrated at the conceptual level.

Such an approach could also be defended as a preferred alternative to the bifurcation of class analysis and ethnic studies into separate subdisciplines, each with its own unique battery of concepts and problems. There is something to be said in favour of a single framework of ideas and a common vocabulary with which to conduct the discourse on structured inequality in all its familiar guises. All this amounts to a general declaration that internal class divisions should be accorded as much theoretical attention as the 'boundary problem' itself; or, more correctly, that the identification of class and communal boundaries should be regarded as aspects of a single problem and should be analysed as such. In the following chapter the framework for such an analysis is proposed, based on Weber's concept of social closure.

## Notes

1 Giddens has shown for example that the notion of the 'new working class' appears to have very different meanings in different national contexts. In French sociology it refers predominantly to qualified technical workers, whose strategic position in the division of labour marks them out for a vanguard role in the working-class movement. Among American sociologists, on the other hand, the term is used to describe the 'ethnic poor' whose exclusion from the ranks of organized labour renders them politically powerless. In British studies the term appears to designate the 'non-traditional' segment of the working class. See Giddens 1973: 192–97 and 215–22. See also the variety of usages in Hörning (ed.) 1971.
2 Lukacs 1971:323.
3 Lukacs 1971:323.

4 Cited in Luxemburg (ed. Davis) 1976:124–25.
5 Cited in Luxemburg (ed. Davis) 1976:127.
6 Weber (eds Roth and Wittich) 1968:389.
7 Weber (eds Roth and Wittich) 1968:389.
8 Lockwood 1970.
9 Glazer and Moynihan 1975:16–17.
10 Bell 1975.
11 As Bell puts it, 'it is clear that "class" and "ethnicity" have been the two . . . dominant modes of coherent group feeling and action, and we can raise the general question, under what conditions has *one or the other* become most salient for action, or under what conditions might the two be fused' (Bell 1975:165–66 (italics added)). This way of posing the question seems to rule out the possibility of the *equal* salience of class and ethnicity, without any 'fusion' of the two. It must be said, however, that Bell, unlike many writers, does emphasize the possibility of *choice* between political identities – even if it is, as for Weber, an either/or choice in any given period.
12 Hechter 1975.
13 Blauner 1972. See, in particular, Carmichael and Hamilton 1967.
14 Boggs 1970:14.
15 Hechter 1975:292. See also, Davies 1973.
16 Westergaard and Resler 1975:351–52.
17 Poulantzas 1974.
18 Boserup 1972:173.
19 Wolpe 1976:215.
20 Luxemburg (ed. Davis) 1976:96–7.
21 Lockwood 1970:64.
22 Nairn 1977:60.
23 Weber (eds Roth and Wittich) 1968:391.
24 Glazer and Moynihan 1975:18.
25 Weber (eds Roth and Wittich) 1968:395.

# 4

# Social closure
# as exclusion

By social closure Weber means the process by which social collectivities seek to maximize rewards by restricting access to resources and opportunities to a limited circle of eligibles. This entails the singling out of certain social or physical attributes as the justificatory basis of exclusion. Weber suggests that virtually any group attribute – race, language, social origin, religion – may be seized upon provided it can be used for 'the monopolization of specific, usually economic opportunities'.[1] 'This monopolization is directed against competitors who share some positive or negative characteristic; its purpose is always the closure of social and economic opportunities to *outsiders*.'[2] The nature of these exclusionary practices, and the completeness of social closure, determine the general character of the distributive system.

Surprisingly, Weber's elaboration of the closure theme is not linked in any immediate way with his other main contributions to stratification theory, despite the fact that processes of exclusion can properly be conceived of as an aspect of the distribution of power, which for Weber is practically synonymous with stratification. As a result, the usefulness of the concept for the study of class and similar forms of structured inequality becomes conditional on the acceptance of certain refinements and enlargements upon the original usage.

An initial step in this direction is to extend the notion of closure to encompass other forms of collective social action designed to maximize claims to rewards and opportunities. Closure strategies would thus include not only those of an exclusionary kind, but also those adopted by the excluded themselves as a direct response to their status as outsiders. It is in any case hardly possible to consider the effectiveness of exclusion practices without due reference to the countervailing actions of socially defined ineligibles. As Weber acknowledges: 'Such group action may provoke a corresponding reaction on the part of those against whom it is directed.'[3] In other words, collective efforts to resist a pattern of dominance governed by exclusion principles can properly be regarded as the other half of the social closure equation. This usage is in fact employed by Weber in his discussion of 'community closure' which, as Neuwirth has shown, bears directly upon those forms of collective action mounted by the excluded – i.e. 'negatively privileged status groups'.[4]

The distinguishing feature of exclusionary closure is the attempt by one group to secure for itself a privileged position at the expense of some other group through a process of subordination. That is to say, it is a form of collective social action which, intentionally or otherwise, gives rise to a social category of ineligibles or outsiders. Expressed metaphorically, exclusionary closure represents the use of power in a 'downward' direction because it necessarily entails the creation of a group, class, or stratum of legally defined inferiors. Countervailing action by the 'negatively privileged', on the other hand, represents the use of power in an upward direction in the sense that collective attempts by the excluded to win a greater share of resources always threaten to bite into the privileges of legally defined superiors. It is in other words a form of action having usurpation as its goal. *Exclusion* and *usurpation* may therefore be regarded as the two main generic types of social closure, the latter always being a consequence of, and collective response to, the former.[5]

Strategies of exclusion are the predominant mode of closure in all stratified systems. Where the excluded in their turn also succeed in closing off access to remaining rewards and opportunities, so multiplying the number of substrata, the stratification order approaches the furthest point of contrast to the Marxist model of class polarization. The traditional caste system and the stratification of ethnic communities in the United States provide the clearest illustrations of this closure pattern, though similar processes are easily detectable in societies in which class formation is paramount. Strategies of usurpation vary in scale from those designed to bring about marginal redistribution to those aimed at total expropriation. But whatever their intended scale they nearly always contain a potential challenge to the prevailing system of allocation and to the authorized version of distributive justice.

All this indicates the ease with which the language of closure can be translated into the language of power. Modes of closure can be thought of as different means of mobilizing power for the purpose of engaging in distributive struggle. To conceive of power as a built-in attribute of closure is at the very least to dispense with those fruitless searches for its 'location' inspired by Weber's more familiar but completely unhelpful definition in terms of the ubiquitous struggle between contending wills. Moreover, to speak of power in the light of closure principles is quite consistent with the analysis of class relations. Thus, to anticipate the discussion, the familiar distinction between bourgeoisie and proletariat, in its classic as well as in its modern guise, may be conceived of as an expression of conflict between classes defined not specifically in relation to their place in the productive process but in relation to their prevalent modes of closure, exclusion and usurpation, respectively.

Moreover, stating the matter this way is equally consistent with that tradition that very properly places the concept of exploitation at the heart of class analysis. That is, in so far as exclusionary forms of closure result in the downward use of power, hence creating subordinate social formations, they can be regarded by definition as exploitative. Exploitation here defines the nexus between classes or other collectivities that stand in a relationship of dominance and subordination, on *whatever* social basis. There is no compelling reason why the term should be restricted to its conventional Marxist usage, referring to the appropriation of surplus value on the part of capital, since this is itself but one important case of the more general phenomenon of exclusionary closure. Collective efforts to restrict access to rewards and opportunities on the part of one social group against another, including one group of workers against another, can be regarded as inherently exploitative even though the relationship is not one of surplus extraction deriving from property ownership. Relations of dominance and subordination between bourgeoisie and proletariat, Protestants and Catholics, whites and blacks, men and women, etc., can all be considered as exploitative relationships in the neo-Weberian sense. The Marxist objection to such an expanded usage is that it violates the scientific status of the concept. According to Wolpe, for example,

'while the concept of exploitation can have a rigorous and explicit meaning in defining class relations, it becomes a vague, descriptive term in the characterization of relations between such entities as racial, national or cultural groups.'[6]

The reason for this is supplied by Bettelheim:

'Because the concept of *exploitation* expresses a *production relation* – production of surplus labour and expropriation of this by a social class – it necessarily relates to *class relations* . . .'[7]

All that this really means, of course, is that Marxists choose to employ the concept in this narrower sense; such a meaning does not inhere in the term itself. To broaden the meaning of the term to encompass relations of dominance and subjection other than those between capital and labour does not thereby signal a shift from a scientific or technical usage to a moral one; exploitation is a morally weighted concept *whichever* way it is used, and it as well to acknowledge this from the outset. This broader application of the concept has particular implications for the analysis of intra-class relations, shortly to be considered. First, though, it is necessary to flesh out these somewhat sketchy remarks with a more detailed exposition of the closure thesis.

## II

As previously noted, exclusion is the predominant form of closure in all stratified societies. Historically, the rise and consolidation of ruling groups has been effected through monopolistic control over valued resources such as land, esoteric knowledge, or arms by a limited circle of eligibles marked out by certain social characteristics. Aristocratic domination and reproduction via the lineage system is the obvious example from European history of this type of closure. Bourgeois forms of exclusion, by contrast, do not typically rest upon the restrictions of descent of similar group membership criteria for their effectiveness, but more upon what Weber somewhat misleadingly calls the 'rational commitment to values'. Thus among non-hereditary examples of closure Weber mentions the use of '. . . qualifying tests, a period of probation . . . election of new members by ballot . . . or [admission] by virtue of achievements open to anyone'.[8] That is to say, the process of class formation and social reproduction of the bourgeoisie is significantly different from that of preceding classes in that the conditions of membership are, in principle at least, attainable by all. Exclusionary rules and institutions must always be justified by universal criteria that are indifferent to the pretensions or stigmata of birth. There is thus a permanent tension within this class resulting from the need to legitimate itself by preserving openness of access, and the desire to reproduce itself socially by resort to closure on the basis of descent.

In modern capitalist society the two main exclusionary devices by which the bourgeoisie constructs and maintains itself as a class are, irst, those surrounding the institutions of property; and, second, academic or professional qualifications and credentials. Each represents a set of legal arrangements for restricting access to rewards and privileges: property ownership is a form of closure designed to prevent general access to the means of production and its fruits; credentialism is a form of closure designed to control and monitor entry to key positions in the division of labour. The two sets of beneficiaries of these state-enforced exclusionary practices may thus be thought of as the core components of the dominant class under modern capitalism. Before taking up the discussion of common class interests fostered by private property and credentials it may be useful to consider each of the two principal closure strategies separately.

It has already been remarked upon how the concept of property has been devalued in the modern sociology of class as a result of the heavy weighting accorded to the division of labour. This has not always been true of bourgeois sociology. Weber was in full accord with Marx in asserting that '"Property" and "lack of property" are . . . the basic characteristics of all class situations'.[9] The post-Weberian tendency to analyse social relations as if the propertyless condition had painlessly arrived is perhaps a natural extension of the use of 'western' or 'industrial' to denote societies formerly referred to as capitalist. The post-war impact of functionalist theory certainly contributed to this tendency, since the proclamation of belief in the ultimate victory of achievement values and the merit system of reward naturally cast doubt on the importance of property as an institution. The inheritance of wealth after all requires notably little expenditure of those talents and efforts that are said to be the only keys to the gates of fortune.

The extent to which property has come to be regarded as something of an embarrassing theoretical anomaly is hinted at in the fact that it receives only the most cursory acknowledgment in Davis and Moore's functionalist manifesto, and even then in the shape of an assertion that 'strictly legal and functionless ownership . . . is open to attack' as capitalism develops.[10] To propose that the imposition of death duties and estate taxes constitutes evidence for an assault upon property rights is somewhat like suggesting that the introduction of divorce laws is evidence of state support for the dissolution of the family. Property in this scheme of things can only be understood as a case of cultural lag – one of those quaint institutional remnants from an earlier epoch which survives by the grace of social inertia.

Several generations earlier Durkheim had reasoned along similar lines in declaring that property inheritance was 'bound up with archaic concepts and practices that have no part in our present day ethics'.[11] And although he felt it was not bound to disappear on this account he was willing to predict that inherited wealth would 'lose its importance more and more', and if it survived at all it would only be 'in a weakened form'.[12] Durkheim was not of course opposed to private property as such, only its transmission through the family. 'It is obvious that inheritance, by creating inequalities amongst men from birth, that are unrelated to merit or services, invalidates the whole contractual system at its very roots.'[13] Durkheim wanted society made safe for property by removing those legal practices that could not be squared with conceptions of liberal individualism and which therefore threatened to cause as much moral and social disturbance as the 'forced' division of labour.

There was not much likelihood of property itself declining as an institution because it was part of the order of things invested with a sacred character, understood in that special Durkheimian sense of an awesome relationship rooted deeply in the *conscience collective*. Although the sacred character of property arose originally from its communal status, the source of all things holy, the marked evolutionary trend towards the individualization of property would not be accompanied by any decline in its divinity. Personal rights to property were therefore seen by Durkheim as part of that general line of social development by which the individual emerges as a distinct and separate entity from the shadow of the group. The individual affirms himself as such by claiming exclusive rights to things over and above the rights of the collectivity. There is more than an echo here of Hegel's dictum that 'In his property a person exists for the first time as reason'.[14] As Plamenatz comments:

> 'It makes sense to argue, as Hegel does, that it is partly in the process of coming to own things, and to be recognised as their owners, that human beings learn to behave rationally and responsibly, to lead an ordered life. It is partly in the process of learning to distinguish mine from thine that a child comes to recognise itself as a person, as a bearer of rights and duties, as a member of a community with a place of its own inside it.'[15]

As Plamenatz goes on to say, however plausible as a defence of personal property this may be, as a defence of capitalist property relations it is 'lamentably inadequate'.[16]

The reason for this is that Hegel, like Durkheim, and many contemporary sociologists, never clearly distinguishes between property as rights to personal *possessions* and property as capital. Parsons is only one of many who reduces all forms of property to the status of a possession; this is understood as 'a right or a bundle of rights. In other words it is a set of expectations relative to social behaviour and attitudes.'[17] If property is simply a specific form of possession, or a certain bundle of rights, then everyone in society is a proprietor to some degree. On this reckoning there can be no clear social division between owners and non-owners, only a gradual, descending scale from those with very much to those with very little. This is well in line with Parsons' usual theoretical strategy of asserting the benign quality of any resource by reference to its widespread distribution. The possession of a toothbrush or an oilfield confers similar rights and obligations upon their owners, so that property laws cannot be interpreted as class laws. As Rose and his colleagues have suggested:

> 'the ideological significance of such a universalistic and disinterested legal interpretation of property in modern capitalist society is two-fold. First, as the law protects and recognises *all* private property, and as virtually all members of the society can claim title to *some* such property, it may be claimed that all members of society have some vested interest in the *status quo*. From such a perspective, therefore, it can be argued that, far from representing an irreconcilable conflict of interests, the distribution of property in modern capitalist society gives rise to a commensurability of interests, any differences being variations of degree rather than kind. The office developer, the shareholder, the factory-owner, the householder and even the second-hand car owner may thus be represented as sharing fundamentally common interests, if not identities.'[18]

What the sociological definition of property as possessions interestingly fails to ask is why only certain limited forms of possession are legally admissible. It is patently not the case, for example, that workers are permitted to claim legal possession of their jobs; nor can tenants claim rights of possession to their homes, nor welfare claimants enforceable rights to benefits. Possession in all these cases is pre-empted by the conflicting claims of employers, landlords, and the state respectively, which are accorded legal priority. Although the law may treat the rights of ownership in true universalistic fashion it is silent on the manner by which only some 'expectations' are successfully converted to the status of property rights and others not.

Even where property is understood in the narrower and politically more significant sense of ownership of the means of production, its importance for class analysis is not thereby affirmed. The reason for this is that the separation of ownership from the control of productive capital is felt to lead to its domestication, as it were, in the modern corporation. It is only when these two functions of ownership and control are fused, as in the case of landed property or the early capitalist enterprise, that property is believed to carry an explosive potential. The transition to the corporate firm apparently defuses capital not only by distributing it more widely but by placing it in the care of a managerial stratum that technically shares the same employee status as all other sellers of labour power. The social embodiments of capital thus merge indistinguishably into the category of labour, so transcending the old distinctions based on pure ownership. So much so that, in Parsons' view, we 'can clearly no longer speak of a "capitalistic" propertied class which has replaced the earlier "feudal" landed class'.[19] Parsons therefore recommends 'divorcing the concept of social class from its historic relation to both kinship and property as such'.[20]

However, it is Dahrendorf rather than Parsons who advances the most explicit and sustained case for making this divorce. By arguing that property is but one historically specific form of a more general phenomenon, authority, Dahrendorf is able to dampen any of those lingering hopes for the attainment of a classless society much in the way that Weber had earlier done, and on roughly similar grounds.[21] However, the effect of reconstituting property as authority is to wrench the analysis of class from its usual societal setting and to place it in a much narrower organizational one. Seen from this angle, a subordinate class exists within the confines of almost any bureaucratic locale, each one institutionally isolated from the rest. The appropriate class image would therefore seem to be 'a sack of potatoes' rather than anything suggestive of a social collectivity.

In Marx's schema, the propertyless are a class in the full sense in so far as the entire weight of the political and legal apparatus bears down upon them in whatever work situation or social setting they are found. In Dahrendorf's schema, the authority-less are a class only in a partial and limited sense in that they shed their subordinate status immediately upon leaving the physical location in which the rules of command and obedience operate. The moment an individual steps outside the 'imperatively co-ordinated association' he is at liberty to assume other roles, including those invested with their own authority. Authority relations do not penetrate into the very pores of society in the way that property relations do, because there are a multitude of social spaces that are not and cannot be colonized by formal organizations. Marx's proletariat has no hiding place because the effects of property cannot be confined within restricted social zones any more than the effects of the market can. It is as a result of this that class is universalized. Redefining property as authority relations *particularizes* class by presenting it as a function of organizational forms that are themselves too fragmented and diverse to yield a general condition of subordination.

The question never seriously posed by Dahrendorf is: for what *purpose* is authority exercised and occasionally challenged? The command structure of a business enterprise is geared directly to the pursuit of profit, and those who staff the key posts are in effect the guardians of capital; they are not concerned with the enforcement of obedience as an end in itself. Similarly, any challenge to managerial authority by organized labour is usually for the specific purpose of redistributing the share between capital and labour. It does not arise from a romantic belief in the psychic benefits of insubordination. In other words, the authority exercised in an organization could be said to derive its meaning from the ends to which the organization is dedicated; authority is not something that is properly understood independently of its uses. That Dahrendorf should select the industrial firm as the paradigm case of his model is decidedly odd, because it is the one locus above all others where authority relations are inseparable from property rights. When workers occupy their factory and lock out management, the offence for which they are liable to be arraigned is not disobedience, which is a mere offence against authority, but unlawful trespass, which is an offence against property.

The fact that class conflict between managers and managed is not always containable or resolvable within the walls of the organization throws doubt on the status of authority as the ultimate cause of conflict. When the chips are down and conflict assumes a less benign character from its routinized version, authority is seen not to reside in the 'incumbency of positions' within the organization; it is seen to reside in the state – an external body charged with the duty of protecting the rights of property and appropriation. Managerial command over labour therefore takes place within a legal framework in which the inviolability of property is already guaranteed. Authority and its exercise may, in other words, be thought of more as an activity that is licensed by the state than as something that creates its own legitimacy from the logic of organization.

The background reality of the state is perhaps far more easily overlooked when the issue is posed as the exercise of authority rather than as rights over property. Clearly no-one would imagine otherwise than that the state would be the principal guardian of property, not the proprietors themselves. The images of the policeman, the courthouse, and the prison cell are almost inseparable from the idea of property. But these images tend to recede when authority displaces property as the leading idea because it does so often appear that industrial and other bureaucracies are self-regulating. It is only on those dramatic occasions that organizations themselves cannot handle that the wholly derivative nature of managerial authority is revealed through the intervention of external powers dedicated to the enforcement of property rights.

The case for restoring the notion of property into the centre of class analysis is that it is the most important single form of social closure common to industrial societies. That is to say, rights of ownership can be understood not as a special case of authority so much as a specific form of exclusion. As Durkheim expresses it, 'the right of property is the right of a given individual to exclude other individual and collective entities from the usage of a given thing'.[22] Property is defined negatively by 'the exclusion it involves rather than the prerogatives it confers'.[23] Durkheim's reference to *individual* rights of exclusion clearly indicates that once again he has possessions in mind, and that, characteristically, he sees no important distinction between objects of personal ownership, and the control of resources resulting in the exercise of power.

It is clearly necessary to distinguish property as possessions from property as capital, since only the latter is germane to the analysis of class systems. Property as capital is, to paraphrase Macpherson, that which 'confers the right to deny men access to the means of life and labour'.[24] This exclusionary right can obviously be vested in a variety of institutional forms, including the capitalist firm, a nationalized industry, or a Soviet enterprise. All these are examples of property that confers legal powers upon a limited few to grant or deny general access to the means of production and the distribution of its fruits. Although personal possessions and capital both entail rights of exclusion, it is only the exclusionary rights embedded in the latter that have important consequences for the life-chances and social condition of the excluded. To speak of property in the context of class analysis is, then, to speak of capital only, and not possessions.

Once property is conceptualized as a form of exclusionary social closure there is no need to become entangled in semantic debates over whether or not workers in socialist states are 'really' exploited. The relevant question is not whether surplus extraction occurs, but whether the state confers rights upon a limited circle of eligibles to deny access to the 'means of life and labour' to the rest of the community. If such exclusionary powers are legally guaranteed and enforced, an exploitative relationship prevails as a matter of definition. It is not of overriding importance to know whether these exclusionary powers are exercised by the formal owners of property or by their appointed agents, since the social consequences of exclusion are not demonstrably different in the two cases. Carchedi and other neo-Marxists may therefore be quite correct in suggesting that 'the manager is capital personified'; but all that needs to be added is first, that this dictum holds good not only for monopoly capitalism, but for *all*, including socialism, systems in which access to property and its benefices is in the legal gift of a select few; and, second, that it

53

squares far more comfortably with the assumptions of bourgeois, or at least Weberian, sociology than with classical Marxist theory.

# III

Of equal importance to the exclusionary rights of property is that set of closure practices sometimes referred to as 'credentialism' – that is, the inflated use of educational certificates as a means of monitoring entry to key positions in the division of labour. Well before the onset of mass higher education, Weber had pointed to the growing use of credentials as a means of effecting exclusionary closure.

'The development of the diploma from universities, and business and engineering colleges, and the universal clamour for the creation of educational certificates in all fields make for the formation of a privileged stratum in bureaus and offices. Such certificates support their holders' claims for intermarriages with notable families . . . , claims to be admitted into the circles that adhere to "codes of honour", claims for a "respectable" remuneration rather than remuneration for work well done, claims for assured advancement and old-age insurance, and, above all, claims to monopolize social and economically advantageous positions. When we hear from all sides the demand for an introduction of regular curricula and special examinations, the reason behind it is, of course, not a suddenly awakened "thirst for education" but the desire for restricting the supply of these positions and their monopolization by the owners of educational certificates. Today the "examination" is the universal means of this monopolization, and therefore examinations irresistibly advance.'[25]

The use of credentials for closure purposes, in the manner elaborated by Weber, has accompanied the attempt by an ever-increasing number of white collar occupations to attain the status of professions. Professionalization itself may be understood as a strategy designed, amongst other things, to limit and control the supply of entrants to an occupation in order to safeguard or enhance its market value. Much of the literature on the professions has tended to stress their differences from workaday occupations, usually accepting the professions' own evaluation of their singularity in creating rigorous codes of technical competence and ethical standards. It is perfectly possible to accept that the monopolization of skills and services does enable the professions to exercise close control over the moral and technical standards of their members, whilst also endorsing Weber's judgment that 'normally this concern for efficient performance recedes behind the interest in limiting the supply of candidates for the benefices and honours of a given occupation'.[26]

It would seem to be the professions' anxiety to control the supply side of labour that accounts, in part at least, for the qualifications epidemic referred to by Dore as the 'diploma disease'.[27] This is the universal tendency among professions to raise the minimum standards of entry as increasing numbers of potential candidates attain the formerly scarce qualifications. The growing reliance upon credentials as a precondition of professional candidature is commonly justified by reference to the greater complexity of the tasks to be performed and the consequent need for more stringent tests of individual capacity. Yet Berg's careful analysis of these claims was able to turn up no evidence to show that variations in the level of formal education were matched by variations in the quality of work performance.[28] Nor was there anything to suggest that professional tasks were in fact becoming more complex such as to justify a more rigorous intellectual screening of potential entrants. Berg's conclusion, in line with Weber's, is that credentials are accorded their present importance largely because they simplify and legitimate the exclusionary process. It is on these grounds, among others, that Jencks suggests that 'the use of credentials or test scores to exclude "have not" groups from desirable jobs can be viewed in the same light as any other arbitrary form of discrimination'.[29]

Formal qualifications and certificates would appear to be a handy device for ensuring that those who possess 'cultural capital' are given the best opportunity to transmit the benefits of professional status to their own children. Credentials are usually supplied on the basis of tests designed to measure certain class-related qualities and attributes rather than those practical skills and aptitudes that may not so easily be passed on through the family line. It is illuminating in this respect to contrast the white-collar professions with the sporting and entertaining professions. What is especially remarkable about the latter is how relatively few of the children of successful footballers, boxers, baseball and tennis stars, or the celebrities of stage and screen have succeeded in reproducing their parents' elevated status. One reason for this would seem to be that the skills called for in these pursuits are of a kind that must be acquired and cultivated by the individual in the actual course of performance, and which are thus not easily transferred from parent to child. That is, there seems to be no equivalent to cultural capital that can be socially transmitted to the children of those

Marxism and class theory

gifted in the performing arts that could give them a head start in the fiercely competitive world of professional sport and show business. Presumably, if the rewards of professional sport could be more or less guaranteed along conventional career or bureaucratic lines serious proposals would eventually be put forward to limit entry to those candidates able to pass qualifying examinations in the theory of sporting science. This would have the desired effect of giving a competitive edge to those endowed with examination abilities over those merely excelling in the activity itself.[30]

The reason why professional sports, and the entertainment professions in general, are likely to be resistant to the 'diploma disease' offers a further instructive comment upon the nature of the white-collar professions. The supreme advantage of occupational closure based upon credentials is that all those in possession of a given qualification are deemed competent to provide the relevant skills and services for the rest of their professional lives. There is no question of retesting abilities at a later stage in the professional career. The professional bodies' careful insistence that members of the lay public are not competent to sit in judgement on professional standards effectively means that a final certificate is a meal ticket for life. In the sporting and entertainment professions, by contrast, the skills and abilities of the performers are kept under continuous open review by the public; those who consume the services are themselves the ultimate arbiters of an individual's competence and hence his market value, as expressed via their aggregate purchasing power. There can be no resort to the umbrella protection of a professional licence when sporting prowess and the ability to entertain are felt to be in decline in the eyes of those who pass collective judgement.

Against this exacting yardstick, then, credentialism stands out as a doubly effective device for protecting the learned professions from the hazards of the marketplace. Not merely does it serve the convenient purpose of monitoring and restricting the supply of labour, but also effectively masks all but the most extreme variations in the level of ability of professional members, thereby shielding the least competent from ruinous economic punishment. The small irony is that credentialist strategies aimed at neutralizing the competitive effects of the market confer most benefit upon that class that is most prone to trumpet the virtues of a free market economy and the sins of collectivism.

The use of systematic restrictions upon occupational entry has not of course been wholly confined to the white-collar professions. Certain skilled manual trades have adopted similar techniques designed to regulate supply, as in the case of the apprenticeship system or certain forms of the closed shop. Some unskilled occupations such as dock work and market-portering have also sought to restrict entry to the kinsmen of those already employed, though this does not normally guarantee control over the actual volume of labour supply. The crucial difference between these attempts at occupational exclusion by manual trades and those adopted by the professions is that the latter generally seek to establish a *legal monopoly* over the provision of services through licensure by the state. Whereas the learned professions have been remarkably successful in winning for themselves the status of what Weber calls 'legally privileged groups', it has been far less common for the manual trades to secure the blessing of the state for their exclusionary tactics. Indeed, the resort to 'restrictive practices' on the part of organized labour is commonly condemned as a breach of industrial morality that should be curbed rather than sanctified by law. Presumably the fact that governments have usually been reluctant to legislate formally against such practices is not unrelated to the awkwardness that might arise in drawing legal distinctions between these practices and the exclusionary devices of the professions, including the profession of law itself.

A further point of difference between professional closure and restrictive practices by trade unions is that the main purpose behind the latter activity has been the attempt to redress in some small part the disadvantages accruing to labour in its uneven contest with capital. Closure by skilled workers has been a strategy embarked upon in the course of struggle against a superior and highly organized opponent, and not primarily with the conscious intent of reducing the material opportunities of other members of the labour force. Credentialism, on the other hand, cannot be seen as a response to exploitation by powerful employers; the learned or free professions were never directly subordinate to an employing class during the period when they were effecting social closure. Their conflict, concealed beneath the rhetoric of professional ethics was, if anything, with the lay public. It was the struggle to establish a monopoly of certain forms of knowledge and practice and to win legal protection from lay interference. The aim was to ensure that the professional-client relationship was one in which the organized few confronted the disorganized many. Under modern conditions, where many professionals are indirectly in the service of the state and occasionally in conflict with the government of the day over pay and conditions, a somewhat better case could perhaps be made for likening the position of professions to that of craft unions, in so far as both could be said to employ closure for purposes of bargaining with a more powerful agency. But however acrimonious relations may become between professional bodies and the state, it is worth noting that the state rarely if ever threatens to take sanctions against professions in the way that would most seriously damage their interests – namely, by rescinding their legal monopoly.

On all these grounds it is necessary to regard credentialism as a form of exclusionary social closure comparable in its importance for class formation to the institution of property. Both entail the use of exclusionary rules that confer benefits and privileges on the few through denying access to the many, rules that are enshrined in law and upheld by the coercive authority of the state. It follows from this that the dominant class under modern capitalism can be thought of as comprising those who possess or control productive capital and those who possess a legal monopoly of professional services. These groups represent the core body of the dominant or exploiting class by virtue of their exclusionary powers which necessarily have the effect of creating a reciprocal class of social inferiors and subordinates.

One of the attractions of defining the principal beneficiaries of exclusion as constituent elements of a single dominant class is that the conceptual parallels are nicely matched at the empirical level. That is to say, those who monopolize productive property and credentials share for the most part a broadly similar political and ideological stance. Throughout all western societies parties of the right appear to be the natural political habitat of both these major groups; there is no demonstrable cleavage of interest or loyalty between propertied and professional status. Conservative parties, for example, rely upon the professional stratum of the bourgeoisie not merely for electoral support but for political leadership at all levels, including the very highest. Again, the social circles within which the elites of industry, commerce, and politics move freely are not notable for barriers set up between those of professional calling and those of wealth. Professional elites may often invest surplus income in property shares, while families of landed or commercial wealth often ensure that their children are expensively schooled in preparation for professional careers. However, this is not to say that the higher professions are part of the modern bourgeoisie *because* they may own shares. They would still qualify as members of this class if they dispersed all their income in riotous living. The manner in which income is spent is hardly a useful definition of class membership. Thus, it is misleading when seeking to define the dominant class to place exclusive emphasis upon the rights of property, as in one version of the Marxist tradition, or upon the power of the new technical and professional experts, of the 'post-capitalist' era, as suggested by Daniel Bell. The dominant or exclusionary class of modern capitalism is a fusion of both these elements.

In some respects perhaps it would be conceptually more economical to define these two key groups as part of the same exploiting class by reference to the single criterion of property ownership, provided that the concept was stretched to encompass both productive capital and cultural capital. Writers like Bourdieu and Berg do in fact suggest that the two forms of property are similar in their capacity for crystallizing class advantages over time:

> 'Educational credentials have become the new property in America. That nation, which has attempted to make the transmission of real and personal property difficult, has contrived to replace it with an inheritable set of values concerning degrees and diplomas which will most certainly reinforce the formidable class barriers that remain, even without the right within families to pass benefices from parents to their children.'[31]

From this standpoint, then, it would seem perfectly acceptable to retain the classical Marxist distinction between propertied and propertyless classes as the basic line of cleavage under modern capitalism. If it is theoretically permissible to expand the original definition of property to include control over, as well as ownership of, productive means, the way seems clear for a further extension of this flexible concept to include a purely cultural component. It is unlikely, however, that Marxists would welcome this additional tampering, given the exegetical difficulties already encountered in reconciling the notion of managerial control with the classical formula of pure ownership. Property even in the revised or neo-Marxist sense still refers to an institution rooted directly in the sphere of production, and thus remains amenable to analysis by reference to the conceptual storehouse of political economy. Cultural capital and credentialism, on the other hand, are notions that do not readily fit into the vocabulary of modes of production, other than as mere epiphenomena. Indeed, they have the suspicious appearance of concepts relating to the distributive system, with all that this implies in the way of Weberian contamination.

However this may be, a more valid objection to conflating the two senses of property is that attention would once again be diverted away from the fact that property defined even in this more inclusive sense still represents but one specific form of exclusionary closure among others. Alternative forms of closure to cultural or productive capital may be just as effective in bringing about class formation and political domination. Two obvious examples here would be the exclusionary powers exercised by the communist party apparatus in socialist states, and the legally supported exclusion of blacks by whites under the *apartheid* system. It would be stretching the concept beyond all recognition to suggest that communist party membership or a white skin should also be treated as forms of property by virtue of the special privileges they endow upon their 'owners'. Such terminological licence is in any case unnecessary, since the vocabulary of closure captures the essential similarity of these otherwise different phenomena quite adequately. It is therefore preferable to retain the conventional, narrower meaning of property as a form of exclusionary closure over productive resources, and to treat credentials, along with party membership, racial characteristics, lineage, etc., as quite separate and distinct bases of closure.

## IV

Closure strategies vary in important ways in the degree to which they serve as a means of class reproduction over time. That is to say, exclusionary practices that secure the position of a given class do not always guarantee the safe transmission of advantage to family descendants. Although it is wholly realistic to suppose that the well-placed in any social system will seek to ensure a similar fate for their children, it need not follow that the apparatus of closure is designed primarily to serve this end. Under some systems it would seem that the 'senior' generation attaches greater priority to the rules that guarantee its own well-being than to those designed to transfer privilege intact to its descendants. This at any rate would appear to be the message conveyed by the class arrangements of modern capitalist societies and, even more clearly, by socialist states. Social systems in which a dominant class is greatly exercised by the wish to ensure its own continuity through the generations are characterized by forms of closure based predominantly on criteria of descent and lineage. Where all avenues to property and power are closed to those lacking the appropriate pedigree, there is bound to be relatively little in the way of class dilution by the penetration of outsiders or by the demise of appointed heirs.

Bourgeois forms of closure, by contrast, are not obviously perfected to bring about this result, *pace* those analyses that find in the processes of social reproduction the central rationale of capitalist relations. In fact, neither property nor credentials are altogether reliable as institutions for preserving family privileges intact over several generations, especially by comparison with the stratagems employed in pre-bourgeois societies. Property in an expanding and commercially energetic society is too volatile to serve as a reliable safeguard against either class demotion of bourgeois offspring or the steady infiltration of parvenus. New families are continually appearing in the proper-tied ranks, flung up by the capitalist wheel of fortune, while established names sink without trace. One reason for this is that wealth and property under capitalism assume a multiplicity of forms, all liable to fluctuation and decline. Landed, industrial, commercial, and finance property each tend to have a different social foundation, so making it difficult for any group based upon one type of property to prevent the rise of new groups based upon a different type. This is a condition markedly different from agrarian society in which land is virtually the only form of productive wealth, thereby enabling the same families to monopolize power over long periods of time.

In bourgeois society it would seem that the ideological commitment to the rights of property is upheld not primarily with the aim of class reproduction but *despite* the class dilution that property can bring about. Thus, evidence presented by Marceau on the pattern of class formation in France indicates that only 28 per cent of the sons of the propertied stratum ('owners of industry and commerce') had succeeded in reproducing their fathers' status. Twenty per cent had become middle-ranking white-collar employees, while 35 per cent were industrial workers.[32] It is difficult to understand how any propertied class with a real sense of its collective destiny could permit such a haemorrhage in the space of only two generations.

Similar doubts arise about the translation of credentials into a form of cultural capital designed to crystallize the advantages of class. The continuous raising of academic hurdles and certification barriers as a means of controlling entry to the professions carries with it a strong element of risk that large numbers of children from professional families will not make the grade. The reliance upon written examinations does, as earlier argued, work in favour of those expensively schooled or otherwise socially advantaged, thereby reducing the hazards of competition quite considerably. Nevertheless, that troublesome factor known as intelligence can never quite be ruled out of the reckoning, especially that unknown quantum of it contributed by the throw of the genetic dice. Dense children of the professional middle class, despite heavy investments of cultural capital, will continue to stumble on the intellectual assault course set up largely for their *parents'* own protection. Conversely, large numbers of bright children of the culturally dispossessed will sail through to claim the prize of professional entry. Thus, although credentialism may have some advantages over property as a device for defending class frontiers, its efficiency in this direction is not all that it is cracked up to be by advocates of the reproduction thesis. The most recent figures for social mobility in Britain show that less than half the sons of the highest professional groups had managed to reproduce their fathers' status, even though the bulk of the remainder did attain some sort of white-collar position.[33] The French study already cited shows a very similar pattern of less than fully efficient self-recruitment. Moreover, penetration into the professional middle class from below also appears to be quite commonplace. In Britain, only about a quarter of the men in top professional and managerial posts have fathers drawn from the same category, fewer in fact than men of proletarian parentage.[34] Miller's conclusion, based on an earlier comparative study, that the transmission of elite statuses is only about 50 per cent successful, suggesting that the well-born 'have no firm perch in the upper tiers of society', is thus complemented by Goldthorpe and Llewellyn's observation that access to these tiers from below is a good deal less restricted than the class reproduction thesis allows.[35]

The fact that about a half of all sons of professional and managerial groups (more if these categories are generously defined) are eventually able to attain similar status themselves, is one that can be interpreted in different ways. Judged against the optimistic claims for equality and social fluidity in the open society these findings can be presented as a shocking reminder of the persistent influence of class inheritance. Examined, however, in the light of those claims concerning the self-reproductive aims and capacities of the bourgeoisie the evidence takes on a rather different meaning. In particular, it raises the crucial question of how dedicated the modern bourgeoisie actually is to its self-perpetuation through the blood line. A class committed to this end could naturally countenance an inward trickle of new blood and some loss of old blood without undue concern; but for it to have allowed the trickle to become a flow in both directions looks like sheer carelessness. Either we must accept that the bourgeois *conscience collective* is guilty of grievous errors and miscalculations in its reproductive designs, or we should acknowledge that self-reproduction has not been the overriding aim.

It has already been suggested that there is a definite tension between the commitment to closure by way of property and credentials on the part of one generation and the desire to pass on benefits to subsequent generations of kith and kin. It is not in the least necessary to deny that most members of the exclusionary class will strive to put their own advantages to the service of their children, while asserting at the same time that bourgeois forms of closure are not exactly tailor-made for self-recruiting purposes. In fact exclusionary institutions formed under capitalism do not seem to be designed first and foremost to solve the problem of class reproduction through the family line. The kinship link can only be preserved as a result of *adaptation* by the bourgeois family to the demands of institutions designed to serve a different purpose; it does not come about as a natural consequence of the closure rules themselves. In systems based on aristocratic, caste, or racial exclusion, families of the dominant group can expect to pass on their privileged status to their own descendants as a direct result of the closure rules in operation, however socially lethargic those families might be. The bourgeois family, by contrast, cannot rest comfortably on the assumption of automatic class succession; it must make definite social exertions of its own or face the very real prospect of generational decline. In other words, although the typical bourgeois family will certainly be better equipped than most to cope with the closure system on its children's behalf, it must still approach the task more in the manner of a challenge with serious risks attached than as a foregone conclusion. Even when it is successful it must face the prospect of sharing bourgeois status with uncomfortably large numbers of parvenus. What kind of system is this to provoke such anxieties in the breasts of those supposedly in command?

The answer must be that it is a system designed to promote a class formation biased more in the direction of sponsorship and careful selection of successors than of hereditary transmission. Although *both* aims might be held desirable, the first takes ideological precedence over the second, so that succession along kinship lines must be accomplished in conformity with the application of criteria that are ostensibly indifferent to the claims of blood. There is nothing especially bizarre about an arrangement whereby a dominant class relinquishes its children's patrimony in order to ensure that the calibre of its replacements is of the highest possible order. It would only appear strange to those unable to conceive that the attachment to doctrine could ever take precedence over the claims of kinship. As Orwell noted in his discussion of communist party oligarchies:

> 'The essence of oligarchical rule is not father-to-son inheritance, but the persistence of a certain world-view and a certain way of life, imposed by the dead upon the living. A ruling group is a ruling group so long as it can nominate its successors. The Party is not concerned with perpetuating its blood but with perpetuating itself.'[36]

There are also powerful forces in capitalist society that are more dedicated to the perpetuation of bourgeois values than bourgeois blood. Ideological commitment to the rights of property and the value of credentials may be just as fierce as any faith in Leninist party principles. Each represents a set of ideals that can be held quite irrespective of the consequences upon the family fortunes of their advocates. The party militant's belief in a system of political selection and exclusion that could tell against his own ideologically wayward children has its counterpart in the liberal's belief in the validity of meritocratic criteria that would find against his not too clever off-spring. It was perhaps examples of this kind that Weber had in mind when referring to patterns of closure distinguished by a 'rational commitment to values'. The same idea is also more than hinted at in Marx's well-known assertion that the bourgeoisie always puts the interests of the whole class above the interests of any of its individual members. These priorities are not, presumably, reversed whenever the individual members in question happen to be someone's children.

To suggest that predominant forms of closure under modern capitalism are in some tension with the common desire to transmit privileges to one's own is to point up politically significant differences of interpretation of bourgeois ideology. The classical liberal doctrine of individualism contains a powerful rejection of those principles and practices that evaluate men on the basis of group or collectivist criteria. The political driving force of individualist doctrines arose in part from the opposition of the emergent middle classes to aristocratic pretensions and exclusiveness centred around the notion of descent. The emphasis upon lineage was an obvious hindrance to those who had raised themselves into the ranks of property by way of industry and commerce, but who lacked the pedigree necessary to enter the charmed circles inhabited by those of political power and social honour. Although non-landed wealth could occasionally be cleansed through marriage into the nobility, the new rising class sought to make property respectable in its own right by divorcing it from its associations with particular status groups. Property in all its forms was to become the hallmark of moral worth without reference back, as it were, to the quality of proprietorial blood. In the individualist credo, property thus assumed the same characteristic as money in the marketplace, where the ability to pay overrides all questions as to the actual source of the buyer's cash.

The 'individuation' of property and the consequent assault upon the purely landed monopoly was accompanied by the bourgeoisie's attack upon the practices of patronage, nepotism, and purchase that governed aristocratic recruitment to the higher civil service, the universities, the officer corps, and the ancient professions. The gradual displacement of these practices by a greater reliance on formal qualifications shifted the balance of advantages away from the men of breeding to those who flourished in the peculiar atmosphere of the examination room. The doctrine that only individual attainment and personal merit could be the proper grounds for allocating honours and benefices was thus a handy moral argument for a class hemmed in by aristocratic tribalism.

While individualism might prove to be a serviceable doctrine in the struggle against an entrenched nobility it seems to run into difficulties once bourgeois ascendancy has been accomplished. It is all too apparent that liberal ideology, notwithstanding its historic opposition to lineage forms of closure, can yield social arrangements conducive to a pattern of class reproduction not wholly dissimilar to those resting openly and explicitly on the blood tie. The restriction upon political rights in force throughout most of the nineteenth century is one instructive example of the perverse uses of bourgeois ideology. Admission to the franchise was governed by the ostensibly individualist criteria of residential and property qualifications and not by the open presumption of class membership. Industrial workers able to meet the minimum registration requirements were admitted to the suffrage whilst men of bourgeois origin who could not were excluded. Political exclusion therefore appeared to be well in line with the liberal distaste for judging individuals by reference to collectivist criteria. Yet the justice of such an arrangement was clearly dependent on the tacit disregard for the inequalities of condition that ensured that only a predictable few would be in a position to meet the standards of political entry. The outcome would not have been dramatically different if workers *had* been excluded purely by virtue of their proletarian status. Individualist criteria could thus be employed to produce a form of closure similar to that brought about by the use of collectivist criteria.

This is similar in many ways to the uses of liberal ideology in the field of education, where individual merit and performance in examinations are held to be the only relevant criteria for selective entry. The maintenance of academic standards and the cultivation of excellence require that all factors other than the individual's measured ability be wholly discounted. Even though it might be shown that successful candidates under these arrangements came disproportionately from middle-class families, this would not damage the moral case for selection since it could plausibly be assumed that differences in intellectual capacity were in fact class-related. On this interpretation, working-class or black children would be excluded not because they were working class or black, but because of their genuinely lesser abilities as individuals. This is not simply analagous to the case of political exclusion but an extension of the same principle – namely, the use of ostensibly individualist criteria to produce a pattern of social closure that quietly discriminates via the collectivist criterion of class or racial membership.

It is not, then, difficult to show that bourgeois ideology despite its formal opposition to ascriptive norms is supportive of a class system having a greater degree of self-recruitment than seems consistent with the liberal doctrine of the open society. However, bourgeois ideology like any other is capable of harbouring more than one political interpretation. There is, in fact, another version which is perfectly hospitable to the idea that all forms of socially inherited advantage are unjust precisely because they pervert the true individualist ethic. This view is reflected in, among other things, the liberal view of property rights. Whereas the ownership and acquisition of wealth resulting from a person's own exertions are deemed fully defensible, the inheritance of wealth is not because it rewards those who have demonstrated no ability other than in their judicious choice of parents. Inheritance, moreover, sets up unfair obstacles and competition to those striving to make their own way into the ranks of ownership.

The objection to educational selection is made on similar grounds. Selection tests are felt to be morally acceptable only on the proviso that all children enter the competition for places on more or less equal terms. Since it is not possible to legislate away cultural advantages inherited through the bourgeois family, the practical alternative is to raise the aspirations and cultural level of the socially handicapped by the aid of interventionist programmes. Only by removing or offsetting class-related handicaps can the race be run according to the rules of fairness.

The essence of this version of liberal ideology is that social closure conforms to the standards of justice only in so far as it discriminates between individuals on the basis of their innate capacities and performances, and that these are not contaminated by the social inheritance of material or cultural goods. The full implementation of this doctrine would tend to produce a class system with a low degree of self-reproduction through time, so corresponding to Durkheim's vision of the ideal society in which 'social inequalities exactly express natural inequalities'.[37] It is the paradigm case of a society in which the dominant class in any period would be more dedicated to the defence of a particular conception of distributive justice than to its own immortality. The duty of the state would be to set up conditions to ensure that class succession went to the gifted and deserving, on the grounds that only this system of inequality has any prospect of capturing the affection of all the people, including the least rewarded. This moral programme opposes itself not only to all collectivist criteria of closure but also to the socialist alternative of the classless society with its implicit promise of doing away with closure in all its many guises. Liberalism finds nothing reprehensible in exclusionary closure *per se*, provided that it is grounded in a genuine and uncompromising individualism and not in the spurious version that masks the ignoble purpose of class reproduction.

## V

Strong elements of both these conflicting interpretations of bourgeois ideology co-exist in modern capitalist society. Consequently, patterns of exclusionary social closure do not conform to any pure type but are a combination of individualist and collectivist criteria. That is to say, although property and credentials are the chief means by which class privilege and domination are legally secured, and on the justice of which both strands of the ideology are in general agreement, the political implementation of exclusionary principles gives rise to the two variants just discussed. The fact that capitalist societies are capable of yielding evidence both for their openness and for their tendencies towards class reproduction is partly traceable to this tension at the very heart of bourgeois ideology.

It can in fact be suggested that exclusionary forms of closure in any social system display a certain 'mix' of collectivist and individualist criteria. In Soviet society, for example, the institution of *nomenklatura* is an exclusionary device that falls decidedly towards the individualist pole. *Nomenklatura* is the practice by which all candidates for elite positions are carefully vetted for their ideological purity and party record quite independently of their technical competence for office. It is a selection procedure that is designed to evaluate a person's political capacities and performances which by their very nature are hardly at all the product of inherited social advantage. In this respect, if no other, it is an arrangement that squares well with the ideal of liberal individualism.

Credentialist forms of closure in Soviet society, on the other hand, show a certain departure from this ideal. Entry to the academies of higher learning and to the top professions is still biased in favour of the children from the intelligentsia, indicating that workers' and peasants' children are still at some disadvantage in selective tests, whatever compensatory efforts may have been made by the state on their behalf. Here too, then, we find the covert use of collectivist criteria creeping in under the guise of a system supposedly designed to test the calibre of individuals irrespective of their social origins. This combination of party nomination through *nomenklatura* and the familiar resort to credentialism suggests that bourgeois society is not alone in setting up conditions making for both class reproduction and class renewal.

One reason for pressing the distinction between collectivist and individualist criteria underlying all forms of exclusion is to suggest that subordinate classes or strata are likely to differ in their political character according to which of the two sets of criteria is predominant. Looked at in ideal-typical terms, purely collectivist types of exclusion, such as those based on race, religion, ethnicity, and so on, would produce a subordinate group of a communal character – that is, one defined in terms of a total all-encompassing negative status. Blacks under *apartheid* or minority groups herded into religious and racial ghettoes are the familiar modern examples. The polar archetypal case would be that of exclusion based solely on individualist criteria, giving rise to a subordinate group marked by intense social fragmentation and inchoateness. The example here is furnished by the model of a pure meritocracy in which class is virtually replaced by a condition of discrete segmental statuses never quite reaching the point of coalescence. In non-fictional societies, of course, individualist and collectivist criteria are usually applied in some combination or other, so producing stratified systems located at various points between these two extremes. This can be depicted in simplified form as follows:

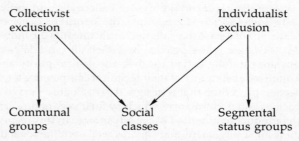

| Collectivist exclusion | | Individualist exclusion |

| Communal groups | Social classes | Segmental status groups |

Thus, of the three major types of subordination, classes are presented as a combination of both types of exclusionary criteria. Schematically, a subordinate class could be located towards either of the opposite poles according to the relative weighting of the two sets of criteria. The proletariat of early and mid-nineteenth century Europe, for example, would approximate to the communal pole by virtue of its wholesale exclusion from civil society arising from the treatment of its members as a *de facto* collectivity. The badge of proletarian status carried with it the kinds of stigmata commonly associated with subordinate racial and ethnic groups. It was a total condition which permitted little leeway for the cultivation of those small part-time identities that bring temporary release from the humilities of servile status. Correspondingly, of course, the proletarian condition under communal exclusion offered fertile ground for movements and ideologies which raised large questions about the nature of the political order and its legitimacy, and not merely about the fact of unequal shares.

It is the very hallmark of the communal condition that subordination is experienced through a myriad of direct personal degradations and affronts to human dignity, encouraged by the submersion of the individual into the stereotype of his 'membership' group. It is largely as a result of this that the politics of communal exclusion so frequently stresses the need for subordinate groups to create an alternative moral identity to that fashioned for them by their oppressors. Although the condition of the early proletariat was never completely of a communal kind, it was not so different from that of a despised ethnic group, if only because the visible signs and trappings of status were as unmistakably clear as racial features. Certainly the mixture of horror, fear, and revulsion felt by the upper classes for the great unwashed was not a far remove from the sentiments usually held by dominant racial or ethnic groups towards those whom they simultaneously exploit and despise.

To speak of a gradual shift in the nature of exclusionary rules, from collectivism to individualism, is thus to point to those tendencies making for the progressive erosion of the communal components of proletarian status, otherwise referred to as working-class incorporation into civil society. Although under advanced capitalism labour remains an exploited commodity, the status of the worker does not derive to anything like the same extent from his immersion in a total collective identity and its accompanying rituals of personal degradation. Mills' portrayal of the pattern of 'status cycles' by which the modern urban worker is able to find escape in class anonymity during leisure periods and vacations may be somewhat overdrawn;[38] but there is a real sense in which the absence of clearly visible and unambiguous marks of inferior status has made the enforcement of an all-pervasive deference system almost impossible to sustain outside the immediate work situation. It would now take an unusually sharp eye to detect the social class of Saturday morning shoppers in the High Street, whereas to any earlier generation it would have been the most elementary task. More to the point, even assuming that a lynx-eyed bourgeois could accurately spot a worker in mufti, what real hope could he now entertain of having any claim to deference actually honoured? A system of deference can only operate effectively when the status of strangers can accurately be judged, and the information required for this is difficult to come by without the aid of a collectivist stereotype. In this respect the personal dignity of the modern worker has been enhanced by the evolution towards individualist exclusion, even though his subordination to capital remains a central fact of life.

As class subordination becomes increasingly less communal in character, the political ideals and programmes that flourish among its members tend to become less inspired by visions of a new moral order and the promise of emancipation, and rather more preoccupied with the issues of distributive justice. Those who deplore the apparent flickering of those energies and passions that produced nineteenth-century socialism might care to reflect on the possibility that this has less to do with the iniquities of working-class leadership than with the system of modern exploitation, in which the engines of political resentment are not so lavishly fuelled by the personal degradations arising from wholesale collectivist exclusion.

# VI

It may be helpful to round off this part of the discussion with a few remarks to explain why the terms 'individualist' and 'collectivist' have been used to describe exclusionary criteria in preference to the more familiar terminology of 'achievement' and 'ascription'. One mild objection to the Parsonian usage is that ascription is normally used to denote status assessments made on the basis of certain social or physical attributes, such as age, race, or sex, that are deemed to be given, in so far as the individuals labelled by these criteria have not voluntarily opted for the status in question. The fact that exclusion on the basis of such ascriptive criteria is often felt to be morally wrong stems from precisely this notion that the individuals discriminated against are consigned to a negatively privileged status group 'through no fault of their own', as Parsons puts it.[39]

However, similar actions are frequently taken against individuals by virtue of their putative membership of status groups that are not simply the by-product of nature. Exclusionary rules directed at Trotskyists, homosexuals, kulaks, Jehovah's Witnesses, 'bourgeois remnants', hippies, and other assorted enemies of the people, all attest to the use of a negative group stereotype that owes little to the idea of involuntary membership. Moreover, it could be argued that even physical or 'natural' characteristics do not in fact impose specific statuses on their bearers because of the certain amount of leeway usually available for the management and presentation of such traits. In this respect, any hard and fast distinction between statuses that have been achieved from those that are ascribed seems to put a misplaced contrast upon the voluntaristic quality of the former and the naturally given quality of the latter. The important question, surely, is whether an individual is defined for exclusionary purposes as a member of some status group or collectivity, not whether the group in question is a natural or a social artefact.

The companion term 'achievement' is even less satisfactory in so far as it implies a mode of social selection based on 'non-discriminatory' criteria. For many sociologists it would seem that the shift from ascription to achievement values is tacitly understood as a mark of moral progress, heralding the arrival of the good society. But to refer to the reward system of modern capitalism as one stressing the virtues of individual achievement shows an alarming confusion of thought, by suggesting as it does that a fairly close relationship exists between the level of personal effort and the level of reward. Clearly, a girl from the black ghetto who succeeds via high school and college in becoming a junior school teacher will have demonstrated far more in the way of individual achievement and effort than, say, the son of a doctor who enters the medical profession. Yet every 'achieving society' will lavish more benefits and honours on the latter than on the former. It is not achievement as such that is honoured but the possession of certificates, quite irrespective of the amount of personal effort invested in their getting. On these grounds alone the term is highly suspect. But more importantly, perhaps, it is unsatisfactory because of the heavy moral overtones it carries of a mode of exclusion that is socially just and acceptable, unlike the discrimination supported by ascriptive criteria. The argument put forward in these pages, however, is that all forms of exclusion are exploitative, by *whatever* criteria they are justified. To speak of a shift in the nature of exclusionary rules along the collectivist-individualist axis is thus simply to denote a change in the basis of exploitation. The twin notions of ascription and achievement are now so firmly embedded in a style of moral discourse to which the concept of exploitation is completely foreign that they cannot usefully be harnessed to the service of class analysis.

## Notes

1 Weber (eds Roth and Wittich) 1968:342.
2 Weber (eds Roth and Wittich) 1968:342.
3 Weber (eds Roth and Wittich) 1968:342.
4 Neuwirth 1969.
5 These arguments were first tentatively sketched out in my 'Strategies of Social Closure in Class Formation' (Parkin 1974). In that publication the two types of closure were referred to as *exclusion* and *solidarism*. This latter term does not, however, satisfactorily describe a mode of collective action

standing in direct opposition to exclusion, since solidaristic behaviour can itself be used for blatantly exclusionary ends. That is to say, solidarism does not properly refer to the purposes for which power is employed. The term *usurpation* more adequately captures the notion of collective action designed to improve the lot of a subordinate group at the expense of a dominant group. Solidarism is simply one means among others to this end. These distinctions are elaborated upon in Chapter Six.

6  Wolpe 1975:240.
7  Cited in Wolpe 1975:240.
8  Weber (ed. Parsons) 1964:141.
9  Weber (eds Gerth and Mills) 1948:182.
10  Davis and Moore 1945:247.
11  Durkheim 1957:174.
12  Durkheim 1957:175 and 217.
13  Durkheim 1957:213.
14  Plamenatz 1975:120.
15  Plamenatz 1975:121.
16  Plamenatz 1975:121.
17  Parsons 1951:119. The entry in the index under 'Property' invites the reader to 'see Possessions'.
18  Rose *et al.* 1976:703.
19  Parsons 1970:24.
20  Parsons 1970:24.
21  Dahrendorf 1959.
22  Durkheim 1957:142.
23  Durkheim 1957:142.
24  Macpherson 1973.
25  Weber (eds Gerth and Mills) 1948:241–42.
26  Weber (eds Roth and Wittich) 1968:344.
27  Dore 1976.
28  Berg 1973.
29  Jencks 1972:192.
30  It transpires that the idea is not so far-fetched after all. The Council for National Academic Awards has recently approved the syllabus for a BA Degree in Sports Studies. Undergraduates will be instructed in 'the variables influencing performance in sport; a science and its sports application; scientific methods, statistics and computing; and wide practical experience in a number of sports.' *Daily Telegraph*, Monday, 28 August 1978, p. 3.
31  Berg 1973:183.
32  Marceau 1974:222, *Table 8*.
33  Goldthorpe and Llewellyn 1977:267, *Table 2*. Many of those downwardly mobile from the top professional stratum do of course succeed in re-entering it at a later stage. Nevertheless, as the authors point out, where this type of 'counter-mobility depends, as it often must, on acquiring a professional qualification or on securing successive promotions within a bureaucratic hierarchy, it is obviously of a far more contingent nature' than status transmission via property inheritance (p. 273). For any one family line, moreover, attrition is likely to be cumulative if in each generation downward mobility takes its usually steady toll.
34  Goldthorpe and Llewellyn 1977:262, *Table 1*.
35  Miller 1960:50; Goldthorpe and Llewellyn 1977:263. These authors suggest that the extent of penetration from below into the professional middle class

invalidates the 'closure thesis'. It is clear from their text that they are using this term to mean 'class reproduction'.

36 Orwell 1949:215.
37 Durkheim 1964a:377.
38 Mills 1956:257–58.
39 Parsons 1969:260.

# 5
# Social closure
# as usurpation

Usurpation is that type of social closure mounted by a group in response to its outsider status and the collective experiences of exclusion. What usurpationary actions have in common is the aim of biting into the resources and benefits accruing to dominant groups in society – a range of possibilities extending from marginal redistribution to complete expropriation. But whatever the intended scale of usurpation it is a form of action that generally draws upon alternative standards of distributive justice to those solemnized by the rules of exclusion. Typical examples would thus include the routine struggles between organized labour and capital, as well as those more ambitious political programmes dedicated to the complete dissolution of this very distinction; it embraces the collective efforts of subordinate ethnic and racial groups to attain civic and social rights, and to similar attempts by women's organizations to achieve full equality with men. What is entailed in all such cases is the mobilization of power by one group or collectivity against another that stands in a relationship of dominance to it. Metaphorically speaking, usurpation is thus the use of power in an upward direction.

One of the important differences between usurpationary closure and exclusionary closure is that the former tends to rely heavily upon the public mobilization of members and supporters, as in the use of strikes, demonstrations, sit-ins, marches, picketing, symbolic vigils, and the like. As a result, usurpationary activities normally stand in an uncomfortable relationship to the legal order. The borderline between lawful and unlawful usurpationary acts is often rather finely drawn, and tends moreover continuously to be redrawn over time, as the chequered history of the right to strike and to 'peaceful picketing' well illustrates. Part of the reason for this is that the type of collective behaviour usually associated with usurpationary closure is difficult to sustain over long periods without the use or threat of sanctions against recalcitrants, which may often infringe upon the state's claim to the legal monopoly of physical coercion.

In addition, the more effective usurpation proves to be, the more serious becomes the challenge to the formal system of distributive justice expressed in the legal endorsement of exclusionary rules and institutions. If the fruits that should rightfully fall to the owners of property and credentials are plucked too freely by those who have neither, but who have some alternative means of access, as it were, then clearly the whole purpose of closure through proprietorship and certification is thrown into question. Hence there can never really be the same degree of legal and institutional backing for usurpationary activities as for exclusionary ones. The effect of such an arrangement would be to confer equal legitimacy upon two contradictory systems of distributive justice. Collective industrial action on the part of organized labour, for example, is frequently anathematized as a form of blackmail, a moral judgement designed to reaffirm the propriety of exclusionary closure over the claims and methods of usurpationary closure.

This immediately raises the question of the limits that are likely to be imposed on usurpationary efforts that fall short of the demand for a total transformation of the social order. Seen specifically in the context of the struggle between capital and labour, the issue is one concerning the extent to which closure on the part of workers can effectively counteract the exclusionary powers of property. One traditional position, endorsed by various liberal economists and Marxists alike, is that there are definite fixed if unspecifiable limits to the share accruing to labour in relation to capital, and that this proportion remains more or less constant over time.[1] The implication would seem to be that organized labour should accept the iron logic of market forces and recognize that strike activity to increase real wages is nothing other than a sort of industrial rain dance; or, alternatively, that labour should endorse the analysis and take the next obvious step of exchanging the commitment to trade union bargaining for the higher political goal of capitalist expropriation.

The conventional view regarding labour's constant share has been challenged recently by Marxist economists seeking to demonstrate, for Britain at least, that militant union action could result in a 'profits squeeze' and a corresponding enlargement of labour's share.[2] This analysis would appear to square quite well with the anxieties and criticisms of trade union power voiced from a different political quarter throughout the past decade. In this interpretation, organized labour and its leaders have become the fifth estate of the realm, an ascendant power in society equivalent to, or greater than, elected government and its agencies. The issue is most sensitively felt in matters pertaining to income distribution, and in particular the use of industrial leverage in support of 'excessive' wage claims. Usurpationary demands of this kind are felt to raise in an especially acute form the Durkheimian problem of how to impose moral constraints upon appetite when no other constraints are available. As Finer puts it: 'Let us stop wondering why this or that group of industrial workers has pitched its demands so high, and ask ourselves instead why it has set any limits on them at all.'[13] The question of voluntary limitation upon the use of power arises only because of the peculiar nature of the power at workers' disposal:

> 'The power of organised labour does not rest in its possession of the means of coercion . . . Nor does it consist in numerical superiority . . . Nor, for that matter, does it inhere in organised labour as a whole, but in certain small specialised groups within it. The power resides not in acts of commission but in acts of omission: in the ability of these special groups to withhold certain services which are, today, critical to the survival of society.'[4]

From the point of view of those who enjoy rewards on the basis of property and credentials, usurpation based upon the threat of sanctions is clearly illegitimate because it does not conform to any accepted principle of distributive justice. Market rules of allocation are held to be self-regulating in so far as the laws of supply and demand limit the levels of reward accruing to any group; coercive power by contrast is held in check by nothing other than the size of the victim's purse.[5]

Seen, however, from the angle of those who raise these usurpationary claims, a certain theory of distributive justice may well be implied along the lines of functional importance. This is not of course the functional importance claimed on behalf of those who carry the awesome burdens of managerial and professional responsibility. A different measure of this elusive quality would be the extent of economic and social dislocation caused by any group following the withdrawal of its labour. Those occupations that caused great disorganization by suspending their activities could, by this token, be said to be of especial functional importance to the community and should be rewarded accordingly; while those whose absence would scarcely cause a ripple on the surface of social life would be deemed to be of least functional importance and should have a correspondingly weak claim on the common purse.

It is not of course suggested that such a theory is consciously articulated by powerful industrial groups. But it could perhaps be thought of as a subterranean theory of distributive justice which provides tacit moral justification for organized labour's attempts at usurpation, and a coherent alternative to the principles supporting exclusionary closure. However this may be, it seems probable that official displeasure at what Professor Hutt calls the 'strike threat system' of allocation becomes especially pronounced when its effectiveness threatens to disturb the balance of power between classes, such that the subordinate groups appear to be making gains at the expense of the dominant.[6] Presumably incomes policies, whether statutory or otherwise, only become a major political preoccupation of governments when the usurpationary powers of organized labour have increased beyond the point that is fully consistent with working-class subordination; that is to say, at the point at which the 'fifth estate of the realm' suddenly appears to be claiming its patrimony.

A logically prior question to this is: what accounts for the apparent increase in labour's usurpationary power in the recent post-war period? Since the sanction of strike action is almost as old as the labour movement itself, other factors must explain its seemingly greater effectiveness. In some respects, the problem could be framed in normative terms by suggesting that what has occurred is the erosion of conventional standards of distributive justice that have, in the past, served to inhibit the full use of power by industrial workers. The present wages 'free-for-all' would then be understood as a manifestation of the collapse of deferential values and the cramped expectations engendered by them. No longer trapped in their own narrow horizons, workers would be morally released to activate that dormant power that has *always* been at their disposal.[7]

The persuasiveness of this argument depends not only on an almost Parsonian faith in the binding force of normative constraints, but also on the prior assumption that no significant change has actually occurred in the instrumental power of organized workers. If, however, we make the opposite assumption, that the industrial leverage available to labour is indeed greater now than at any previous period, then the very recognition of this fact by workers would quite adequately account for their change in conduct. On this reckoning, workers' apparent deference to the official version of distributive justice in earlier times would be explained not as a product of normative housetraining, but as a response to a condition of comparative powerlessness. Whether or not any significant increase in labour's usurpationary power has in fact occurred is a question that cannot be answered with anything approaching complete assurance, because of the obvious dearth of that kind of evidence that puts sociological minds to rest. There are, however, certain circumstantial arguments and observations that would lend support to the view that workers' bargaining position has improved over the long term. Chief among these is the argument to the effect that the greater the capital-intensive nature of production, the more damaging the consequences of industrial action, and hence the greater readiness by management to settle on labour's terms, even without the latter's resort to strike action. The long-term trend towards capital-intensive production processes thus enhances labour's bargaining capacity. Second, the more the economy is geared to international markets and foreign competition, the more punishing are the effects of labour stoppages on any firm with tight delivery deadlines. Finally, to the extent that an advanced capitalist system produces an ever more complex and inter-locking division of labour, the greater the disruptive potential endowed upon various key groups at the very heart of the productive system.

On all these different counts, then, the development of capitalism would seem to have enhanced the bargaining power of large sectors of the organized labour movement in the post-war period – a shift in the balance of power that has *preceded* the disturbances to traditional expectations and the conventions of status. These disturbances are most probably initiated by the action of those groups whose disruptive potential is of a high order; the success of their usurpationary claims then serves to provide inspirational example to other groups whose own leverage is considerably weaker. It is as though once capital is shown to be vulnerable at certain tender points, labour as a whole becomes more confident of its usurpationary potential.

Thus, what used to be thought of as a free bargaining relationship between capital and labour, when labour was relatively weak, has now been redefined by one academic authority as the 'crude exercise of power bargaining based upon the capricious ability to inflict damage on industry and the community'.[8]

'Under conditions of advanced technology involving high capital-labour ratios, low levels of intermediate stocks, and ever more closely integrated production and distributive processes, the balance of bargaining power has tipped in favour of groups who are prepared to exploit this critical strategic situation.'[9]

Hence the need to pose the rhetorical question: 'Can society stand the strain of the extension of uninhibited collective bargaining?'[10] To rephrase the question somewhat, it is not so much a matter of whether that convenient abstraction called 'society' can stand the strain, but of whether the exclusionary class can. Undoubtedly this class has felt itself to be under quite considerable and unaccustomed strain in recent times. Certain trends in income distribution, for example, would suggest that organized labour has been rather more successful in combatting the effects of inflation on real wages than have many managerial and professional groups.

*Figure 1*

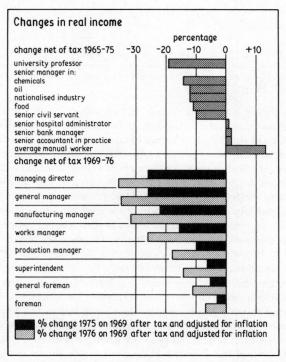

Source: G. D. Newbould and J. R. Sparkes, 'Managers' Pay', *New Society* 17 February 1977, p. 337.

As *Figure 1* indicates, between 1965 and 1975 the real income of various professional employees declined quite substantially (between 8 per cent and 19 per cent) compared with an increase of 13 per cent in the real wages of the average manual worker. The same general trend is revealed in the figures presented by the Royal Commission on the Distribution of Income and Wealth, in which the pre-tax earnings of manual workers are compared with those of middle and higher management over the period 1970 to 1975.

This would certainly seem to suggest that the changing usurpation-

Marxism *and class theory*

Table 1 *Trends in pre-tax incomes (males) 1970–75 at constant 1970 prices (1970 =
100)*

|      | Median earnings Manual men | Median earnings Non-manual men | Middle Management | Higher Management |
|------|------|------|------|------|
| 1970 | 100 | 100 | 100 | 100 |
| 1973 | 113 | 107 | 101 | 89 |
| 1974 | 112 | 106 | 95 | 82 |
| 1975 | 117 | 111 | 96 | 83 |

From *Royal Commission on the Distribution of Income and Wealth*, Report No.3
(1976), *Table 25*, p. 55

ary capacity of organized labour is not wholly a figment of the
middle-class imagination. Indeed, it is difficult to see what more
useful index of shifts in the balance of class power there could be than
a measure of changes in the outcome of distributive struggle. Needless to say, small shifts in the balance of power are not necessarily an
indication of a progressive trend culminating in the dominion of
labour. It is altogether possible that the present tendency could be
reversed and labour's gains gradually wiped out. In a society still
largely dominated by the exclusionary institutions of property and
credentials it would be paradoxical in the extreme if the relative shares
accruing to this quarter were permitted to decline too sharply as a
result of successful closure from below.

In addition, of course, any shifts that have occurred in the overall
balance of class forces would not affect all sectors of organized labour
to the same degree. The long-term developments in the productive
system already mentioned confer greater bargaining strength on
some groups than others, so possibly giving rise to new sources of
inequality within the working class comparable to those that have
traditionally existed between skilled and unskilled workers. It is
rather surprising that the co-existence of two quite separate sources of
inequality among wage labourers has not been fully acknowledged,
even in class analyses rooted in the Weberian tradition. This could
well be because the concept of 'market situation' is felt to be sufficiently encompassing to include all possible conditions and types of
bargaining capacity associated with the division of labour. Yet, if only
on grounds of conceptual clarity, a distinction should be made between the ability to command resources on the basis of skill and
market scarcity, and the ability to command resources on the basis of
'disruptive potential'. Since the two sources of industrial leverage
vary independently, any given group's total bargaining capacity

should be determined by its rating on both these counts. It is equally important to maintain this distinction because of the difference in the degree of legitimacy that each can claim. Demands raised by virtue of skill are fully compatible with market principles of reward and are therefore unlikely to meet with as much moral obloquy from the dominant or exclusionary class as demands based upon disruptive potential. The existence of two quite different sources of power is, by this same token, liable to exacerbate those ever-present tensions within the organized labour movement over the vexed question of the maintenance of traditional differentials.[11]

This is one way of highlighting the fact that closure attempts on the part of labour are always hampered by competitive struggles over distribution within the ranks of the working class. Attempts at usurpation of a purely class nature are especially difficult to sustain on the industrial front because of the tendency towards fragmentation along occupational lines. Industrial forms of closure, moreover, are designed to combat the *effects* of exclusion and are rarely aimed at dismantling the institutional apparatus of exclusion itself. On this score the activities of organized labour have remained faithful to Lenin's account of them as incorrigibly economistic. However, to the extent that the ancient Marxist belief in the potential power of labour now perhaps *for the first time* has a ring of plausibility, any renunciation of the use of this power for expressly political and not merely economic ends does raise anew the entire question of workers' 'loyalty to the system'. Marxism has tended to muddy this issue by assuming that the proletariat was endowed with massive usurpationary powers more or less from its inception, so that the 'problem' always to be accounted for was why workers failed to actualize it for their own political ends. This paved the way for a succession of Marxist theorists, from Lukacs and Gramsci to the Althusserian and Frankfurt schools, offering a diagnosis implying in the most oblique and scholarly manner that the proletariat was suffering from a kind of collective brain damage.

But if the usurpationary capacity of the working class is judged in terms of its decisive position in the productive process (and not on its ability to supply cannon fodder in an insurrectionary romance) then a good case can be made for saying that its actual potential for bringing the system to a permanent halt was never all that great before the era of highly advanced capitalism. It is only now that the question of voluntary restraints upon the use of power for political ends becomes of genuine interest and importance. That is to say, it is only within the context of contemporary capitalism that labour's willingness or otherwise to give moral endorsement to the social system is in the least problematic, because political acquiescence is less easily accounted for as a response by labour to its collective weakness in the face of organized capital. When labour can seriously challenge capital without reliance upon the superhuman personal qualities of workers, then the latter's sufferance of capitalism *is* explicable only by reference to a set of beliefs about this system and its possible alternatives.[12] And in this respect the role of labour's leadership is likely to be of some significance. If Finer is only even partly right in suggesting that 'the critical limit upon union power lies in *sentiments*', the part played by those charged with the responsibility for articulating such sentiments is bound to be an increasingly fateful one.[13]

In the light of all this, it is not altogether surprising that the leaders in question have been subject to that special kind of flattery at which the state excels when seeking allies among its potential adversaries. The fact that so many contemporary commentators have managed to detect signs of a 'corporatist' solution to social unrest is attributable above all to government's reliance upon trade union officialdom in spreading the doctrine of self-denial among those whose active goodwill capitalism for the first time requires in abundance.

# II

The integrative burdens shouldered by trade union and labour organizations become especially onerous when the ability of the system to honour its tacit commitments is thrown into open question. Capitalism more than any other social order derives its legitimacy from its capacity to fulfil the promise of abundance for all. The prospect of uninterrupted improvements in the material quality of life makes for the conditional acceptance of those political and economic arrangements that seek to give inequality a good name. Provided the least advantaged class is conscious of its own gradual betterment, and remains optimistic about the prospects for further modest advancement, there is no great need for elaborate exercises in moral persuasion. The Durkheimian assumption that contractual relations alone cannot guarantee social order, but require supplementation by some form of secular faith, is one that finds little support in the example of successful capitalism. The stability of this system should not really be read as a success story in the art of moral persuasion, whether the storyteller is Parsons or Gramsci. Stability has been more a function of continuous economic growth that has enabled minimum expectations to be satisfied and the potentially explosive issue of redistribution to be defused. That is to say, the always contentious matter of the size of relative shares accruing to different classes becomes muted when the absolute size of that slice of the national cake going to the subordinate class is always slowly increasing, even though the increase may be disproportionately less than that going to the dominant class. Modern capitalism has banked heavily upon its capacity to sustain economic growth as the most effective way of forestalling usurpationary claims. Through continuous growth, the struggle over distribution can usually be confined to the marginal, incremental increase in the national product, rather than directly affecting the total system of allocation. Capitalism's conviction of its ability to maintain this performance indefinitely would seem to be well illustrated by the leading role accorded to commercial activities like advertising and promotion, expressly designed to realize the Durkheimian nightmare of appetite creation. To impose moral constraints upon material expectations, far from being necessary to the stability of the system, would threaten to stall one of its most powerful engines.

The awkward moment arrives when increased appetites must be satisfied from a cake that, for whatever reason, has failed to get bigger. At this point, expectations can only be met by the net transfer of resources from one group to another. Usurpationary claims by the working class are inevitably contested by the prospective losers, so that the entire apparatus of distribution then becomes the centre of political attention. It is at this belated stage that moral appeals take on a sudden urgency as organized labour is called upon to elevate the interests of society above those of class. It now becomes necessary to try to convince workers to adopt a *comparative* class perspective by recognizing that the decline in their own position is matched by that of the dominant class. Fairness entails that sacrifices should be borne by all, which means abandoning the commitment to the maintenance of absolute standards. Thus, whereas expansive capitalism has nothing to gain by encouraging the open comparison between class and class, stagnant capitalism has everything to lose by failing to encourage it. If workers insist on preserving or increasing their absolute share even when the cake is shrinking, the fate of the privileged minority begins to look precarious. Because workers are not usually moved politically to contest the relative advantages of the bourgeoisie, so long as their own position is felt to be improving, it should come as no surprise that a sudden worsening in the bourgeois condition would not usually be regarded by these same workers as grounds for accepting a corresponding diminution in their own share. In other words, the absence of a comparative class perspective, which has been the despair of radicals and a stabilizing force in a period of growth, actively fuels usurpationary demand and gives them a sharper political edge in a period of economic stagnation.

The really serious problem faced by declining capitalism is that usurpationary demands cannot be met by the transfer of resources from the exclusionary minority on a continuous basis, since the gains would be spread too thinly among the majority. The net result is that stagnant capitalism is an unusual form of social system that gives rise to serious resentment and discontent among *both* the major classes. This is its distinctive and politically unsettling feature. In previous periods of crisis, as in the inter-war years, the working class shouldered virtually the entire burden through mass unemployment and depressed wages; the condition of the middle class improved if anything as a result of low prices for goods and services. The fact that in the modern version of the crisis the bourgeoisie has been directly exposed to its punishing effects is in itself some indication of the relative shift in the balance of power between the classes.

This is not to suggest that the costs of economic stagnation are evenly borne by the two classes; a relative decline from a high plateau still leaves room for social manoeuvre and adjustment not available to those already near or at the bottom. The important point is that when both classes experience relative deprivation this does not appear to produce any sense of cameraderie or a temporary cease-fire in the class war, so much as an intensification of the struggle. In the 1930s the bourgeoisie, largely unaffected by the crisis, could express heartfelt sympathy for the plight of the unemployed and the hunger marchers. In the 1970s, directly affected themselves, the prevailing bourgeois sentiment is one of antipathy, since the organized working class and its leaders are now singled out as the main cause of the crisis. The outcome is a heightened form of class conflict in which a relatively more powerful proletariat confronts a middle class *enragé*. The resolution of this conflict can obviously take a variety of political forms, though the odds in favour of a purely Durkheimian solution would seem to be the slimmest of all.

# III

Usurpationary forms of social closure occur, of course, in contexts other than those of a purely class kind. The collective efforts of women or racial and ethnic groups to seek either full inclusion into civil society, or some degree of secession from the existing nation state, are generically similar to the countervailing actions of a subordinate class. Although the nature of these claims may differ in important respects, the attempt to mobilize power against a legally defined and state-supported dominant group is the crucial point of similarity. Differences in political aims are always secondary to the overriding fact of the directional use of power.

One of the important contrasts between usurpationary closure on the part of an exploited class, and similar action by other exploited social groups, is that a class has at its disposal a set of potentially injurious sanctions with which to back up its claims. Ethnic minorities or women, on the other hand, do not typically occupy strategic positions in the division of labour that would endow them with the ability to bring things to a halt. Their members are usually dispersed throughout the labour market, so that any concerted withdrawal would not be especially disruptive. Typically, in any case, they tend to occupy the low-paid jobs spurned by workers in the dominant ethnic or sex group which, almost in the nature of the case, are positions weak in industrial leverage. Moreover, of course, when unemployment rates are high they are to be found disproportionately among the members of the dole queue, that least commanding of all bargaining positions.

In the absence of any industrially based sanctions these exploited groups are forced to rely far more heavily upon collective mobilization of a purely social and expressive kind in order to press their claims. That is to say, when a group has little or no capacity to disturb the operation of the system at its vulnerable points, it is thrown back on a strategy that depends for its effectiveness upon the activation of political energies and moral sentiments. One common, if slightly paradoxical, form this takes is the attempt to manipulate the belief system of the dominant group by pointing up the inconsistencies between its advertised doctrines and its actual conduct. Civil rights movements and feminist groups have tended to lay considerable store on the vulnerability of key sections of the exclusionary group to moral appeals that articulate the high ideals of the formal ideology – in particular those centred around the flexible notion of equality. In this manner even those who have no resort to instrumental sanctions are sometimes able to mobilize proxy power, as it were, by gaining the support of influential sectors of the dominant group. Legislation aimed at removing certain types of exclusion against blacks or women, for example, appears to have resulted more from the exercise of moral persuasion over powerful members of the white and male populations, respectively, than from the ability to back usurpationary demands with punitive sanctions. Naturally the success of this strategy depends upon there being a stratum within the exploiting group that is sufficiently committed to the high ideals of equality and allied values to react politically against their blatant infringement. In bourgeois society, at least, it would seem that the phenomenon of 'white liberalism' has its analogue in all situations of collectivist exclusion, whatever their bases, so that usurpationary claims grounded in moral appeals are not wholly without effect.[14] Bourgeois society is perhaps more vulnerable than most to this type of moral pressure from below because of the radical, or at least reformative, potential of liberal ideology. As Marx recognized, this ideology is a versatile weapon that can be directed with good effect against its manufacturers.[15]

It should nevertheless be recognized that inconsistencies between conduct and proclaimed values, be they ever so glaring, do not of themselves generate remedial political action by the high-minded. It is still necessary for the subordinate and exploited groups themselves to achieve their own social closure by forging a common political identity and some measure of collective consciousness before they are in a position to exert moral leverage. In the absence of any such initial concerted action it seems unlikely that even modest usurpationary gains would be forthcoming. Indeed, even when some degree of closure has been accomplished, and the moral claims duly launched and accepted, the promised transfer of resources is not usually of avalanche proportions. This is not simply due to the fact that usurpation resting solely upon the manipulation of moral sentiments is less effective than claims backed up by the threat of sanctions, but also because any major redistribution is likely to be opposed by those groups that will be more adversely affected by it than the liberal bourgeoisie. Workers, in particular, may take a less benign view of redistributive measures that assuage the liberal conscience but which reduce the workers' own share of resources. This theme is developed in the following chapter as part of a more general discussion of exclusionary practices arising within that social class that is itself the historical product of exclusionary closure.

## Notes

1 Blackburn 1965:142–45.
2 Glyn and Sutcliffe 1972.
3 Finer 1975:329.
4 Finer 1975:329.
5 According to Professor C. K. Rowley, the relationship between capital and

labour is now 'most effectively defined as extortion' on the part of organized labour. 'The term "extortion" refers to such an act of obtaining payments in return for not imposing harmful effects on other citizens.' Rowley 1978:91.

6 Hutt 1973.

7 John Goldthorpe, for example, has suggested that the greater readiness of British trade unions to 'punch their weight' arises in large part from the 'weakening of the inhibitions formerly imposed by the status order'. That is to say, 'one may see the decay of the status order as having released, as it were, distributional dissent and conflict at a new level of intensity . . .' Goldthorpe 1978:200 and 201. Goldthorpe connects the decay of the old status order to social and demographic changes, in particular those combining to produce an exceptionally 'mature' working class unfettered by pre-industrial status conceptions. Increasing class maturity is thus thought to mitigate against normative incorporation – a reversal of the standard thesis that 'immature' workers, first-generation recruits from agrarian life, are the most politically volatile elements among the proletariat and the most susceptible to radical ideas.

8 Roberts 1972:269.

9 Roberts 1972:266.

10 Roberts 1972:269. The same question appears to have exercised the minds of the Conservative Party leadership. A committee under the chairmanship of Lord Carrington produced a 'secret report' warning that 'a future Conservative Administration would be unable to defeat trade unions with the power to throttle the physical and economic life of the country, such as the miners and the power workers, should they confront the government. . . Strong unions and the advanced technology operated by their members, particularly in fuel and power industries, mean that no government these days can "win" in the way Mr Baldwin's Cabinet triumphed during the General Strike of 1926, by maintaining essential supplies and services.' Reported in *The Times*, Tuesday, April 18 1978, p. 1.

11 It would be further necessary to distinguish between the ability to disrupt the *productive system* in a way likely to damage profits and to result in lay-offs in associated industries; and the ability merely to inflict *public inconvenience*. Strikes by firemen, postmen, hospital staff, dustmen, and other service workers result in the discomfort of large numbers of individuals who are thus required to 'absorb' the effects personally; the productive system is more or less unscathed by such activities, rendering them less effective for bargaining purposes.

12 This question of political alternatives is discussed in the final chapter, The Dictatorship of the Proletariat and Social Democracy.

13 Finer 1975:329.

14 Van den Berghe has claimed that the political and legal gains made by American blacks in the 1960s were 'the result of mass militancy and of the adoption of unconventional methods of protest such as passive resistance and civil disobedience by the oppressed minorities, rather than of magnanimity and benevolence from the Federal government or the dominant group at large'. Berghe 1967:93. Undoubtedly, collective political action by the blacks was a *precondition* for such reforms as were eventually forthcoming; but could it seriously be suggested that such action would have been sufficient to bring about change if the dominant racial group and the state had been determined to prevent it? Closure by blacks has produced political results precisely because whites have not been uniformly opposed to the dismantling of exclusionary institutions.

15 'The bourgeoisie recognised that all the weapons which it had forged
against feudalism could have their points turned against itself; that all the
means of education which it had created were rebels against its own
civilisation. . . It had become aware that all the so-called civil liberties and
instruments of progress were menaces to its own class dominion, which
was threatened alike at the social base and at the political apex – that is to
say, they had become "socialistic".' Marx 1926:73.

# 6

# Dual closure

In the light of the foregoing remarks it should be clear that the conceptual categories of exclusion and usurpation are not altogether synonymous with the more familiar distinction between capital and labour. Although there is a considerable overlap in their usage (and given the nature of the substantive issues being raised it would be peculiar if this were not so) the Weberian schema directs attention to certain issues that are not easily brought into the Marxist embrace. Of particular relevance here is the fact that exclusionary social closure is an aspect of conflict and cleavage within social classes as well as between them. That is to say, exclusion strategies aimed at what Weber calls the 'monopolization of opportunities' are frequently employed by one segment of the subordinate class against another, most usually on the basis of race, sex, ethnicity, or some other collectivist attribute. This is also a way of saying that exploitation occurs within the subordinate class as well as against it, since the forms of collective action involved entail the use of power in such a way as to create a stratum of socially excluded inferiors. Clearly the notion that, say, industrial workers may adopt formal practices of exploitation against others is one that can hardly be made consistent with orthodox Marxist categories, given the narrower definition of exploitation as the appropriation of surplus value by the owners of capital. But if property is regarded as but one form of exclusionary relationship, and hence but one form of exploitation, the possibility must be recognized that other monopolistic rules and practices, unrelated to ownership, also fall under the same moral classification.

Examples of such exploitative practices within the working class are common enough; they would include the organized resistance of men against equal employment opportunities and legal rights for women; the efforts of Protestant workers in Ulster to exclude Catholics from skilled jobs and from political office; the action by white workers in the United States to deny blacks equal access to schools and housing; or the attempt by one language group, as in Belgium or Canada, to monopolize key posts and resources, and so forth. These are all examples of exploitation in the neo-Weberian sense in so far as they entail the use of power in a downward direction, so creating a stratum of subordinates, rather than the use of power against those who occupy a more privileged place in the distributive system. It is not, then, the social location of those who *initiate* collective action that determines whether the action is exploitative or not but the location of those against whom it is directed.

Now although social closure within a class arises for the most part from the direct activities of the intended beneficiaries, it is not invariably the case that the latter themselves are the prime movers. The relationship between the indigenous West European working class and the migrant workers who make up an important segment of the unskilled labour force is a case in point. It is clear that the migrant workers are placed in an extremely weak bargaining position as a result of the punitive legal restrictions placed upon their activities by the various European governments. In terms of pay and social conditions they form a virtual sub-proletariat beneath the indigenous workforce. But it can hardly be argued that the French, Swiss, German, and British workers are themselves immediately responsible for the depressed condition of immigrant labour. This is due largely to the action of state and business interests in seeking to maintain a supply of relatively cheap and pliable labour that is easily disposed of during recessions, and which is a minimum drain on welfare resources. The point is, however, that although the indigenous workforce has not itself directly created a category of socially excluded labour it has, equally, displayed little readiness to flex its political muscles in order to improve the conditions of migrant workers by incorporating them into the organized labour movement.[1] In fact, of course, indigenous workers gain certain tangible benefits from the exclusion of immigrants from full citizenship; and to this extent they could be said to be engaged in 'exploitation by proxy' by reaping the rewards of exclusionary closure initiated in a different quarter.

More commonly, though, closure by one group of workers against another is prompted directly by the beneficiaries themselves, with or without the backing of other agencies. The history of early labour movements in industrial societies is replete with examples of militant working-class action designed to exclude the entry of foreign workers as potential competitors for jobs and resources. The Australian labour movement, for example, played a leading role in shaping the White Australia policy aimed at excluding Asian labour from the domestic market.[2] Similarly, in the late nineteenth century, workers on the west coast of Canada and the United States formed the Working Men's Protective Association, a movement that 'made Chinese exclusion a major plank in its political platform'.[3] The closure activities of the early labour movements in South Africa were especially vigorous:

'By means of trade union combination, political pressure, strikes and physical violence, they secured for white miners and artisans sheltered employment which cut them off from their fellow African worker and filled them with overweening racial pride and arrogance. The Labour party pandered to this sentiment, agitated for an all-white franchise, and fought elections on a platform of white supremacy. It was the party's proud boast that it had been the first to propose total racial segregation. And indeed, by entering into a coalition with Afrikaner nationalism in 1924, Labour enabled the Nationalist party to take office and lay the foundations of apartheid.'[4]

Exclusionary activities of this kind by the white working class were not of course triggered off simply by xenophobia or uncomplicated racial prejudice. Rather, they can be understood as a rational response to their own exploited condition, which the importation of cheap labour onto the market threatened to make worse. Frequently, the attempts at exclusion by organized labour were in direct conflict with the aims of employers who naturally favoured an expansion in the labour supply. In this respect, then, closure by the indigenous working class against potential competitors, especially those thought willing to accept lower wages, has represented an oblique form of class conflict. It is collective action designed to prevent the creation of an 'industrial reserve army' that would weaken labour's usurpationary potential against capital. The political lethargy displayed by the present-day European working class towards the plight of migrant labour is thus part of a long tradition of well-founded suspicion of capitalists' motives in encouraging the 'dilution of labour'.

This usefully illustrates the important general point that organized workers frequently resort to *dual* forms of closure: usurpationary activities against employers and the state, combined with exclusionary activities against other less organized groups of workers, including ethnic minorities and women. The adoption of exclusion devices is naturally made easier if the target group can be defined as alien, and as therefore not included within the moral compass of the labour movement. But even within a context of racial homogeneity social closure by one sector of the workforce against another has been a common feature, most notably in the case of the labour aristocracy. The apprenticeship system of the skilled craftsmen served similar ends to the use of credentials by the professions in ensuring that tight control was exercised over the supply of labour and market scarcity preserved intact. Mackenzie notes that craftsmen in the United States employed a variety of strategems for restricting access, including stiff examinations, citizenship requirements, and prohibitive initiation fees.[5] Bauman has suggested that the overriding aim of the labour aristocracy in Victorian England was 'to ensure that the skilled worker achieved a legally protected occupational status similar to that possessed by the members of the liberal professions'.[6]

> 'The idea of restricting the labour market gradually became an obsession with the "new model" unions. It was the prism through which union leaders viewed all problems concerned with the workers, and it provided them with guidelines for settling every sort of problem and argument. Unskilled and unorganised workers existed for them only in so far as they constituted an element that could interfere with the market privileges of their particular trade.'[7]

Exclusionary practices by the labour aristocracy may also be seen as a quite rational response on the part of a group that was itself excluded by capital. By monopolizing the market in skills it was better placed to conduct the usurpationary struggle against employers, even though the bargaining capacity of other workers might be diminished as a result. Closure along these lines was not of course directed against any specific, identifiable subgroup within the labouring poor, any more than white-collar credentialism has a particular exclusionary target. Undoubtedly, though, exclusionary attempts within the working class are most frequently directed against socially visible target groups. One obvious reason why specific groups should be singled out for closure purposes is that workers are not usually in a position to employ impersonal criteria of property ownership or credentials as a means of excluding others from opportunities and rewards. Consequently, they commonly resort to collectivist criteria that, from the perspective of liberal ideology, are regarded as illegitimate – i.e. 'discriminatory'. And, as already mentioned, it is the moral objection to such collectivist rules of exclusion by a stratum of the dominant class that can often be tapped by the excluded minorities in mounting their own countervailing actions.

It should not be assumed that all exclusionary acts are of equal significance in the formation of class and allied forms of inequality. Indeed, if all forms of exclusion were put on the same social and political footing it would hardly be possible to speak of a class system at all. The picture presented would bear a close resemblance to the caste system – that is, a hierarchy of strata arranged in descending order of inferiority in which the share of resources, material and symbolic, became parcelled out in ever-dwindling proportions. To retain the perspective of class it is therefore necessary to suggest some line of demarcation and conflict that is more fundamental, socially and politically, than other sources of division and antagonism. Unless such a basic line of cleavage is assumed it would obviously make little sense to speak of internal class conflict as a phenomenon in its own right. For definitional purposes, then, the dominant class in a society can be said to consist of those social groups whose share of resources is attained *primarily* by exclusionary means; whereas the subordinate class consists of social groups whose *primary* strategy is one of usurpation, notwithstanding the occasional resort to exclusion as a supplementary strategy.

It is within the terms of this general formulation that the issue of internal class divisions is best understood, and in particular the tendencies toward exploitation within the subordinate class just alluded to. Attempts at exclusionary social closure by one section of the subordinate class against another are, for the most part, secondary or supplementary strategies. They are actions taken in addition to the primary aim of biting into the share of resources held by the dominant class. The usurpationary struggle against an exclusionary class is the defining feature of workers' class position since it is the fluctuating outcome of this permanent struggle that overwhelmingly decrees their material and social fate. The rewards that also accrue as a result of exclusion against ethnic minorities or women are, in the typical case, marginal additions to the primary source, and not equivalent values.

If this were not the case, and industrial workers in effect gained as much or more as a result of exclusionary practices than from usurpationary struggle against the dominant class, then on the present definition such workers could not be said to constitute part of a subordinate class at all; exclusion would be their primary strategy not a mere secondary or supplementary one, and on this account they would rank as part of a dominant class. The paradigm case here is that of the white South African workers whose privileged place in society owes more to their systematic closure against the blacks than to usurpationary claims upon the white bourgeoisie. As Davies has argued, 'it is clear that a section of the labour-force will tend to become most fully tied to the bourgeoisie when it benefits from the extraction of surplus value, in other words when it participates in the exploitation of the majority of the working class'.[8] In South Africa

> 'Black workers are . . . the victims of a super-exploitation, which
> has tended to increase rather than to diminish . . . Since the
> average white wage is a significant amount above the "surplus
> free wage", and since it is not based on higher productivity, the
> inescapable conclusion is that the white mine workers benefit
> from the surplus value created by blacks; in other words they
> indirectly share in the exploitation of blacks, via their political
> support for the State and the economic privileges they receive
> from it in return.'[9]

This nicely illustrates the point that the status of industrial worker
is not synonymous with membership of a subordinate class, although
typically of course this is the case. It is not a group's position in the
division of labour or the productive process that determines its class
location but the character of its primary mode of social closure. White
industrial workers in South Africa must be regarded as part of the
dominant class by virtue of the fact that exclusion is their chief mode
of operation and the source of their privileges. Closure on racial
grounds thus plays a directly equivalent role to closure on the basis of
property and credentials. Black workers, by contrast, conduct their
struggle almost wholly upon usurpationary lines, bringing them into
conflict not only with the representatives of capital but with exclusionary white labour also.

Whether or not the exclusion of one group of workers by another
becomes the primary rather than secondary or supplementary political goal is no doubt partly a question of the relative size of the two
sub-populations. Where, as in the South African case, blacks are the
largest proportion of the total workforce, they contribute sufficiently
to the national wealth to support an exploitative white workforce as
well as a white bourgeoisie. Under these conditions it may be seen as
perfectly rational for white workers to align themselves with their
own bourgeoisie rather than make common cause with the black
proletariat in order to share the spoils of usurpation. Where, on the
other hand, the dominant ethnic group makes up a large majority of
the population, as is normally the case, the subordinate group would
clearly be unable to generate sufficient surplus to make exclusion by
the former a realistic primary strategy.

The situation is naturally more complex in societies where the
subordinate ethnic group is a large minority, as in the case of Catholics in Northern Ireland. Exclusionary closure on the part of Protestant
workers yields certain tangible advantages in the shape of an established monopoly of skilled and better-paid jobs as well as other
material and symbolic perquisites that flow from the control of political office. Against this has to be offset the possible gains that might

accrue to Protestant workers if they were to join forces with Catholic workers in making usurpationary demands on the bourgeoisie. One familiar interpretation of the Ulster situation is that the religious cleavage is equally damaging to the class interests of both communal groups and that a unification of forces would improve labour's share in general, including that of Protestant workers. The latter's heavy commitment to closure against the Catholics is thus seen as evidence of that peculiar kind of working-class irrationality known as false consciousness.

However, this assessment of the common benefits likely to result from united class action might be more persuasive to the Protestant workers if the evidence from societies with a homogeneous proletariat was an unambiguous story of success. Paradoxically, it is the chief exponents of the false consciousness doctrine who are usually loudest in their proclamations of the failure of organized labour in *all* capitalist societies, whatever their social make-up, to mount a serious offensive against the bourgeoisie. Workers who opt for closure against a minority group can hardly be declared guilty of irrationality in choosing to retain the proven benefits of exclusion in preference to the uncertain or doubtful pay-off resulting from combined usurpation. Only if united class action elsewhere had fulfilled political expectations would it be necessary to feel puzzled by the Protestant workers' failure to embark upon the same course. It probably always requires considerably less expenditure of political energy to effect exclusionary social closure against a visible and vulnerable minority group than to mount collective usurpationary action against a powerful dominant class.

One important reason why this should be the case is that collectivist exclusion on the part of one group of workers against another is usually facilitated by the past or present policies of the state. Ethnic minorities, for example, that have at some time or other been deprived of political and civil rights by the state are the natural target for exclusionary moves by the lower strata of the dominant cultural or racial group. Weber's account of the closure process is extremely misleading on this crucial point. In discussing the criteria by which certain groups come to be defined as 'outsiders' he argues that 'it does not matter which characteristic is chosen in the individual case; whatever suggests itself is most easily seized upon'.[10] But obviously this is not so. It is *never* the case that exclusionary criteria are simply plucked out of the air in a purely arbitrary manner. In all known instances where racial, religious, linguistic, or sex characteristics have been seized upon for closure purposes the group in question has already at some time been defined as legally inferior by the state. Ethnic subordination, to take the commonest case, has normally occurred as a result of territorial conquest or the forced migration of populations creating a subcategory of second-class citizens within the nation-state. The groups singled out for exclusion by the labour movement of the culturally dominant group are therefore those that *already* suffer the disabilities of marginal political status, and whose own organizing and defensive capacities are seriously diminished. Although with the passage of time political and legal handicaps may formally be removed from the subject group, their place in the economic and status order tends to remain low and their inherited disadvantages continue to mark them out as victims in the distributive struggle. Precisely the same point could be made in relation to the exclusion of women: their vulnerability to closure practices on the part of men is in good measure attributable to the state's own systematic treatment of women as political and legal inferiors.

Proletarian exclusion against definable social groups thus only appears to occur in the wake of a similar policy conducted via the state by the dominant class itself. Indeed, it is only through the action of the state that cultural groups become hierarchically ranked in a manner that enables one to effect closure against another. If it were merely a matter of one group 'seizing upon' some attribute or other, as suggested by Weber, it would not be possible to explain why Catholics in Northern Ireland failed to bring about closure against Protestant workers, instead of the reverse; or why blacks in the Deep South did not seize upon white skin colour as a criterion of exclusion, or why female workers did not monopolize employment opportunities at the expense of men. None of these possibilities could be realized because the dominant class and the state had not already paved the way by creating the appropriate legally and politically vulnerable category. There is thus nothing in the least arbitrary in the selection of exclusionary criteria.

If exclusion by workers or other lower social groups only follows upon the state's own negative treatment of the target group, political problems seem bound to arise where the state, for whatever reason, seeks to end this type of discrimination by incorporating the previously excluded group into civil society. It is at this point that workers in the dominant cultural group tend to enter into direct conflict with the state, since formerly accepted closure practices are now looked upon as illegitimate. The resort to physical resistance against the new integrationist measures (bussing, power sharing, etc.) is a measure of the sense of betrayal felt by lower strata at the state's withdrawal of its erstwhile connivance in their exclusionary prerogatives.

Although it is conventional to speak of the *state* coming belatedly to the aid of subordinate ethnic and other social groups, it would probably be more correct to identify the source of this concern in the ranks of the liberal bourgeoisie. It is this stratum of the exclusionary class above all that is most likely to mobilize political sentiment against purely collectivist forms of exclusion. The willingness of government to respond favourably to this line of moral argument is naturally helped by the recognition that in dismantling these particular forms of closure no disturbance is caused to the even tenor of bourgeois life and institutions. The exclusionary rights of property and credentials are not in the least impaired by the removal of restrictive social practices founded on 'irrelevant' criteria. An important strand in liberal theory is that sexual, racial, and similar forms of discrimination act as a fetter upon the creative and productive capacity of society by inhibiting the fullest use of individual talents. On this interpretation, capitalism has nothing to fear, and a great deal to gain, from the release of energies bottled-up by outmoded tribal practices. Far from the bourgeoisie reaping any political benefit from a communally divided working class, as Marxists would claim, the liberal diagnosis dwells upon the dysfunctions of this arrangement and the technical and moral superiority of a more rationally ordered class system based purely upon individualist exclusion.[11]

It is this line of reasoning, and the introduction of anti-discriminatory legislation following from it, that sets the scene for those sporadic clashes between the state and organized labour already alluded to. The strong class overtones of the conflict make themselves heard in the accusation by workers and the 'respectable poor' that they are expected to bear the entire social costs of minority-group incorporation, because the middle-class advocates of reform are carefully shielded from the social impact of their own recommendations. Any gains made by blacks or other formerly excluded groups are felt to encroach on the already modest quantum of jobs, housing, and education held by lower-class whites, leaving the preserves of the suburban middle class comfortably intact. Liberal support for minority-group usurpation is thus seen to be a case of that happy form of moral rectitude which calls for no personal sacrifice on the part of its sponsors. The general point of interest here is that once the state withdraws its open or tacit support for a particular set of exclusionary practices it becomes more difficult for lower-class groups to sustain these practices by their own organizational efforts. They are then obliged to rely on the same kinds of cumbersome solidaristic tactic that normally accompany usurpationary claims, instead of relying on the distant, magisterial, and respectable forces of law and state.

## II

The fact that exlusionary aims may also be pursued by the methods of mass mobilization and direct action suggests the need to draw a clearer distinction than has so far been made between the general mode or type of social closure on the one hand, and the actual strategies or tactics employed in their pursuance on the other. As will be clear from what has gone before, the two main practical strategies are, first, those that seek to win the backing of the state and the support of law; and, second, those that rely more heavily upon the public display of solidarism and the political drama of direct action. Exclusionary closure normally goes hand in hand with a *legalistic* strategy, as for example in the professions' pursuit of a lawful monopoly, and property's reliance upon the policeman. Usurpationary closure, by contrast, typically makes use of *solidaristic* tactics, which, though not necessarily illegal, are not always genteel and frequently result in brushes with the law. However, this symmetry is by no means invariable since attempts at usurpation via legislation, on the one hand, and exclusion via solidarism, on the other, are not uncommon.

The latter combination has been discussed briefly in reference to the resistance displayed by white working-class communities to the attempted social integration of blacks. American society in fact provides a number of variations on this theme. The most familiar case of solidarism being harnessed to exclusionary ends is the successful attempt by low-status whites to maintain the social degradation of Southern blacks by the systematic use of violence. Direct collective action and the resort to illegality through organizations such as the Ku Klux Klan were locally sanctioned means for deterring blacks from attempting any encroachment upon the precarious economic and social status of the poor whites. Solidarism on the part of the latter was the only means of preserving the exclusive rights over blacks that had been guaranteed by the state prior to the Civil War and abolition, and which successive legal enactments and Supreme Court rulings had slowly whittled away. The social mobilization of whites and the use of physical repression were made considerably easier than would normally be the case by the fact that the South was virtually a state within the state, permitting the more violent forms of solidarism to take place under the protective canopy of the forces of law and order. It is difficult to conceive of solidaristic activities on such a scale persisting in the absence of some degree of connivance from the agency that is usually so jealous of any infringement upon its monopoly of physical coercion.

The pattern of exclusion in the northern cities illustrates this point. There the use of violence to prevent black encroachment on lower-class white schools and neighbourhoods is usually sporadic and highly focussed; it does not take the form of a permanent political organization and the salutory use of random terror, not least of all because there are no local white enclaves in which the writ of the Federal state does not run. Even the 'white vigilante' groups that patrol the borders of working-class suburbs and the black ghettoes find it necessary to make much of their law-abiding ways. Nevertheless, the riots against bussing or the arrival of black neighbours are reminders that any threat to long-standing exclusionary practices can call forth a collective wrath that cannot always be contained within the orderly routines of law and party politics.

Perhaps one of the most successful applications of solidaristic tactics for exclusionary ends has been that conducted by Protestant workers in Ulster against the British government's insistence on the full political inclusion of Catholics. The general strike called and conducted by the Protestant workers' organizations paralysed the province and scuttled the power-sharing agreement worked out by the Westminster and Stormont governments. The fact that it also led to the collapse of the Northern Ireland parliament has not apparently provoked the theoretical interest that might have been anticipated, given that it is one of the very few cases on record of workers in an advanced capitalist society bringing down a government by direct action. Presumably this has something to do with the fact that this long-awaited event was performed for exclusionary ends rather than for the expected usurpation of capital by labour.[12]

# III

Usurpation does not always draw upon the social resources of solidarism any more than exclusion invariably assumes a legalistic form. Organized labour often attempts to enhance its bargaining power over capital through the enactment of laws that strengthen the foundations of collective action. The close relationship between the trade union movement and the Labour Party found in most western countries make legalistic strategies especially attractive and feasible when social democratic governments are in office. The introduction of laws in support of the closed shop, or extending the scope of picketing, are recent examples of the use of the parliamentary statute book to give a

modest tilt to the balance of class power in labour's direction.[13]
Increasingly, in fact, governments of all shades, though social democratic ones in particular, appear willing to enter into an exchange
relationship with organized labour or its representatives, by which
trade-union-inspired legislation is enacted in return for a limited
period of industrial peace and wage restraint. In times when inflation
is seen as the most pressing of all domestic problems this trading
relationship is likely to be of particular mutual benefit. On the government side, control of the wages element in inflation will be
regarded as an essential step in bringing down or containing prices,
so that pro-labour legislation appears a reasonable payment to make
to secure the temporary breathing space necessary for electoral survival. On the trade union side, the political embarrassments and difficulties of selling wage restraint to the workers are offset by the
knowledge that the holding operation is for a limited period only,
whereas the gains made by way of the statute book represent permanent improvements in the condition of organized labour.

It is the awareness of these long-term statutory advantages accruing to labour in exchange for purely temporary concessions that
provokes the complaint by capital's spokesmen that the unions have
exceeded their proper function by trespassing upon political territory.
Nothing less than the sovereignty of parliament and democracy itself
are felt to be threatened by this new tendency for powerful unions to
dictate to governments the conditions of their co-operation. This is
the understandably plaintive cry of those for whom the hallowed
special relationship between capital and the legislative arm is part of
the natural order of things, and for whom labour's rough intrusion
into the affairs of state is tantamount to a breach of constitutional
etiquette. No doubt it is anxiety about the possible consequences of
legally supported usurpation that causes grave public doubts to be
expressed in Britain about the quality of political institutions that have
hitherto been felt to serve the custodians of privilege faithfully and
well. Suddenly it seems there is an urgent need for a new, written
constitution to safeguard the people against abuse by arbitrary powers; suddenly the electoral system requires a thorough overhaul to
forestall the possibility of minority governments introducing radical
reforms for which they have 'no mandate'. There could be no more
telling illustration of how seriously certain sections of the exclusionary class look upon organized labour's increasing reliance upon a
legalistic strategy of usurpation than the fact that they should now
contemplate changing the rules of the constitutional game.[14]

Access to the statute book, and the long-term advantages it brings,
has not of course been conferred on labour as an act of political grace.
As already pointed out, it arises from the state's reliance upon work-

ers' leaders to promote the idea of self-sacrifice in the interests of a supposedly greater good. This in turn suggests that the effectiveness of a legalistic strategy depends very much on the prior effectiveness of time-honoured practices of a solidaristic kind. It is probably not until labour has the latent threat of disruptive potential at its disposal that it is called upon in the first place to play the role of partner to capital and the state. In the absence of any such threat moral appeals for restraint would be unnecessary, and so therefore would be the requirement to make recompense via the statute book. Whenever organized labour has in the past been granted certain statutory rights and protection, these have usually come about as a result of moral appeals to certain principles of justice rather than from the ability to back up demands by the threat of negative sanctions. But since the system of laws in any society will tend to be fairly responsive to gradual shifts in the balance of power between classes, it follows that labour's impact on the statute book could be expected to grow in line with improvements in its real bargaining position. Thus, usurpation by legal means is initially dependent upon the proven effectiveness of usurpation via solidarism, though the consequence of legislative gains is to give a sharper cutting edge to solidarism itself.

One important difference between the two tactics of usurpation is that solidarism arbitrarily favours those sections of the labour movement with most industrial muscle, and therefore to some extent reinforces ever-present tendencies towards fragmentation and divisiveness. Legalism, on the other hand, always acts as a unifying force in so far as statutory changes affect the entire movement equally, including the weakest groups. If reforms favourable to the trade unions now usually occur more in response to the dictates of *realpolitik* than to the tenderheartedness of government, then the power that the latter is responding to is not that of organized labour as a whole but, in the last resort, to those sectors that have the capacity to make or break government policy. In other words, it is the latent power of the strongest groups that is ultimately responsible for extending the protective legal canopy beneath which *all* branches of the movement can shelter. In this respect, at least, trade union particularism is transcended by the common interests of class.

# IV

The phenomenon of dual closure is not confined to the ranks of industrial workers but is a common feature also among those white-collar groups ordinarily referred to as the lower or semi-professions. These are the occupations that make claims to rewards on the basis of formal qualifications, but which have been unable to secure full professional closure by establishing a legal monopoly or control over the number and quality of entrants. Partly as a result of this incomplete professional closure these white-collar groups are also liable to resort to the tactics of industrial solidarism as a means of advancing their claims. The theoretical interest of the semi-professions thus resides in the fact that they seek to combine the exclusionary devices of credentialism, by an emphasis upon their expert and 'professional' attributes, with the familiar usurpationary methods of organized labour by acting in a 'trade-union' capacity. In recent times this latter type of activity appears to have become especially pronounced as traditionally quiescent vocational groups have assumed a more combative bargaining stance. Consequently, interest has centred on the related questions of (a) why the semi-professions have been unsuccessful in accomplishing full social closure comparable to law, medicine, and similar professional monopolies; and (b) the reasons for the recent upsurge in militancy and the prospect this opens up for semi-professional incorporation into the ranks of organized labour.

One notable attempt to answer the first of these questions starts from the position that schoolteaching, social work, nursing, and the like, are to be regarded as 'failed professions' – that is, occupations that have inappropriately set themselves the task of attaining full professional status, a goal that is actually beyond their reach. One of the chief obstacles to complete social closure is felt, in some quarters, to be their lack of a sufficiently developed 'knowledge base'. Goode, for example, argues that complete professional status is only possible for occupations that have a complex body of esoteric or technical knowledge at their disposal.[15] Occupational groups that have only a slender knowledge base cannot compensate for this deficiency by concerted efforts of an organizational kind. As Etzioni puts it, there are 'powerful societal limitations on the extent to which these occupations can be fully professionalized', suggesting that there are certain inherent features of the division of labour itself that promote or hinder the possibility of closure.[16]

These restrictions upon closure are thought to be compounded, moreover, by the fact that the lower professions tend to be disproportionately staffed by women. That is, the marginal status of these groups is regarded partly as a function of the low status attaching to women generally. So much so that, in Etzioni's judgement, the 'cultural values of professions, organizations, and female employment are not compatible'.[17] More specifically, a preponderance of women in an occupation is felt to jeopardize the attainment of 'autonomy', which is regarded as one of the defining hallmarks of a profession. The Simpsons spell out the logic of this argument as follows:

'The predominantly female composition of the semi-professions strengthens all . . . forces for bureaucratic control in the organizations in which they work. The public is less willing to grant autonomy to women than to men. A woman's primary attachment is to the family role; women are therefore less intrinsically committed to work than men and less likely to maintain a high level of specialized knowledge. . . For these reasons, and because they often share the general cultural norm that women should defer to men, women are more willing than men to accept the bureaucratic controls imposed upon them in semi-professional organizations, and less likely to seek a genuinely professional status.'[18]

The alleged link between female submissiveness and inability to achieve full professional closure assumes particular importance because of the fact that the semi-professions are usually subject to quite close external controls by state and local authorities. That is, they are typical examples of what Weber refers to as 'heteronomous' organizations, in contrast to fully 'autonomous' organizations such as established professions.[19] The Simpsons suggest that one of the main reasons why the semi-professions remain bound by external controls, and hence fail to win full closure and autonomy, is precisely because of the prevalence of that sex for whom obedience is part of the natural order of things. In the light of these ineradicable defects, Etzioni recommends that the semi-professions should renounce their 'inauthentic aspirations' to achieve full professional standing and simply 'be themselves'.[20]

Two observations need to be made about this analysis. First, the case for a complex and codified 'knowledge base' as an indispensable prerequisite for professional closure is taken as self-evident rather than as a case to be argued. That is, the proposition is never formulated in such a way as to encourage dispassionate judgement of those elevated claims made by the professions themselves concerning their command of specialized knowledge. In particular, no distinction is made between forms of knowledge that might be thought to constitute the operational core of professional work, and those various accretions that have scant practical application but are more in the way of ritual embellishments that prolong the period of training, thereby protecting market scarcity.[21] It is part of credentialist strategy to insist that *all* the knowledge tested by examinations is indispensable to the eventual performance of tasks. However, the observer's willingness to suspend disbelief in this judgement should not be carried to the point where the professionals' own claims take on the status of sociological truths. One possibility that deserves to be toyed with is that once a professional monopoly has been established, the way then becomes clear for the elaboration of those purely ceremonial conventions by which access to specialized knowledge is carefully monitored and restricted. Moreover, to the extent that any given knowledge base is recognized as being to some degree *socially* defined, and not altogether an intrinsic feature of the division of labour, the more scepticism is called for regarding those assertions that professional closure is linked in a straightforward way with some unspecified quantum of expertise.[22]

Scepticism also seems to be the proper response to that strand in the argument that identifies the sex composition of the lower professions as a key factor in forestalling closure. It is one thing to say that women are handicapped in their career activities by virtue of the additional domestic burdens they are usually expected to shoulder. But it is quite another to state that women who occupy similar places to men in the occupational order exhibit distinctively 'female' patterns of behaviour when it comes to matters of a professional and organizational kind. In white-collar employment generally, there is no evidence to show that women are more resistant to the appeals of trade union or professional association membership than are men employed in similar work conditions.[23] Nor has it been demonstrated that female employees are less militant or strike prone than their male colleagues. If 'submissiveness' really had such a debilitating effect upon women's organizing capacities as has been suggested it would surely make itself felt in a greater reluctance to act in opposition to managerial authority. The implication is, of course, that if the semi-professions were staffed largely by men they would be far more likely to attain full professional autonomy and closure – what might be called the *machismo* theory of professionalization. It might come as an interesting piece of news to workers in the mining, docks, and construction industries that their routine submission to managerial command is a characteristically feminine trait. But perhaps it is only the white-collar version of manhood that is so staunchly resistant to the importunities of authority and all encroachments upon personal autonomy?

A more plausible explanation for the sex composition of the lower professions is that these, for whatever reason, have not been especially prized by men and that exclusionary devices against women have therefore not operated with the same degree of rigour as in the established professions, except at the highest levels. If the heteronomous nature of the lower professions arises from the fact that they are closely interlocked with local and national government bureaucracies, then the obstacles to full professional autonomy can be seen as quite independent of the sexual composition of employees. Indeed, this could be one of the reasons why aspiring men would be inclined to see these occupations as unattractive and not seek to monopolize them, much in the way that indigenous manual workers abandon the least attractive jobs to immigrant labourers. Although the factors making for the success or failure of professional closure are varied and complex, and by no means fully understood, the emphasis upon sex composition seems the least promising point of departure.

An altogether different approach to the problem is one that includes the semi-professions in the general drift towards 'white-collar proletarianization'. This thesis implicitly endorses the view that the semi-professions lack the necessary attributes for full member-ship in the professional middle class, suggesting that collective action on the industrial model is the compelling alternative. The main impetus behind this development is seen to be the steady erosion of autonomy at the workplace as bureaucracy tightens its grip, so gradually removing one of the most rewarding aspects of semi-professional life and moving it one step nearer to the condition of industrial labour.

'In such occupations, the proletarian form begins to assert itself and to impress itself upon the consciousness of these employees. Feeling the insecurities of their role as sellers of labour power and the frustrations of a controlled and mechanically organized workplace, they begin, despite their remaining privileges, to know those symptoms of dissociation which are popularly called "alienation" and which the working class has lived with for so long that they have become part of its second nature.'[24]

Braverman's statement finds an echo in Oppenheimer's view that 'the income position, employment picture and job condition of the increasingly bureaucratically-located professional is helping to create "proletarian" conditions'.[25] The new-found willingness to resort to previously despised forms of collective action arises from the fact that, 'In the process of having autonomy taken away by adminis-trators, the professional becomes proletarianized; in defending what remains of autonomy, further proletarianization results'.[26] Marcus's study of militancy among schoolteachers in the United States draws upon broadly similar arguments, concluding that teachers 'will be the prototype of the new and emerging professional because the changes they have undergone and the problems they have confronted in the past two decades are just now beginning to be experienced by other professionals'.[27]

The proletarianization thesis is thus presented as an explanation for the recent trend among the lower professions towards collective action of a markedly different kind from that associated with credentialism and legal monopoly. But the question raised by this account is how far the change in conduct is due to the loss of autonomy set in train by the drift towards bureaucracy. It is worth remembering that Weber's anguish at the bureaucratization of everything was expressed more than half a century ago. Although there are no doubt some small corners of modern society still awaiting its touch, a little more exactitude is surely now required in speaking of an *increase* in bureaucratic control, especially in the case of occupations that have never exactly revelled in autonomy. The proletarianization thesis assumes the existence of a golden age of semi-professional independence now abruptly shattered by newly imposed external controls. In fact, of course, many of the lower professions were virtually the *creation* of bureaucracy, having been set up as government agencies for the administration of the welfare state. It seems unlikely, to say the least, that the shift towards an 'industrial strategy' has been sparked off as a reaction to the unexpected encounter with officialdom. Who, it may be wondered, enters any of the lower professions believing them to be anything other than tightly constrained by the policies, budgets, and dictates of local and state authorities?

# V

A more obvious reason for the novel behaviour of these groups in recent times is to do with their equally novel experience of inflation. As was pointed out in an earlier chapter, these occupations tend to be in the front line of government campaigns to reduce public expenditure. It is the welfare professions above all that have suffered from the sudden contraction of those prospects and conditions normally thought to give them an edge over even the best paid manual workers. The fact that the semi-professions are heavily concentrated in the public sector producing non-marketable goods renders them especially vulnerable to those solutions to the 'fiscal crisis of the state' that seek to divert resources into the manufacturing and productive sectors. Thus, it is probably not so much the loss of autonomy and the alienation effect that accounts for the new militancy, so much as the confrontation with budget-conscious state authorities. Subordination to such authority is nothing new; what is new is the unexpected deterioration in conditions of work and life-chances following hard on a period of comparative munificence.

Direct action of a solidaristic kind therefore recommends itself as an appropriate strategy for defending jobs and improving pay and working conditions. Professional closure is a long-term goal that promises to yield dividends at some unspecified and distant time. But under inflationary conditions the concern with distant prospects is likely to take second place to the immediate preoccupation with current income. This is especially the case when bargaining takes place within the restricted time limits imposed by the annual wages round, since those groups that fail to exert sufficient pressure at the appropriate time may find it difficult to make up for lost ground in the subsequent round. Inflation thus creates a moral climate in which the struggle over pay tends to occupy the collective mind to an extent that leaves little room for the cultivation of professional decorum. When the immediate protection of living standards becomes the order of the day, the old reluctance to engage in the less genteel form of collective action may begin to seem like a costly self-indulgence.

The thesis of white-collar proletarianization assumes a continuous and irreversible process of decline in the condition of intermediate groups, since it is hardly on the cards that bureaucracy could be rolled back sufficiently to permit the lower professions to regain the autonomy they have allegedly lost. However, if it is not the loss of professional autonomy that is at the heart of the matter, but the impact of inflation and public spending cuts, there need be nothing irreversible about the trade-union orientation of these groups, unless perhaps inflation itself were to become a permanent condition of capitalist economies. Under a less stringent economic regime they could quite plausibly revert to a pattern of activity in which the goal of professional closure assumed greater importance. It is a characteristic of these intermediate groups that they strive to maximize their advantages by adjusting the balance between *both* types of closure activity, according to changing circumstances. This fact has often been obscured by the tendency to present the two types of activity as a contrast between 'status' versus 'class' orientations. The striving for professional qualifications and standards is viewed as an attempt to enhance the membership's occupational dignity and similar intangibles of status; whereas direct bargaining over incomes and the attendant threat of conflict is defined as class action.[28] However, it seems more realistic to conceive of both strategies as attempts to improve *material* conditions, broadly conceived, in so far as the credentialist approach also has important market consequences, although of a longer-term kind than direct industrial action. The difference between professional and trade union action is not a difference between status and class concerns, but between long-term and immediate gains.[29]

The class versus status distinction stems partly from the view that trade unionism is the expression of collectivist attitudes and sentiments that come naturally to the working class, but which contrast strongly with the individualist outlook of the middle class. However, as the earlier discussion of professional closure made clear, bourgeois strategies yield little to those of the proletariat in their reliance upon co-operative and concerted action. Exclusionary groups would hardly be able to assert themselves in defence of privilege if they were less capable of acting collectively than usurpationary groups. Indeed, the very notion of closure only makes sense as a form of common action, even though the actual criteria adopted for exclusionary purposes may be of an individualistic kind. It would therefore be greatly confusing to set up a contrast between the 'collectivism' of trade unionism and the 'individualism' of professions. Common or concerted action is required of both; what is at issue is whether such action is directed towards exclusionary or usurpationary ends.

This does not amount to saying that there is some necessary incompatibility in pursuing the exclusionary objectives of professional closure simultaneously with those activities normally associated with usurpation. Attention has recently been drawn to the emergence of so-called 'professional unions', which combine aspects of both types of organization.[30] Similarly, Lansbury has pointed to the tendency among some lower professional groups to seek membership in professional associations *and* trade unions, suggesting on the basis of his own study that this practice is 'increasingly regarded, particularly by the marginal professional groups, as complementary rather than contradictory'.[31] It is this desire to place a 'bet each way', as Lansbury puts it, that more probably accounts for the current popularity of the trade union option than the sudden acknowledgement of proletarian status. Since there are no indications of the semi-professions abandoning their hopes in credentialism it would seem premature to consign them unequivocally to the subordinate class.

Although intermediate white-collar groups may fruitfully combine exclusionary and usurpationary strategies, it seems likely that the latter will be adopted with some reluctance, and only if the attempt to establish full closure fails to come off. Complete professional status is probably always regarded as the more desirable goal, if only because there are very few social costs incurred in maintaining a legal monopoly once it has been accomplished, compared with the continuous organizational efforts and costs incurred in the ever-recurring cycle of usurpationary claims. The possibility, too, of confrontation with the law and its guardians is not likely to recommend itself as an attractive alternative to a strategy that carries the full blessing of the law. As Roberts and his colleagues have shown in their account of the evolution of draughtsmens' and technicians' unions, the transition from exclusionary to usurpationary closure was undertaken only with the greatest reluctance:

'Draughtsmen had discovered an occupational identity at the end of the last century; they had quickly acquired prestige and commanded a scarcity rent in the labour market . . . But hopes entertained for the creation of a professional occupation sustained by the device of strictly controlled entry faded with the changing structure of industrial organisation and the pattern of demand for draughtsmen. . .'[32]

'The market strategies of both draughtsmen and the other technicians' associations moved towards a greater acceptance of collective bargaining on behalf of "all working at the tools" and away from attempts to create closed professional associations.'[33]

The semi-professions of the welfare state have not travelled as far down this path as the draughtsmen and technicians, *pace* the confident predictions of their imminent proletarianization. They remain archetypal intermediate groups by virtue of their continuing commitment to both main strategies of closure. In neo-Marxist terms they would no doubt qualify for candidature among those occupations in a 'contradictory class location', having one foot in each of the two great classes. However it should again be said that there is nothing necessarily contradictory in pursuing two different strategies in an attempt to maximize rewards; complementarity would seem to be the more appropriate term.

The theoretical purpose behind classifying intermediate positions as contradictory is to suggest their inherent instability due to unmanageable cross-pressures that must ultimately be resolved by the acceptance of 'full' class membership. In Marxist theory the social arena between the two main classes resembles a field of magnetic forces pulling all elements in opposing directions in unceasing flux and motion. There can be no permanence or stability in this zone, governed as it is by the forces of attraction and repulsion emanating from opposite class poles. As a consequence, Marxist theorists from Marx himself through to Trotsky and Poulantzas have consigned intermediate class groupings to a political and ideological limbo; their history is made for them, not by them, and it is a story told without a future tense.

The closure thesis, on the other hand, asserts that class formation and class conflict derive from opposing principles of distributive struggle, summed up in the metaphorical notion of the directional use of power. And this is perfectly consistent with the idea that any particular social or occupational group may draw upon each of these two opposing sets of principles in varying degrees without thereby entering a state of internal confusion and disarray. Social groups, no less than individuals, appear to be quite capable of acting upon general principles, which, at some level of abstraction, seem so apparently at odds as to lead only to self-annulment or paralysis. Contradictory class locations, as with so many of the widely advertised contradictions of capitalism, seem to be especially glaring in the immaculate realm of theoretical construction but noticeably less troublesome to those being theorized about.

# VI

Whereas the lower or semi-professions of the welfare state tend to adopt dual forms of closure, in which exclusionary and usurpationary elements are of roughly similar importance, the same could not be said of the full professions, despite their recent skirmishes on the wages front and their occasional resort to direct industrial action. At first blush it might appear that strike activity and allied forms of public protest by hospital doctors and consultants, higher civil servants, university teachers, and the like, dissolve all useful distinctions between professional exclusion and trade union usurpation as alternative strategies of distributive struggle. Moreover, the greater readiness of certain professions now to affiliate to the TUC after a history of resistance to such a move, appears to blur the distinction even more in so far as a formal attachment to the industrial wing of the labour movement has generally been thought of as an index of 'unionateness', with all that this implies in the way of a working-class outlook and commitment.

However, the fact that some of the full professions have affiliated to the TUC would seem to indicate not so much a shift in the class outlook of these groups as a sign that affiliation to the organized labour movement is no longer a useful index of class attachment, however serviceable it might once have been. Such a move by the professions is more plausibly understood as an attempt to *prevent* any slide towards proletarian status and a further narrowing of the earnings gap, by forging tactical links with a powerful body whose support may often be decisive in salary negotiations with government. In so far as it reflects any sharpening of class consciousness it is probably in the direction of a keener awareness of middle-class identity.

The same could be said of strike activity on the part of professionals; it would seem to be less an indication of a new or emergent working-class alignment than a last ditch attempt to forestall it. This raises the interesting question of whether professional strikes are in some sense different from strikes by industrial workers for whom they are part of the standard repertoire of the bargaining process. That is to say, can direct industrial action, and similar shows of solidarism, be said to differ in an analytical sense as between those groups for whom exclusion is the predominant form of closure and those that rely primarily on usurpation? It is necessary to suggest that any distinction should be on analytical grounds, since it would not be very illuminating to be told that professional strikes were in some way different simply *because* they were by professionals, even though in all other important respects they were identical to strikes by industrial workers. Against the appealingly no-nonsense view that a strike is a strike is a strike, the hypothesis advanced here is that solidaristic industrial action by normally exclusionary groups will differ in one highly significant way from similar action by usurpationary groups. Namely, that in the case of the latter, the withdrawal of labour will typically be accompanied by the institution of picketing, whereas in the case of the former it typically will not. The crucial significance of picketing is that it represents an appeal for active support and a show of solidarity from organized labour in general. It is thus one of the most important symbols of contemporary *class* action, expressing as it does an appeal to workers in all other occupations to give direct assistance by refusing to cross the invisible moral boundary staked out. It represents in other words an appeal to the working-class movement as a whole to honour the claims of usurpation over those of exclusion. Moreover, in making such an appeal, those on the picket line give an unspoken commitment to honour subsequent claims made upon them by other groups of workers in dispute. Thus, under inflationary conditions most occupations may be willing to strike, including the full professions; but not all are willing to resort to even the peaceful variety of picketing, thereby incurring political and social debts to the organized labour movement. Direct action by the professions is thus likely to be kept within tightly circumscribed limits in which the assistance of industrial workers or other occupational groups is not openly and routinely sought. It would certainly be paradoxical if the members of a dominant, exclusionary class were to seek and to receive regular backing from the social groups whose own subordination they indirectly guaranteed.

## VII

By way of concluding this part of the discussion, it might be appropriate to offer some general remarks on the explanatory status of the closure model. This model, like any other, recommends the use of a particular sociological vocabulary and an attendant battery of concepts that contain barely disguised moral assumptions about the nature of class society. It is not strictly speaking a 'theory' of class but a way of conceptualizing it that differs from that proposed by other variants of bourgeois sociology or by Marxism. Most of what we conventionally call theories of class are in fact conceptual methods of this kind. They are, for the most part, take-it-or-leave-it moral classifications, not sets of propositions that stand or fall under the impact of evidence. What conceivable social facts could destroy either the Marxist conception of class as an exploitative relationship, or the liberal conception of class as an exchange relationship? Since conceptual models are ways of presenting social reality, it follows that the preference for one presentation over another entails a personal judgement of some kind about the moral standing of class society.

On this score, the closure model is almost bound to appear defective by liberal and Marxist theorists alike. Liberal theory endorses a contractual view of class, in which the notion of mutual interest and harmony is the essential ingredient. Marxism, on the other hand, assumes not merely the absence of harmony and common class interests, but, more importantly, the presence of irresolvable antagonisms that drive the system to ultimate breakdown. The neo-Weberian position advanced here is that the relation between classes is neither one of harmony and mutual benefit, nor of irresolvable and fatal contradiction. Rather, the relationship is understood as one of mutual antagonism and permanent *tension*; that is, a condition of unrelieved distributive struggle that is not necessarily impossible to 'contain'. Class conflict may be without cease, but it is not inevitably fought to a conclusion. The competing notions of harmony, contradiction, and tension could thus be thought of as the three broad possible ways of conceptualizing the relation between classes, and on which all class models are grounded.

Since class models are not subject to direct empirical assault, the case for advancing the cause of one in preference to another rests partly on the claim that it draws attention to a set of problems and issues that are otherwise obscured. Thus, one of the attractions of the closure model is that it highlights the fact of communal cleavage and its relationship to class, and seeks to analyse both within the same conceptual framework. More generally, it proposes that intra-class relations be treated as conflict phenomena of the same general order as inter-class relations, and not as mere disturbances or complications within a 'pure' class model. Hence the extension of the concept of exploitation to cover both sets of phenomena. There is, in addition, a recommendation that social classes be defined by reference to their mode of collective action rather than to their place in the productive process or the division of labour. The reason for this is that incumbency of position in a formally defined structure does not normally correspond to class alignment where it really counts – at the level of organized political sentiment and conduct. This serious lack of fit between all positional or systemic definitions of class and the actual behaviour of classes in the course of distributive struggle, is not due to any lack of refinement in the categories employed. It arises from the initial theoretical decision to discount the significance and effect of variations in the cultural and social make-up of the groups assigned to the categories in question. Models constructed upon such formal, systemic definitions require of their advocates much ingenuity in accounting for the continuous and wholesale discrepancies between class position and class behaviour. A good deal of the intellectual energy of western Marxism has been dissipated in wrestling with this very problem which is of its own conceptual making.

If the mode of collective action is itself taken to be the defining feature of class, as proposed by the closure model, it follows that problems of this kind do not arise. There is no independently defined structure of positions for class action to be discrepant with. The predictable objection to this line of approach is to say that all forms of collective action are related to logically prior material factors, so that these factors should be the principal focus of theoretical concern. From a Marxist point of view, any given set of closure strategies could in principle be understood as mere responses to the material pressures and forces set in play by the capitalist mode of production. Now such an objection would carry considerable weight if it were in fact the case that, say, exclusionary social closure on the grand scale was unique to societies governed by the capitalist mode of production. However, the fact that it is found in all large-scale societies, including all known varieties of socialism, makes it altogether plain that collective action to bring about closure is not dependent upon any one specific set of productive relations or material factors. Credentialism flourishes as well in command economies as in market systems; the exclusionary rights attaching to productive property are a prominent feature of capitalist, socialist, feudal, slave, and caste societies and their associated modes of production; collective social closure on the basis of sex and ethnicity shows a similar indifference to the type and quality of the material substructure.

Although it would be perfectly true to say that closure practices are related to material factors, it would also be banal. There is a world of difference between the truism that the institutions of closure usually emerge in response to material forces of *some kind or another*; and the claim that such institutions are a response to *one specific set* of material forces. The first statement simply says that any form of organized closure in any type of society will arise on the basis of certain economic and social factors, which can always be intelligibly described in the particular case. The second statement says that closure is a phenomenon of that unique constellation of social and economic factors known as capitalism – and is thus patently false. There might be a case for reducing patterns of social closure to some prior materialist conception if past and present productive systems in all their manifold variety could somehow be incorporated into a single theoretical schema – a kind of universal mode of production akin to 'deep structural grammar'. It would then presumably be possible to explain all forms of social closure in all types of society by reference to general material laws, instead of resorting merely to the descriptive analysis of economic and social factors. But the likelihood of Marxism ever producing such a general schema should not be rated very high, not least of all because its traditional preoccupation with capitalism has badly stunted its generalizing capacity. The conceptual artillery constructed for the assault upon private property and the market-place turns out to be virtually obsolete against the very different targets presented by contemporary socialist societies. Even the notion of a socialist mode of production remains thoroughly obscure, which is not the best advertisement for an ostensibly materialist theory claiming wide explanatory powers.

Nor does it seem likely that historical materialism, ancient or modern, could account for the structure and origins of communal conflict. The answer to the question, why does exclusion and domination assume a predominantly racial form in one society, a religious form in another, and a largely class form in yet a third, is only explicable in historical terms. There is no general *theory* that could explain why some societies and not others experienced the migratory and demographic movements that finally resulted in communal divisions. These have to be treated as 'just so' historical facts, not as events to be incorporated into some jumbo social theory. The events leading up to any particular system of domination can of course always be described, analysed, and otherwise made intelligible. And Marxism, like Weberian sociology, offers its own special package of concepts for carrying out the exercise of making things intelligible. But a conceptual package or model is not a theory about how or why things came to be as they are; it is a moral vocabulary that reconstructs past and present social reality in an unavoidably slanted way.

The choice, in other words, is not between a sociological or Weberian class model on the one hand, and a Marxist class theory on the other; the choice is between competing models, each containing its own built-in recommendations as to the proper way to understand and pronounce judgement upon the forms and varieties of structured inequality and oppression. It is perhaps unlikely that Marxists would be willing to concede that what is commonly presented as a powerful global theory is in effect only one morally loaded conceptual model among others; in which case we shall have to go on waiting for the curtain finally to rise on that grand explanatory performance for which so much of western Marxism seems like a permanent dress rehearsal.

## Notes

1 As Castles and Kosack point out, 'National trade union policy has always called for equality, but in the absence of any practical programme to combat discrimination it has remained purely abstract and has had little effect at the local and plant levels.' Castles and Kosack 1973:145. These authors document numerous cases of the refusal of indigenous European workers to support industrial action taken by immigrant workers, even where both groups were members of the same union. See pp. 152–79.
2 Yarwood 1964; Palfreeman 1971.
3 Price 1974:135.
4 Simons and Simons 1969:618–19. The slogan of the early communist movement in South Africa was 'Workers of the World Unite – To Defend a White South Africa!'. Adam 1971:19.
5 Mackenzie 1973:172–3.
6 Bauman 1972:99.
7 Bauman 1972:91.
8 Davies 1973:49.
9 Davies 1973:51.
10 Weber (eds Roth and Wittich) 1968:342.
11 Capital 'requires racism not for racism's sake but for the sake of capital. Hence at a certain level of economic activity . . . it finds it more profitable to abandon the idea of superiority of race in order to promote the idea of the superiority of capital. Racism dies in order that capital might survive'. Sivanandan 1976:367.
12 Note, in this respect, Perry Anderson's somewhat premature judgement that, 'As a political weapon, strikes are nearly always profoundly ineffectual. No general strike has ever been successful'. Anderson 1967:266.
13 In the eyes of some observers the tilt has been anything but modest. According to Professor Grunfeld, 'The TUC has the legislative bit now

firmly between its teeth. Its change in attitude towards law dates from the realisation in 1969 that the Cabinet room itself could be penetrated. . . . Once the TUC realised it could control the law-making process itself, its attitude towards labour law made a U-turn'. Grunfeld 1978:97. No estimate is given of the date at which the representatives of capital are thought to have 'penetrated' the Cabinet room.

14 Johnson 1977. In this diagnosis of the times, the power of organized labour is singled out as one of the factors contributing to 'the atrophy of constitutional habits' (p. viii).

15 Goode 1969.

16 Etzioni 1969:vii.

17 Etzioni 1969:vi.

18 Simpson and Simpson 1969:199.

19 Weber (eds Roth and Wittich) 1968:49–50.

20 Etzioni 1969:vii.

21 Elliott's work suggests that the established professions in Britain were well on the way to securing a legal monopoly *before* a 'knowledge base' had been systematically cultivated. Elliott 1972:29–32.

22 As Perrucci argues, 'while expert knowledge may be a factor in initiating the power of an occupational group, that same power is also used to maintain exclusive control over the knowledge of the profession and the legal right to use that knowledge in practice. Thus, while the knowledge base of an occupational group may be critical for creating a profession with the power to control its activities, the knowledge base is not a sufficient explanation for the continuation of this power'. Perrucci 1973:123.

23 On the unionization of women, see Lockwood 1958:151–3; Bain 1970: 40–3.

24 Braverman 1974:408.

25 Oppenheimer 1973:223.

26 Oppenheimer 1973:225.

27 Marcus 1973:192.

28 See, for example Prandy 1965.

29 As the Parrys point out, 'Unionism and professionalism may be seen as alternative occupational strategies which are concerned with the collective manipulation and control of particular types of market capacity'. Parry and Parry 1976:251.

30 Dickens 1972.

31 Lansbury 1974:299.

32 Roberts, Loveridge, and Gennard 1972:231.

33 Roberts, Loveridge, and Gennard 1972:232.

PART TWO

# Class and state

# 7

# Social cleavages and the forms of state

The sombre reality of the state as a political force has always been fully appreciated by Marxists, but it is only in quite recent times that the state has been thought to pose a serious theoretical problem. Lenin's terse definition of the state as 'bodies of armed men' seemed serviceable enough to an earlier generation committed to its revolutionary seizure and overthrow. For contemporary Marxism, on the other hand, the state is at once a much more shadowy and omnipotent creation; like the holy spirit, its manifestations are everywhere. And like the holy spirit, too, about the last thing it lends itself to is physical seizure. In Miliband's words, ' . . . "the state" is not a thing . . . it does not as such exist'.[1]

Much of contemporary bourgeois theory also seems predicated on the assumption that the state does not 'as such' exist. Pluralist theory in particular has little room in its explanatory model for a social agency so heavily laden with the trappings of power. Power in the pluralist model is a political resource that does not readily lend itself to such storage and concentration; rather, it is subject to continuous dissipation and self-cancellation through the push and pull of competing veto groups. Since in any case pluralism is part of that tradition that has sought to map out a terrain called 'society' it would naturally encounter some difficulty in incorporating a foreign body conventionally thought to be above society. David Easton's pronouncement that 'neither the state nor power is a concept that serves to bind together political research', and that in his own analysis of the political system the very term state would 'be avoided scrupulously' on the grounds that 'clarity of expression demands this abstinence', was simply a formal statement of tacitly accepted pluralist practice.[2]

It may be worth recalling that this particular form of abstinence was to some extent a reaction to what was felt to be a tedious and fruitless harping on the state theme by earlier generations of western theorists. The notion of the state advanced by many nineteenth-century writers was closely bound up with contemporary movements of national unification and the drawing and consolidation of territorial boundaries. The unity of the state served as an attractive doctrine in the struggle against local particularisms as well as against the claims of the universal church. In addition, of course, the symbols of state could be harnessed to the drive for internal cohesion against the schismatic appeals of class and sectional interests. Loyalty to the state could be presented as the ultimate moral commitment, transcending loyalty to any particular set of leaders, institutions, or interests. Theorists of the state were thus in some respects busy concocting a shining ideological rationale for the sometimes grubby territorial and nationalist aspirations of their political masters. Given this background of events it is not altogether surprising that the state should often come to be portrayed as the noblest and best of man's creations, a form of adulation reaching its apogee in that strange Hegelian love affair with the state idea.

One of the most striking things about this is how few takers there now appear to be for the positive doctrine of the state. Who today, it might be asked, has a good word to say for the state? Conservative, anarchist, liberal, and Marxist theorists, each in their different way, present the state as a malevolent force squatting like a toad on the backs of men, stifling all human potential and independent spirit. The term has come very largely to be used as a derogatory substitute for the more benign 'government' or 'society' on the part of those who have not quite learned to love their rulers or their social structures.[3]

Part of the reason for this is that the concept of the state, in the western world at least, has become to some extent divorced from the concept of nation, with which it was once closely allied. A homely connotation was introduced by the hybrid usage 'nation-state', in that the concept of nation, implying as it does a cultural community, is not quite so contaminated with those ideas of force and violence with which the concept of the state is impregnated. As Weber pointed out, although nation and state refer to quite different social categories, which are by no means congruent, they do tend to require one another for mutual survival. Weber saw the main source of national identity in the language community, the primary vehicle of cultural expression and collective sentiments. The state on the other hand was a political force laying claim to powers on a specifically territorial basis. Nations needed to become states in order to defend the boundaries of the cultural community against erosion or assault by powerful neighbours. States needed to become nations in order to provide the moral foundations of internal unity.

It is significant that Weber's writings on the state are largely concerned with its use of power in a purely territorial capacity, reflecting no doubt the German preoccupation with unification and the sensitive issue of the eastern borders. He says comparatively little about the role of the state in relation to class structure and the distributive system. The state is decidedly not one of the 'aspects of the distribution of power' within the stratification system.

In contemporary Marxism, by contrast, the state is considered in almost no other light. Its function is one of purely internal social control, and any mention of the use of state powers for the defence of national boundaries is something of a rarity. Marx's reference to the state as an instrument adopted by the bourgeoisie to safeguard their 'internal and external purposes' has not really been pursued with equal seriousness on both counts.[4] For Marxism in the era of peaceful co-existence the only serious threats acknowledged by the state appear to be those that come from within its borders. And, for the capitalist state in particular, the use of power in a territorial capacity is understood only in that very special sense of the territory on which class struggles take place.

## II

Contemporary Marxist theorizing on the problem of the state is preceded as a rule by two preliminary observations: first, that Marx himself never developed a fully fledged theory of the state – an omission that, given the encroachment of the central powers in modern times, is felt to be in urgent need of repair. And, second, that Marx's occasional treatment of the state as a working political entity appears to be at some variance with his more lofty and programmatic statements, at least in terms of a changed emphasis upon the independent role of the state in the distribution of power.

The classic statement at the conceptual level is of course the elliptical pronouncement in the *Communist Manifesto* in which the capitalist state is likened to an executive committee charged with the workaday task of managing the affairs of the bourgeoisie. The state acts in a fairly uncomplicated way as the direct spokesman and protector of the exploiting class. Marx's own dismissive comment in *The German Ideology* that the state is 'nothing more than' this, seems to squash quite firmly any idea that it raised problems of any real theoretical import.[5]

However, in his account of the Bonapartist state, Marx abandons the broad brush strokes of historical generalization in favour of a detailed and finely drawn sketch. And in this, the relationship between state and dominant class is shown to be one of considerable complexity and tension. Marx portrayed the state under Louis Bonaparte as the saviour of the bourgeoisie, notwithstanding the fact that the *coup d'état* stripped the bourgeoisie of parliamentary power and elevated Bonaparte to the standing of a personal dictator. The bourgeoisie, Marx implies, actually needed this form of rule, despite their formal opposition to it, in order to hold on to their social and economic privileges.

The French bourgeoisie of the period were depicted as weak and disorganized, unable to destroy the vestigial power of the old aristocracy and riddled with anxieties about the political demands of the newly emergent proletariat. Trapped and apparently ineffectual between these two opposing forces the bourgeoisie felt a collective need for a more protective state than parliamentary democracy could offer. Bonaparte's dictatorship fitted the bill; it made safe the rights of property, though at the heavy cost of suspending traditional political liberties and parliamentary rule. The bourgeoisie, it seems, wept all the way to the bank. Thus, in Marx's reading of events, the state rules in the general interests of the dominant social class but is in no sense their 'executive committee'.[6]

It is this second version of the state – as an agency serving the collective purposes of an exploiting class while not acting as its direct representative – that provides the usual entry point for Marxist analysis of the modern capitalist state. Far from being dismissed as a non-problem, the bourgeois state now appears to qualify for the same kind of theoretical treatment and elaboration meted out to the Bonapartist state. That is to say, those peculiarities of the state identified by Marx as the outcome of a somewhat unusual condition of class stalemate have now come to be regarded as intrinsic features of almost any kind of state, including the modern capitalist variety.

Although the Bonapartist model undoubtedly provides the inspiration for much current Marxist writing on the state, it is noticeable that the original emphasis on unstable class equilibrium has been quietly dropped. The equilibrium thesis was stated in general terms by Engels in the course of his discussion on the origins and evolution of the state: 'By way of exception periods occur in which warring classes balance each other so nearly that the state power as ostensible mediator acquires for the moment a certain degree of independence of both.'[7] This idea of opposing classes reaching a point of temporary balance or equilibrium is logically implied in the classical Marxist emphasis upon the ascendancy of new, and the decline of old or degenerate, class forces. The very imagery of decline and fall naturally suggests the occurrence of brief historical interludes in which a class in the ascendant has not quite reached its social climax, but still hovers on the brink of evicting the sitting political tenant. It is under this temporary condition, when history holds its breath, that the state is felt able to emerge from the shadows as a force in its own right, filling the vacuum created by class stalemate. Trotsky's metaphor nicely captures the idea:

'As soon as the struggle of two social strata – the haves and have-nots, the exploiters and the exploited – reaches its highest tension, the conditions are established for the domination of bureaucracy, police, soldiery. The government becomes "independent" of society. Let us once more recall: if two forks are stuck symmetrically into a cork, the latter can stand even on the head of a pin. That is precisely the schema of Bonapartism.'[8]

Whatever parallels contemporary Marxism finds between Bonapartist and bourgeois states the idea of delicately balanced classes is not one of them. The standard account of the modern capitalist state is of a system in which the bourgeoisie swamps totally the life and mind of the proletariat. One of the intriguing things about this account is that distinctive and decisive powers are accorded to the state under social conditions that do not remotely approach class equilibrium. Hence the organizing concept around which Marxist analysis of the modern state revolves is not that of balance or equilibrium, as it was for earlier theorists, but of 'relative autonomy' – that is, the capacity of the state to break free of its role as a mere executive committee and to win some measure of independence from the class whose destiny is so intimately bound up with its own.

The state's need for, and ability to gain, relative autonomy is felt to be necessary on a number of grounds. Most important among these is its function of organizing and replenishing the conditions that make bourgeois hegemony possible. It seems that, left to its own devices, the dominant class would be unable to make secure its political and social pre-eminence. In Poulantzas' view, for example, 'because of the isolation of socio-economic relations and because of the break-up of the bourgeois class into fractions, etc., the dominant classes are more often than not unable to raise themselves by their own efforts to a hegemonic level vis-a-vis the dominated classes.'[9] This is a view echoed in Miliband's remarks to the effect that a prime responsibility of the capitalist state is to resolve conflicts within the bourgeoisie, a task it can only properly perform if some measure of autonomy from this class is guaranteed.[10]

Another beneficial effect for the dominant class of the state's separation is that the state is better placed to accomplish necessary political and social reforms which, although appearing to conflict with bourgeois interests, actually serve to shore them up. The introduction by the state of universal suffrage, the Factory Acts, the legal recognition of trade unions, and so forth, was almost everywhere accompanied by intense opposition from the capitalist class, even though in retrospect it can be seen that these reforms contributed greatly to its very survival. It is, in other words, as if the state acts as the 'intelligence' of the bourgeoisie; by virtue of its social distance from the class it serves, the state is all the more able to orchestrate and plan the strategies for bourgeois survival. The bourgeoisie itself is caught up in the day-to-day struggle against the working class and therefore tends to be conscious only of its immediate, short-term interests. The state, on the other hand, being well removed from the front line, can take the long-term, strategic view.[11]

This idea of the state as a kind of intelligence is not a specifically Marxist one, as writers of Hegelian persuasion make clear. Bosanquet, for example, speaks of the state as 'an intelligent system' that appeals 'by reasoning and persuasion to the logical will'.[12] Durkheim, too, from a very different tradition, elaborates on the same theme:

> 'The State is the centre . . . of a particular kind of consciousness, of one that is limited but higher, clearer and with a more vivid sense of itself. . . The representations that derive from the State are always more conscious of themselves, of their causes and their aims. These have been concerted in a way that is less obscured. The collective agency which plans them realizes better what it is about. . .
>
> 'To sum up, we can therefore say that the State is a special organ whose responsibility it is to work out certain representations which hold good for the collectivity. These representations are distinguished from other collective representations by their higher degree of consciousness and reflection. . . Strictly speaking, the State is the very organ of social thought . . . Its principal function is to think.'[13]

Needless to say, for Durkheim all this vital thinking is performed for the good of the collective whole, not for the good of something as unimaginable as an exploiting class. Nevertheless, his definition of the state as 'a special organ whose responsibility it is to work out certain representations which hold good for the collectivity' needs to be qualified only by that final crucial term to stand as a faultless summary of the neo-Marxist view.

This is because present fascination with the modern capitalist state centres much less upon its brutish aspects than upon its apparent capacity to win the hearts and minds of those who, on any rational view, should find the state and all its works repulsive. That is to say, attention is now directed to the state's attempt to dress itself in Durkheimian clothing by seeking to transform class representations into collective representations. And, once again, the task of accomplishing this difficult feat of normative persuasion is thought to be considerably eased when the state can keep its distance from the class whose values it is attempting to universalize.

The greater its show of detachment from the dominant class, especially by way of its ability to force through concessions to the underdogs, the more resounding is felt to be the state's success in winning the moral allegiance of the subordinate classes. Workers and other exploited groups become prone to look upon the state as *their* champion, their defence against the ravages of a soulless dominant class, much in the way that the French peasantry were deluded into believing that Bonaparte was their champion against other powerful interests.[14] Legitimacy for the system would be far more difficult to win if the state were seen blatantly to be acting in the interests of one class at the expense of all others – i.e. as the former's executive committee. The state thus performs its highest service for an exploiting class when, as Miliband expresses it, it acts *'on behalf* of that class rather than at *its behest'*.[15]

The conception of the state as the higher intelligence of the bourgeoisie bears more than a passing resemblance to the Leninist conception of the vanguard party as the political intelligence of the proletariat. There too we find the assumption that, left to its own devices, the working class would give an extremely poor account of itself; hence the need for a separate agency of more refined political consciousness to serve on its behalf. Such an agency, in virtue of being for the working masses but not directly of them, would not be hampered or side-tracked by any of those debilitating concerns for immediate, short-term economic gratification at the expense of the ultimate political goal. The vanguard party too, then, can only operate effectively if an area of social space is preserved between itself and the class it represents. One of the most pressing of all problems for Marxism, practical as much as theoretical, is how to account for the process by which the relative autonomy of the vanguard party tends to develop into full autonomy after the seizure of power. What in other words explains the party's transition from the status of a mere 'agency' to a political power in its own right? Similarly, once the state is emboldened to act as something more than another group's executive committee, how and by whom are political limits imposed upon its independence? Why are such important political relationships always thought to freeze at the stage of *relative* autonomy?

## III

The social fact of relative autonomy tends to be demonstrated by reference to the tensions and occasional conflicts that arise between state and bourgeoisie. These are believed to emerge in the course of the state's attempt to grant concessionary reforms to the working class that encroach on bourgeois rights and privileges. The state appears to become caught up in a byzantine set of political arrangements in which the aid of the subordinate class is enlisted in the struggle against the bourgeoisie – a struggle that, paradoxically, is fought in the best interests of the bourgeoisie itself.[16] The curiously antagonistic relationship between state and dominant class is brought out with particular clarity in that formulation that draws a firm conceptual distinction between power as embodied in the state, and the power originating in social classes:

> 'one of the main reasons for stressing the notion of the relative autonomy of the state is that there is a basic distinction to be made between class power and state power, and that the analysis of the meaning and implications of that notion of relative autonomy must indeed focus on the forces which cause it to be greater or less, the circumstances in which it is exercised, and so on. The blurring of the distinction between class power and state power . . . makes any such analysis impossible.'[17]

Once it is acknowledged, as it is here by Miliband, that the state is founded on a separate and possibly competing basis of power to that of social classes, then indeed the state does pose a serious problem, though the most awkward questions are addressed to Marxism itself.

Conceptions of the state that start off from the idea of a separate, independent source of state power are, after all, plentiful enough; but they stem from traditions completely alien to Marxism. There is, for example, an established school of thought that views the state as an exploitative agency in its own right, concerned only with its self-aggrandizement, pursuing interests at variance with those of all other groups or classes. Plamenatz has argued, in the course of his critique of the Marxist position, that although members of the state apparatus may be of bourgeois stock there is no reason to suppose that they will necessarily put the interests of this class above their own corporate interests as state officials.[18] Seen from this perspective, the state may not merely make the transition from relative to full autonomy but may in certain circumstances rise to a position of ascendancy over all social classes, including the dominant.

The notion of the state as a corporate interest group is, of course, more than hinted at in Weber's discussion of bureaucratic powers, usefully summarized by Beetham as follows:

'Though in theory only an impersonal apparatus, a bureaucracy formed at the same time a separate group within the state, with its own special interests, values and power basis. Its separate interests lay in the maintenance and extension of administrative positions and power; its distinctive outlook lay in a belief in its own superior objectivity in interpreting the national interest free from party bias; its power lay in its knowledge and experience and in the cloak of secrecy with which it concealed its operations. While these features were important to its effectiveness as a technical instrument, they also helped mould a bureaucracy into a special group within the state, with its own separate interests.'[19]

Although Weber speaks of bureaucracy as a corporate group within the state, it is only a small step to combine the two in the concept of a state bureaucracy, denoting a powerful stratum distinct from social classes. This usage is of course to be found in the classical liberal view of the state, still kept alive in the writings of von Hayek and propagated by economists of the Chicago school. This is the picture of the state as a modern Leviathan trampling roughshod over cherished bourgeois values and institutions. The unchecked expansion of the central powers is felt to lead to the steady erosion of the moral core of bourgeois ideology, especially the ideals of self-help, market freedom, and individualism – ideals that are displaced by their very opposites: state welfare, central planning, and collectivism. It is Leviathan itself, not the working class, that is here singled out as the implacable enemy of the bourgeoisie.

This vision of the state as a bureaucratic monster that has wrenched itself free of class control to become parasitic upon the rest of society cannot easily be squared with the unshakable Marxist assumption that the only natural habitat of power is in social classes. Thus, Marxists, of whatever vintage, never go so far as to entertain the possiblity of a fully autonomous state. Yet to press a distinction between class power and state power is to travel willy nilly quite a long way down that path that leads to the forbidden land of bureaucratic theory. This theory and its offshoots is, as has been seen, perfectly at home with the idea of power existing independently of, and even above, social classes. Indeed, there is something to be said for the view that much of the appeal of bureaucratic theory rests precisely on its usefulness as a counterweight to the Marxist model of the distribution of power. On this count it is a little surprising to learn from Poulantzas that 'the specific problem that the State apparatus presents . . . is *the problem of bureaucracy*'. That is to say, 'the State apparatus forms an objective system of special "branches" whose relation presents a *specific internal unity* and obeys, to a large extent, *its own logic*'.[20] A state that operates as a unified entity, and in accordance with a logic of its own, does not seem to be at a far remove from a state acting in its own corporate interests. Here too, then, there is more than a hint of state power as an element quite distinct from class power.

One of the difficulties faced by neo-Marxism is that of showing just what are the peculiar interests of the state and its agents that are even partially discordant with those of the bourgeoisie. In the absence of any genuine conflict of interests between the two the fierce insistence on the 'separation of powers', as it were, loses most of its point. The fact that Marxist accounts of the relations between capitalist state and dominant class are more or less unanimous in stressing their ultimate symmetry and concord suggests that the only meaning that can be attached to the notion of relative autonomy is that of mere functional differentiation. That is, the offices of state – in the form of government, judiciary, civil service, armed forces, police, etc. – are institutionally separate from the dominant bourgeois class simply by dint of being specialized functions in the division of labour. The relative autonomy of the bourgeois state is, in other words, nothing much more than the relative autonomy enjoyed by virtually any 'executive committee' *vis-à-vis* the wider constituency or body whose purposes it serves. Present-day Marxists have indulged in much huffing and puffing in trying to discard the classical or vulgar concept of the state, only to have ended up with a thinly disguised version of the same thing.

To impart as much significance to the idea of relative autonomy as is claimed for it by contemporary theorists could be done only by developing fully the tentative and unorthodox suggestion concerning the ability of the state to generate its own power. However much Marxist writers flirt with this suggestion they invariably pull back from its full implications. Whatever autonomy the state enjoys is always thought to be circumscribed in the long run by the parameters of class-based power. That is to say, the modern capitalist state is, in effect, conceived of as an executive committee with wide discretionary powers, answerable in the last resort to its bourgeois constituency. After all, what could the capitalist state possibly do for the bourgeoisie by virtue of its 'relative autonomy' that it would be *unable* to do in its capacity as a sophisticated 'executive committee'?

## IV

At the root of all these difficulties is the current fascination with Bonapartism, that peculiar condition of the state that Marx, rightly or wrongly, diagnosed as the outcome of class stalemate. What is now felt to distinguish one type of state from another is simply the degree to which it departs from the pure Bonapartist model.[21] The question of the day thus becomes 'how much' relative autonomy is enjoyed by this or that state, a question that serves as the basis for a classificatory system of different types of state. Bourgeois and fascist states, for example, can be said to differ from each other on the grounds of their varying degrees of relative autonomy – the fascist state approximating more closely to the pure Bonapartist model by virtue of its greater degree of independence from the dominant class.

However, instead of assuming that modern states enjoy a measure of autonomy as of necessity, it might be more useful to reformulate the problem by attempting to specify the structural features that actually govern the relations between state and class. It would in fact seem profitable to juxtapose state power and class power only when two conditions are fulfilled: first, when the incumbents of state offices form a corporate political elite with distinct aims and interests of its own; and, second, when there also exists alongside this corporate elite a dominant or exploiting class in some broadly accepted sense. Questions raised by the notion of relative autonomy are pertinent only when both these social ingredients are present. If state power is not in the control of a distinct corporate elite it is theoretically barren to juxtapose state and dominant class; if state power *is* monopolized by such an elite, but there is no exploiting class, the juxtaposition is clearly redundant. The two variables can be combined to give the following classification:

## Marxism and class theory

| Corporate political elite | Dominant class | Type of system |
| --- | --- | --- |
| + | + | Absolutist; fascist |
| − | + | Bourgeois |
| + | − | Socialist |
| − | − | 'Full communism' |

On this classification the neo-Marxist concept of the state would be applicable only to the first of the four theoretical possibilities – that is, a political system in which a corporate state elite exists in conjunction with a dominant social class. Absolutist and fascist states do seem to lend themselves quite well to that kind of analysis that draws upon the Bonapartist imagery of mutual attraction and repulsion between state incumbents on the one hand and a dominant class on the other. Bourgeois society, by contrast, does not lend itself to such analysis because the bourgeois state is not in the grip of a corporate group with distinct interests over and above those of the bourgeoisie. Socialist society is also not amenable to such analysis, because although state power is certainly monopolized by a distinct political elite, it cannot be counterposed to the power of any dominant class recognizable to Marxism.

All judgements as to the usefulness or otherwise of the Marxist theory of the state presumably carry more weight if the state in question is seen within the context of a class analysis congenial to Marxism. To find the Marxist theory of the state wanting purely by reference to bourgeois definitions of social reality would be a somewhat pointless exercise. In what follows, therefore, it should be borne in mind that the brief statements about the nature of absolutist, fascist, bourgeois, and socialist systems are not offered as definitive or commonly agreed upon versions of political reality, but as specifically Marxist constructs. Anderson's account of the absolutist state is the first case in point.

Anderson suggests that absolutism is to be understood as a political system developed by the European landed nobility as a response to the decline of serfdom. Once the peasantry had escaped from direct subjugation by the land-owning class at the village or manorial level – mainly through the commutation of labour services into rents – the nobility sought to re-establish and consolidate their control by the use of coercion at the level of the state. At the apex of this system of social control stood the monarchy vested with absolute powers.

The particular point of interest for the present discussion concerns the uneasy relationship between the nobility as the dominant class of the period, and the monarchy as the embodiment of absolute state power. Anderson chronicles numerous episodes that demonstrate the eruption into open conflict of the ever-present tension between aristocratic landed interests and the royal power. This 'nobiliary revolt against the consolidation of Absolutism' is shown to have been especially fierce in France:[22]

> 'The objective contradictions of Absolutism here unfolded in their plainest form. The monarchy sought to tax the wealth of the nobility, while the nobility demanded controls on the policies of the monarchy: the aristocracy, in effect, refused to alienate its economic privileges without gaining political rights over the conduct of the royal State.'[23]

Yet however deep the antagonisms between royal and aristocratic interests might have run, they were never likely to result in a destructive conflict *à l'outrance*. The dominant landed class was all too well aware of the political threat posed by usurpationary groups among the peasantry and the nascent bourgeoisie of the towns. It was therefore willing to suffer the profligacy and arbitrary powers of the monarchy rather than risk the possibility of complete expropriation which would almost certainly have followed the collapse of the royal state apparatus. There could never be a 'full scale, united aristocratic onslaught on the monarchy, for the two were held together by an umbilical class cord'.[24]

In Anderson's presentation, the landed nobility under absolutism thus appear to occupy a somewhat similar position to the French bourgeoisie under Bonaparte in Marx's portrayal. The bourgeoisie reluctantly condoned the exercise of political power by a dictator who was not directly of themselves in order to secure their economic ascendancy over the masses. In Marx's striking phrase, the bourgeoisie in order 'to save its purse must lay aside its crown'.[25] In similar vein, the nobility under absolutism could only make sure of their dominance as a class by agreeing, as Anderson puts it, 'to deposit power with the monarchy'.[26]

The essential feature of this type of account is that the dominant social class of the epoch is counterposed not against an abstraction called the state, but against a definable political elite with specific interests of its own which has *control* of the agencies of state. The notion of relative autonomy has some meaning here in so far as it points up the tense and ambivalent relationship between the incumbents of state power and an exploiting class that is the indirect beneficiary of state rule. It is a relationship between two groups, each powerful in a different way, locked together in a kind of love-hate bondage, and sustained only by the mutual fear of a more terrible fate. It is precisely this schema too, of course, that sums up the standard Marxist account of fascism.

Fascist regimes are usually interpreted as a response to an especially acute crisis of monopoly capitalism, in which parliamentary and
democratic institutions are unable to provide a political framework
capable of guaranteeing the class sovereignty of the bourgeoisie. Due
to the internal contradictions of a system in decay, which are exacer-
bated by the general international crisis and increasing political militancy on the part of the working class, the normally stable foundations of exploitation are badly shaken. In desperation, influential
sections of the bourgeoisie, above all the representatives of monopoly
capital, reluctantly opt for a 'strong' political regime capable of shor-
ing up the crumbling edifice of capitalism in its final phase. This is
achieved by dispensing with the luxuries of parliament, political
parties, and civil liberties, and by reducing to naught the usurpationary capacity of organized labour. In Mandel's paraphrase of Trotsky:
'The historical function of the fascist seizure of power is to change
suddenly and violently the conditions of the production and realization of surplus value to the advantage of the decisive groups of
monopoly capitalism.' But at the same time, 'fascism has only been
able to perform this function by the extensive political expropriation
of the bourgeoisie'.[27]

Once again, Marx's metaphor of crowns being exchanged for
purses seems appropriate. In this case the crown of political authority
is passed from the capitalist class to the fascist party apparatus, a
corporate body with quite definite ideas and purposes all its own. The
fascist party assumes control of virtually the entire machinery of
government, law, and coercion; it staffs all key positions of state with
its chosen members and supporters, and insinuates its own unique
doctrines into social policy and the circulation of ideas. The state
becomes relatively autonomous of the bourgeoisie by virtue of the fact
that all the important agencies and functions of state have become
inextricably fused with the fascist party apparatus. Where a
hegemonic party has its hand on all the levers of political and social
control, yet continues to respect bourgeois rights of property and
expropriation, then the stage seems set for a genuine display of that
delicate and taut relationship between state power and class power
that so excites the Marxist imagination. Under fascism it can indeed
be said that the state is no mere executive committee of the
bourgeoisie. The experience of the Italian and German bourgeoisie
under fascism drove this point home in the sharpest manner:

> 'Having helped the dictators to rob all other classes, and notably
> the working classes, of any semblance of power, they found their
> own drastically curtailed and in some crucial areas, notably for-
> eign policy, altogether nullified. This is not a situation which an

economically and socially dominant class, however secure it may feel about the ultimate intentions of its rulers, can contemplate without grave qualms, since it introduces into the process of decision-making, to which its members have been used to making a major contribution, an extremely high element of unpredictability.'[28]

This presumably is the price to be paid by the bourgeoisie when the state rules 'on its behalf' but not 'at its behest'. If this distinction is offered as anything more than a terminological nicety the very fact that it can readily be accepted as an apt description of fascist rule necessarily weakens its application to the condition of bourgeois rule, where no equivalent price has to be paid because the bourgeoisie does *not* relinquish effective control over the state. The advantage of bourgeois democracy for the dominant class is surely that the state does rule largely at its 'behest' and not merely on its 'behalf'.

## V

The Marxist analysis of the state grounds itself upon that unchartered social space between the institutions of state and an exploiting class. From this position Marxism seeks to observe the antagonisms and occasional conflicts that mark the fruitful tension between the two powers. However, in the important case of bourgeois society, what are taken to be manifestations of tension between state and dominant class turn out on closer inspection to be manifestations of tension within the bourgeoisie itself. It is not the state acting as the organized intelligence of the bourgeoisie that drives through social and political reforms against the shortsighted opposition of this same class; the reforms in question are championed and set in motion by those whom Marxist historiography would judge to be the shrewder elements among the exclusionary class itself, in the teeth of opposition from their less politically astute brethren. The protracted and often bitter struggles over the piecemeal programme designed to incorporate labour into civil society were fought out within the ranks of that class whose members shared a common interest in the survival of capitalism.

As suggested in the discussion of social closure, antagonisms within the dominant class frequently revolve around differing interpretations of liberal ideology, in particular those touching upon the delicate matter of class reproduction and the moral basis of exclusion. A shared commitment to property ownership, rights of appropriation, and a market economy by no means precludes intense disagreement over the practical translation of these values into social policy. The variety of labels used to denote contending factions within the bourgeoisie – Whig and Tory, Liberal and Conservative, progressive and reactionary, etc. – would seem to suggest that ideological cleavages are inseparable from the history of this class. Once the antagonisms over social reform are perceived in the light of this chronic internal class division the need to invoke an additional explanatory factor in the guise of the state quickly evaporates. It is not the state acting as some 'third force' that settles the issues of the day, but the most powerful section of the bourgeoisie acting directly through parliament and the legislative machinery.

The only third force that Marxism would find it necessary to introduce is that of the working-class movement. It could be argued with all plausibility that it is only in response to pressure from below that the liberal and reforming spirits within the bourgeoisie are set loose to do their work, inspired by the formidable combination of charitable sentiment and political prudence. Social reform within capitalist society could therefore easily be thought of as the outcome of a continually changing balance of class forces, both within the bourgeoisie and between this class and the proletariat. It could be predicted that small and gradual shifts in the balance of power to labour's advantage would eventually give rise to a demand for political or social reforms, some of which would be found quite acceptable to the liberal wing of the bourgeoisie. A not unusual political line-up would therefore consist of a temporary alliance between organized labour and the liberal bourgeoisie against the conservative elements in that same class.

To the extent that such an alliance could be said to have smoothed the passage of laws whose overall effect was to domesticate the working class, then it might indeed by claimed that the bourgeoisie had, and still has, an 'intelligence' at its service. But this intelligence emanates not from the state but from influential sections of the exclusionary class itself. The oddity is that Marxists should have brought their heaviest theoretical equipment to bear on the problem of the modern capitalist state, when it is this type of state above all others that requires little in the way of special understanding beyond that provided by orthodox class analysis. It is partly, perhaps, because Marxism tacitly assumes that conflicts internal to a class are never quite as real as conflicts between classes that the bourgeois state is thought to take on decisive powers of its own. Imbued with a reality *sui generis*, it can then be represented as one of the protagonists in a conflict that is felt to be too profound to divide a class against itself.

To draw upon the notion of a separate and distinct state power is really to imply that the workings and the contours of the distributive system cannot properly be accounted for by reference to the power generated by class forces. The leading assumption would seem to be that serious discrepancies exist between the formal power of a social class and the actual share of resources accruing to it – discrepancies that are accounted for by the intervention of an exogenous force, in the shape of the state, that distorts or upsets the distributive effects of unimpeded class struggles. Hence, in the interpretation of fascism, the share of surplus going to the capitalist class is held to be greatly in excess of what it would have gained under conditions of parliamentary democracy and institutionalized class struggle; given its grave political weaknesses the bourgeoisie would probably have come off very badly in an outright and open conflict with the organized working class. The difference between what the bourgeoisie actually gained under fascism, and what it would probably have got merely as a result of its own unaided collective efforts, is the product of direct intervention by the fascist party-state on its behalf. It is the fact of that crucial something extra – a bonus or 'political rent', as it were, accruing to a class – that is the telltale sign of the state's direct entry into the distributive arena as a force in its own right.

On Marxism's own reading of class struggles in modern bourgeois society it would be extremely difficult to cite comparable instances in which the share of spoils were attributable to something in addition to the relative power of capital and labour. The handsome surplus granted to the bourgeoisie under fascism, in excess of its own exploitative capacity, was made possible precisely because the benefactor was not the bourgeoisie's 'own' state. It was the reparation, so to speak, made by the fascist party to the bourgeoisie for so rudely relieving the latter of state power. When, however, a dominant class is in control of the state, such that no other corporate group stands between it and the levers of power, it makes little sense to think of the state as a separate agency in the distributive system; the allocation of rewards follows directly from the distribution of power between classes. All declarations as to the state's intervention on behalf of this or that class can usually be rephrased to read 'intervention by a section of the exclusionary class' without much loss of meaning – a restatement that certainly could not be made in the case of fascism. It could therefore be said that whereas, under fascism, state and party are virtually one, under bourgeois democracy, state and dominant class are virtually one: in neither case can anything of much explanatory value be gained by driving a notional wedge between the two.

## VI

The juxtaposition of class power and state power is uncalled for in the analysis of bourgeois society, because the state lacks a separate corporate reality. In the analysis of socialist society, on the other hand, such a juxtaposition is uncalled for on reverse grounds: namely, the absence of formal class powers. Marxism recognizes no unambiguously exploiting class in socialist society that could stand in a relationship of fruitful tension with the state. The concept of proletarian dictatorship does certainly suggest the possibility of a state ruling on behalf of workers and peasants, even if not directly controlled by them, somewhat akin to the role assigned to the fascist state in relation to the bourgeoisie. But few western Marxists, any more than bourgeois theorists, would be willing to concede that the proletariat in modern socialist societies enjoyed such a position of comparable class dominance under the benevolence of the communist party apparatus. There is rather too much evidence to show that the distributive system of contemporary socialism is, on almost all counts, far more generous to the intelligentsia than to workers and peasants.

Equally, though, Marxist critics of Soviet socialism and its offshoots are not generally inclined to think of the intelligentsia as a dominant or exploiting class either, notwithstanding its undoubted social advantages. Thus, one of the crucial differences between fascist and socialist systems, as seen through western Marxist eyes, is that although both have hegemonic parties that are closely interlocked with the state, socialism has no obvious candidate for the role of a dominant class basking in the protective, if irksome, warmth of state omnipotence.

The communist party-state, it might be said, strives to maintain the uneven equilibrium between intelligentsia and proletariat through a conscious manipulation of the distributive system. That is to say, the party permits white-collar experts and technocrats to accumulate a disproportionate share of social rewards, while at the same time ensuring that the gulf between this group and the workers does not widen to the extent that it might under an open market system. So although the socialist intelligentsia might fare as well in comparison with workers, in terms of disposable income, as do their western counterparts, they would nevertheless tend to be at a relative disadvantage to the western bourgeoisie in so far as their ability to translate income into high-quality personal services and the accoutrements of status is somewhat reduced.

Higher-income groups naturally thrive best within a system in which valuable personal services as well as consumer goods are treated as cash commodities. Where, on the other hand, resources such as housing, education, medicine, transport, recreational facilities, and the like, are withdrawn from the marketplace and allocated by purely social criteria, the advantages of high income are less pervasive, being largely confined to the purchase of domestic trinkets and other consumer goods. In this respect it could be said that the exclusionary privileges granted to the intelligentsia by the communist party-state are rather less consequential in their social effects than are the equivalent rights guaranteed to the western bourgeoisie by its very own state.

It would naturally follow from this that the condition of the socialist proletariat is, in comparative class terms, more favourable than that of the western working class, even though measured in absolute terms workers in the socialist camp might be worse off than their western equivalents. On this interpretation the socialist state could be seen as actively inhibiting the intelligentsia from transforming itself into a dominant class, while simultaneously underwriting such privileges as it enjoys. Conversely, the state might be said to acquiesce in the subordination of the proletariat while also creating the conditions that shield labour from the harsh economic climate of market rationality and commodity exchange.

Ironically, then, the modern socialist state, in the tight grip of the communist party apparatus, would appear to be the closest realization of that theoretical possibility sketched by Engels of a state suspended above classes. The party-state, impelled by aims and purposes of its own, seeks to make secure its own dominion and to preserve political stability by playing off one class against another. In Engels' schema the state succeeds in winning its independent power as a consequence of class stalemate or equilibrium; state power fills the vacuum created by the temporary suspension of class power. In the socialist reality, however, the causal sequence is reversed. It is state power that brings about the suspension of class power, and on anything but a temporary basis. The party-state strips away the capacity of social classes to organize in defence of their collective interests and replaces open distributive struggle by a centralized system of allocation. Under such an arrangement there may well exist a privileged class, but not an exploiting, dominant class. Whether or not this picture of the socialist state as one approximating to Engels' model of a power risen above classes would be endorsed by western Marxists cannot really be known, for the multitude of urgent questions raised about the nature of the socialist state have been answered for the most part by an almost unbroken silence.[29]

# VII

The foregoing discussion seems to harbour a poorly concealed belief that the problem of the state could be allowed to wither away without undue loss to Marxism or bourgeois social theory. The term itself, of course, is indispensable as a means of describing the cluster of administrative, judicial, military, and coercive institutions that the term government does not adequately capture. But a descriptive term, however serviceable, has no automatic claim to be elevated to the status of a conceptual problem. There is in other words something to be said for Marx's own refusal to take it too seriously.

Questions about the state mainly become interesting when framed as questions about the nature of the social group that monopolizes the offices of state. Considered independently of this, as an abstraction or an entity 'in itself', the state is no more inherently problematic than any other institution. If the state is conceived of as an instrument of social domination and control, the important question must surely be: who controls this instrument? And the answer always turns out to be some social or political group – be it class, race, party, military junta, or whatever – that can be defined quite independently of the state instrument itself.

This suggests that the Marxist conception of the state as the servant and protector of a dominant class is far too narrow; the state can equally well serve the interests of a dominant racial group, a dominant religious community, or a dominant party. State powers can, in other words, be harnessed in support of many forms of exclusionary closure, not only those that promote and sustain class exploitation. The closure model conceptualizes the state as an agency that buttresses and consolidates the rules and institutions of exclusion governing all relations of domination and subjection. Indeed, a class, race, sex, or ethnic group only accomplishes domination to the extent that its exclusionary prerogatives are backed up by the persuasive instruments of state.

It follows from this that the political character of the state will tend to vary according to the type of exclusionary closure that predominates in a society. That is to say, the kind of state sanctions employed in the enforcement of communal closure are likely to differ from those generally employed in the enforcement of closure along class lines. The South African state and the Orange state, for example, draw more freely upon direct coercive methods in securing the domination of whites and Protestants, respectively, than upon those more delicately persuasive methods favoured by the modern bourgeois state in maintaining the domination of class by class. The fact that the modern bourgeois state is not routinely called upon to control the working class by the same heavy-handed means as those typically used to control subordinate communal groups should not be taken as indicative of the special properties of the bourgeois state *per se*; it is indicative only of the fact that class antagonisms are themselves less politically intense and less morally encompassing than antagonisms between opposing communal groups. The combination of coercive, normative, and material sanctions drawn upon by the state will thus tend to be different in the two cases.

As this argument implies, the state can be thought of as a mirror that reflects the pattern of relations between exclusionary and usurpationary groups. If and when this relationship changes, so too does the activity of the state. Thus, if the modern bourgeois state comes to play an increasingly interventionist role in economic and social life, this is not because the state itself, wallowing in its 'relative autonomy' initiates such a course of action; it is because the balance of power between the classes has changed in some significant degree. It results from the fact that the usurpationary class is able to mount more effective demands for the supply of public goods and services that are of special benefit to its members, and which large sections of the exclusionary class would prefer to be supplied on a market basis. The nature of the state can, in other words, be 'read off' from the balance of forces in civil society.

State power is felt by Marxists to be especially problematic under that set of circumstances in which the major exclusionary group in society is not in direct control of the very agencies that legitimate and enforce its closure practices. The bourgeoisie under fascism, and the intelligentsia under socialism, are each dependent for their exclusionary privileges on the monolithic party that controls the state machine, and whose own social closure is governed in the main by strictly political and ideological considerations. However, what in Marxist analysis is usually presented as a social tension between state and privileged class, can be better understood as a tension between *party* and class. The tension arises from the use of the same state powers to enforce and sanctify exclusionary practices designed to accomplish the 'reproduction of the party', and for the simultaneous endorsement of quite different closure practices designed to maintain the privileges of class. The political friction between Falangists and some sections of the Spanish bourgeoisie at the close of the Franco era, or between the communist party apparatus and sections of the intelligentsia in eastern Europe, does seem to suggest that special problems arise whenever state powers are employed in the service of two quite differently constituted exclusionary groups. Bourgeois society is not faced with the same difficulty, since direct access to state powers is not governed by exclusionary criteria that differ in any important way from the means by which the dominant class itself is constituted.

Classical Marxism is by no means the best guide to all this. A recurring theme in Marx's work is that the disjunction between social and economic power on the one hand, and political power on the other, sets up tensions throughout the system that cry out for resolution. It is as if there were a natural strain in any social system towards a merger of economic and political power in the body of a single social class. If, moreover, it is assumed that the legitimate heir apparent to the political throne is always a materially dominant class, then the place of the state in the general scheme of things would not occasion much puzzlement. The state merely becomes the locus and the crystallization of those antagonisms arising within civil society that are channelled upwards for resolution.

This conception of the state as the political locale or the distillation of class antagonisms holds reasonably well for bourgeois society, or indeed for any type of society in which distributive struggle between contending interests is accorded open political expression. The state can then be represented as a dependent variable, responsive to the pressures emanating from class or communal forces and the changing balance of power in civil society. The state cannot be represented in quite this way, however, where the tensions and conflict in civil society are held in political suspension, as in the case of societies controlled by a hegemonic party. The *de facto* fusion of party and state means that the party-state becomes the independent, not the dependent, variable; its political activities can no longer be understood as responses to the changing power relations between classes. The classical Marxist conception of the bourgeois state is thus quite unable to survive translation to a social order dominated by the twentieth-century creation of the omnipotent party. Any understanding of the hegemonic party-state must start from the acknowledgement that certain forms of political power can be generated independently of class power and can indeed annihilate the power of social classes. Some of the convolutions of the neo-Marxist theory of the state reflect a nervous dalliance with this idea that always falls short of its final endorsement.

# Notes

1 Miliband 1969:49.
2 Easton 1953:106 and 108.
3 Thus, current expressions such as 'fiscal crisis of the state' could easily be rendered as the fiscal crisis of 'government' without any loss of meaning. This is by no means to say that the two terms can always be treated interchangeably – what might be regarded as the 'Weimar fallacy'.
4 Marx 1965:78.
5 Marx 1965:78.
6 Marx's analysis is echoed in Weber's equally scathing account of the German bourgeoisie under Bismarck. Weber suggested that the German bourgeoisie, although the economically dominant class, were content to let the Junker aristocracy monopolize state power. Again, this 'cowardice of the bourgeoisie in the face of democracy' was put down partly to an (unjustified) fear of the working class, and partly to the political immaturity of the bourgeoisie – what Weber derided as its 'will to powerlessness'. See the excellent discussion in Beetham 1974:157–61.
7 Engels 1972:160.
8 Trotsky 1975:263.
9 Poulantzas 1973:287.
10 Miliband 1973:85, footnote 4.
11 As Miliband puts it, 'the clear perception of the interests of a class in no way betokens a clear perception of the ways in which these interests may best be defended'. As a matter of 'historical fact, privileged classes have very often been short-sighted in this respect, and have needed the skills and adroitness of agents acting on their behalf but with a sufficient degree of independence to mitigate if not to overcome the shortsightedness of their masters'. Miliband 1977:31–2.
12 Bosanquet 1920:173.
13 Durkheim 1957:50–1.
14 Poulantzas 1973:285.
15 Miliband 1975:316; see also Miliband 1977:74. O'Connor has similarly argued that 'A capitalist state that openly uses its coercive forces to help one class accumulate capital at the expense of other classes loses its legitimacy and hence undermines the basis of its loyalty and support . . . The state must involve itself in the accumulation process, but it must either mystify its policies by calling them something that they are not, or it must try to conceal them. . .'. O'Connor 1973:6.
16 Poulantzas refers to social policies that have been '*imposed* on the dominant classes by the state, through the pressure of the dominated classes', an imposition giving rise to 'hostility between the state and the dominant classes'. 'Thus, in fulfilling its political function, the capitalist state comes to rely on dominated classes and sometimes to play them off against the dominant classes.' Poulantzas 1973:285 and 286.

17 Miliband 1973:88.
18 Plamenatz 1963:370–71.
19 Beetham 1974:72.
20 Poulantzas 1969:73 and 75. Only at a much later stage in the debate does Poulantzas seem to become fully aware of the direction this argument is leading to. His retraction takes the form of a strong denial that the state is capable of generating its own power in the manner suggested by bureaucratic theory. See Poulantzas 1976:72–4.
21 Miliband is openly critical of the promiscuous use of the term Bonapartism to describe features of the modern capitalist state. Nevertheless, his own position is in complete accord with the *leitmotif* of all analyses that draw upon the Bonapartist model – namely that the function of relative autonomy is to enable the state to save the bourgeoisie from itself.
22 Anderson 1974:54.
23 Anderson 1974:109.
24 Anderson 1974:54.
25 Marx 1926:74.
26 Anderson 1974:41.
27 Mandel 1975:xix and xx.
28 Miliband 1969:93.
29 Miliband, one of the few academic Marxists to confront the problem of the socialist state, has recently declared that this type of state '"represents" no single class or group and is the instrument of no such class or group; the collectivist character of the society precludes it from being such an instrument . . . Instead, the state may be taken to "represent" the collectivist society or system itself. . .'. Miliband 1977:114. Such a Durkheimian conception of the socialist state appears to rule out the possibility that the state could serve as the instrument with which the party secures *its own* hegemony. This is all the more curious in the light of Miliband's recognition that '"The state" effectively means here the leaders of the Communist Party'. Miliband 1977:114.

# PART THREE

# Class and party

# 8
# The transition
# to socialism

Of all the doctrinal schisms with which Marxism has continually been beset, none has had such fateful political consequences as that surrounding the theory of transition from capitalism to socialism. The question of the displacement of bourgeois society by the proletarian state, and the means by which this was to be brought about, provoked one very distinctive set of answers which can be taken to mark the passage from Marxism to Marxism-Leninism. With Lenin's formidable entry into the arena, conflicting interpretations of the classical texts became crystallized around two diametrically opposed worldviews whose final outcome was the permanent political bifurcation of the western working-class movement.

Although the uniquely Leninist contribution to the theory of socialist transition could be said to centre on the decisive role accorded to the vanguard party, it is clear that the conception of the party and its tasks arises naturally from Lenin's prior rejection of the orthodox interpretation of Marxism as an 'organic' theory of political and social change. The organic interpretation, associated above all with the works of Kautsky, picked out those various and many strands running through Marx's writings that portrayed the demise of capitalism as following inexorably from the social and political ascendancy of the working class. In this view of things, the assumption of state power is not regarded as especially problematic; it is seen as the final act of a lengthy drama whose *dénouement* has been clearly signalled by preceding events in the shape of social and economic victories notched up by the newly emergent class. Political power simply follows from, and makes manifest, the power already contained in emergent socio-economic forces.

## Marxism and class theory

The interpretation of Marxism as an organic theory of change thrived abundantly upon Marx's curious fondness for gynaecological imagery when discussing the process of transition. His frequent allusions to embryos, wombs, and midwives did much to bolster the view that societies move through a sequence of phases – from infancy through to maturity, and to eventual senility and decline – in which the notion of gradual evolution has far more place than that of sudden and violent alterations of condition. Moreover, the resort to this kind of imagery serves to accentuate the apparent *similarity* between different types of transition, suggesting in particular that the process of change from capitalism to socialism would not be of a very different order from that of previous forms of transition. The embryo of the new society, be it feudalism, capitalism, or socialism, invariably matures in the womb of the old, eventually displacing it only to spawn its own successor. There is no hint from Marx that the birth of socialism would depart from this cycle of events, nor that the delivery would be attended by more than the usual expenditure of blood and sweat.

The fact that Marx was not here wholly engaged in a fanciful play upon metaphor is clearly indicated by his attempt to discover incipient forms of socialism within capitalist society – living signs of the embryo nestling within the womb. As Avineri has suggested, Marx attached considerable importance to two particular lines of development that appeared to exemplify early forms of property and productive relations that might come to replace bourgeois property relations.[1] The first of these was the rise of the joint stock company. Marx felt that the separation of ownership from control acted as a corrosive force upon capital; and while this did not in itself amount to the liquidation of private property, it was to be understood as a 'necessary transitional phase towards the reconversion of capital into the property of producers, although no longer as the private property of the individual producers, but rather as the property of associated producers, as outright social property. . .'.[2] As Marx saw it, this development heralded 'the abolition of the capitalist mode of production within the capitalist mode of production itself' and could thus be understood as a 'mere phase of transition to a new form of production'.[3]

A second and parallel development was the growth of the workers' co-operative movement. Marx argued that this movement brought into being a new set of property relations in which 'the antithesis between labour and capital is overcome'.[4] The co-operative factory system demonstrated 'how a new mode of production naturally grows out of an old one, when the development of the material forces of production, and of the corresponding forms of social production have reached a particular stage. Without the factory system arising out of the capitalist mode of production there could have been no co-operative factories'.[5]

It seems clear from all this that his resort to the imagery of the delivery theatre was no mere indulgence on Marx's part; it was a device for illustrating in a vivid and simplified form a schema of social transformation that occupied a central place in his general theory. The fact that neither of the two tendencies he singled out proved to have very startling social consequences in no way detracts from the importance of his methodological intent in seeking to reveal traces of the new order pre-formed within the body of the old. It is as though, for Marx, such traces were taken to be not merely advance signs of a new social order and a new set of productive relations, but the very pre-condition for the ascendancy of a new class. The future hegemony of the proletariat was guaranteed not by virtue of anything as crude as its sheer numerical weight but, as in the case of its great predecessor, by the fact that it was the social embodiment of new productive forces. Marx's effort to locate these new productive forces, parallel to existing bourgeois forms, was therefore a very necessary exercise if it was to be shown that the ultimate triumph of the proletariat did not hinge on anything so capricious as political fortune.[6] If early traces of new property relations could never be revealed within capitalism the outlook for proletarian sovereignty would be somewhat bleak; it would be as if history had ground to a halt at the bourgeois stage of development – one stop too soon before the terminus. Such a self-evidently absurd proposition meant that for those who treated Marxism as an organic theory of change the socialist future was virtually assured; because capitalism had no unique claim to immortality there was no imaginable alternative but its eventual displacement by socialism.

Almost the entire intellectual weight of Leninism is directed against this interpretation of Marx's theory of transition and its confident prognosis. Lenin's alternative reading systematically plays down the vocabulary of organic growth into socialism in favour of the equally authentic language of violent transformation. The imagery of wombs and embryos gives way to that of the Phoenix; socialism emerges not through a slow process of maturation, gradually supplanting its progenitor – it arises from the ashes of a capitalist order destroyed in the flames of the class struggle. Nothing could be further from the spirit of the organic model of transition than Lenin's relentless underlining of those passages by Marx and Engels that exult in the creative possibilities of political violence. References in the classical texts to the need to smash the state, destroy all existing institutions, suppress the former ruling class, and generally get quite rough, are plentiful enough to enable Lenin to construct a model of transition and change that is no less quintessentially Marxist than the organic alternative. The gynaecological metaphor could quickly be dispensed with once it was assumed, as it certainly was by Lenin, that the body of capitalism had become far too diseased to give forth a healthy socialist infant.

These differing interpretations of the transition to socialism are matched by equally divergent views concerning the nature of the preceding stage of transition to bourgeois society. The point of disagreement is over the question of what kinds of parallel can be drawn between bourgeois and proletarian revolutions and whether both conform to the same general laws. Somewhat paradoxically, perhaps, exponents of the organic theory generally argued that the transition from absolutism to bourgeois society was an unusually traumatic and violent affair, compared to which the transition from capitalism to socialism would be extremely peaceable. According to Kautsky, the bourgeois revolution 'had far greater obstacles to overcome, far more difficult problems to solve than are today connected with the conquest of political power by the proletariat under democratic conditions'.[7] Bourgeois revolutions were violent and dramatic episodes because of the unyielding character of feudal institutions; lacking the capacity for innovation and internal reform, the clumsy and rigid apparatuses of absolutism had to be dismantled by force. The 'liberal organizations of modern society are distinguished from those', Bernstein suggested, 'exactly because they are flexible, and capable of change and development. They do not need to be destroyed, but only to be further developed'.[8]

Kautsky and Bernstein thus pay a handsome double tribute to the bourgeoisie, comparable to Marx's own eulogy of capitalist achievements: first, for successfully challenging the organized might of autocracy by way of revolutionary struggle; and, second, for setting up a political and social order that, unlike all previous systems, was so versatile as to allow for its own radical transformation without the resort to violence. Kautsky felt it to be a huge misconception to 'imagine the coming revolution after the style of the old', or that 'armed insurrection, with barricades and similar warlike incidents will nowadays play a decisive part'.[9] One of the chief reasons for Kautsky's later insistence upon defining the Bolshevik revolution as a bourgeois revolution was precisely because of its violent character; the use of force was the unmistakable sign of the non-proletarian status of any revolution.

The Kautskyist school of Marxism argued in effect for the uniqueness of the socialist transition on the grounds that it marked a clear departure from the pattern of violence established by all previous forms of transition. The Leninist school of Marxism also endorsed the argument for uniqueness, though on opposite grounds: namely, because the transition to socialism called for a much *greater* show of force than was necessary at any former stage of development. In pursuing this line of argument, Lukacs suggests, in contradistinction to Kautsky and Bernstein, that the tasks of the bourgeois revolution were far less onerous than those now facing the revolutionary working class. The foundations of absolutism had already been comprehensively undermined by capitalist property and market relationships, so creating an extremely rickety political superstructure that could be toppled without undue difficulty. Indeed, the delivery of the final *coup de grâce* hardly qualified for the title of anything quite so grand as a revolution:

> 'The ability of bourgeois revolutions to storm ahead with such brilliant *élan* is grounded socially in the fact that *they are drawing the consequences of an almost completed economic and social process in a society whose feudal and absolutist structure has been profoundly undermined politically, governmentally, juridically, etc., by the vigorous upsurge of capitalism*. The true revolutionary element is the economic transformation of the feudal system of production into a capitalist one so that it would be possible in theory for *this* process to take place *without a bourgeois revolution*, without political upheaval on the part of the revolutionary bourgeoisie. And in that case those parts of the feudal and absolutist superstructure that were not eliminated by "revolutions from above" would collapse of their own accord when capitalism was already fully developed.'[10]

The victorious bourgeoisie, far from corresponding to Kautsky's portrait of an heroic class struggling against the odds, are here depicted as a class that takes power by stealth rather than by storm; the defences of absolutism, that Kautsky and Bernstein found so formidable, appear to have been flattened in advance by the heavy guns of capital. Lukacs shares Lenin's low regard for the quality of bourgeois revolutions by suggesting that, *typically*, the representatives of capital become a hegemonic class without going through the ordeal of a 1789-style revolution.

As both Lenin and Lukacs well recognized, most European bourgeois revolutions were of the 'failed' variety – 1848 being the symbolic year rather than 1789. Although the western bourgeoisie does not, in the standard case, successfully storm the local equivalent of the Bastille, its eventual displacement of absolutism is nowhere denied. Thus, in so far as the degree of political mastery enjoyed by the modern French bourgeoisie does not appear to be remarkably greater than that enjoyed by the bourgeoisie of neighbouring western states that did not experience their own 1789, it could reasonably be concluded that the dramatic revolutionary act was not quite the decisive watershed that countless historians have claimed it to be. There is in other words a lot to be said for Lukacs' iconoclastic view that the bourgeoisie is normally carried to power on the crest of an economic wave, understood in the broadest sense, and not as a result of some grand political showdown – even one precipitated by the clash between the 'forces of production' and the 'social relations of production'. It was because the bourgeoisie's record as a *political* force did not seem to match up to the glowing account given of it in orthodox Marxism that Lenin advocated the strenuous intervention of the Russian proletariat and peasantry to make the 'democratic revolution' on behalf of the Russian bourgeoisie. Only under the sharp prodding of the former could the latter be driven forward to consummate its revolution and not settle for a shabby 1848-style compromise with autocracy.[11]

In underlining the point that bourgeois ascendancy owed more to invisible economic forces than to political organization and struggle, Lenin and Lukacs serve notice upon the idea that the transition to socialism follows the same pattern as the transition to capitalism. In his critique of what he felt to be Rosa Luxemburg's 'tendency to overestimate the organic element in history', Lukacs reckoned that one of the most serious errors arising from this tendency was that she imagined 'the proletarian revolution as having the structural forms of bourgeois revolutions'.[12] Their structural forms could not be similar because the foundations of capitalism do not suffer internal erosion by anything that could remotely be called a socialist mode of production. Although the system of large-scale capitalist manufacture lends itself to social reconstruction along entirely new lines, it smacks of 'a utopian fantasy to imagine that anything tending towards socialism could arise within capitalism. . .'.[13] Unlike the bourgeoisie, then, the proletariat would get no special assistance in ushering in the new order from any of those underground forces that Marx had been so keen to discover. The historical responsibilities of the proletariat would thus fall directly on the shoulders of the class itself, demanding of its individual members more in the way of purely human effort and political will than had been required of any previous revolutionary class.

The proletariat was felt to be unique in the annals of class struggle in that one of the preconditions for its eventual triumph was the ability to become politically conscious of its historic mission. Lukacs suggests that all previous ascendant classes were exempt from this requirement because there was no great discrepancy between the pursuit of their immediate economic and social goals on the one hand

and the goal of political dominion on the other. The individual and short-run interests of the bourgeoisie correspond closely with their collective and long-term interests as a class; in striving to satisfy their immediate personal ambitions they were, *nolens volens*, acting in furtherance of their general class destiny. There was, therefore, no pressing need for the bourgeoisie to raise itself to a high pitch of political consciousness and awareness; doing what came naturally was all that was required.[14]

Lukacs' estimation of the lesser importance to the bourgeoisie of a system of beliefs, consciously articulated, contrasts unusually with his more familiar emphasis upon the hypnotic powers of bourgeois ideology. However, these two views are not incompatible, since it could presumably be argued that bourgeois ideology only comes to full efflorescence *after* capitalist ascendancy is an accomplished fact. That is to say, a complex belief system might be less necessary as a prelude to bourgeois rule than as a subsequent means of legitimating the new system once it becomes a going concern. This need would no doubt be especially pressing when capitalism itself came to be challenged by an alternative set of ideas stemming from the working-class movement.[15]

However this may be, it is the need of the proletariat to raise itself to a high peak of class consciousness prior to its emancipation which Lukacs sees to be a unique feature of the transition to socialism. In pursuing their immediate and individual interests workers, unlike the bourgeoisie, do not thereby automatically advance their collective interests as a class.[16] Quite the contrary; the path to immediate gratification appears to run off at an alarming tangent from the main route to political power. Consequently, workers need access to a set of ideas that enable them to grasp the essential nature of the capitalist system in broad theoretical terms in order that the larger design should not become obscured by the routine demands of everyday life. What is needed above all is a clear picture of an alternative system if the class that really counts is not to find itself hopelessly entangled in the coils of capitalism's own restrictive logic.

Even those Marxists of the Second International who normally seized upon any of Marx's ideas suggesting the possibility of an organic growth into socialism could not readily accept that class consciousness would simply develop as part of the natural order of things. It was Kautsky who first formulated the controversial thesis, later appropriated by Lenin, that workers could not by themselves become fully conscious of their political destiny, unaided by instruction from the radical intelligentsia. As might be expected, however, Kautsky did not regard this as a serious stumbling block cluttering up the path to socialism. Although the proletariat might not be able to produce socialist ideas on its own account, there was no doubting its ability and readiness to imbibe these ideas once they had been suitably bowdlerized by the party intellectuals. So even if the expansion of working-class consciousness called for the provision of certain interventionist services not actually sanctioned by Marx, the ability of the movement to provide these services was no more a question in Kautsky's mind than was the imminence of a socialist dawn.

It is against this comfortable belief in the capacity of the proletariat to absorb socialist ideology that much of Lukacs' analysis is directed. His notion of an 'historical lag' between the objective conditions of capitalist crisis and the subjective conditions of class consciousness is an early statement of a theme on which many variations later come to be played as the renewable death sentence imposed upon western capitalism fails to be carried out by its appointed executioner. As Lukacs properly points out, the concept of an historical or ideological lag is totally foreign to the orthodox Kautskian view of a natural correspondence between the level of productive forces and the content of political beliefs. From this perspective, the continued presence of sedimentary layers of bourgeois ideology in the mind of the proletariat would be taken 'simply as proof that the objectively decisive crisis of capitalism had not yet appeared'.[17]

For Lukacs, as for so many latter-day Marxists, the lines of connection between the material and ideological realms are subject to intense disturbance and noise; the suggestion of anything as clear-cut as a determinate relationship between the two, other than of the most circuitous kind, is dismissed as laughably simplistic. The material and ideological domains are deemed to follow separate and peculiar rhythms of their own, producing an overall effect of tonal discord rather than plain harmony. Consequently, the problem of class consciousness, its fluctuating and uneven quality, can be posed more or less separately from the problem of economic crisis. More correctly, if the 'crisis of capitalism' is treated as an historical constant, then variations in class consciousness, both within the proletariat and between the proletariats of different capitalist societies, need to be accounted for by social factors that are not reducible to the material substructure. The lines of argument opened up in this direction by Lukacs and Gramsci appear to culminate in Althusser's attempt to stake out the general territory of what might be thought of as a Marxist sociology of the superstructure.

The starting point of this exercise is the familiar lament that the contradictions of capitalism, however glaring and acute, do not necessarily, or even typically, provoke the appropriate response at the conscious political level. Althusser's diagnosis of the problem suggests that the classical notion of 'contradictions' in what used to be thought of as the base, must now be extended to the region of the superstructure.[18] That is, because the legal, political, ideological, and other elements that comprise the superstructure do not always evolve at the same pace or along the same lines, serious discontinuities or contradictions are liable to occur between these various elements. These contradictions ramify throughout the social structure, threatening its entire equilibrium; conversely, social stability is more or less assured when the component parts of the superstructure show a good measure of congruence and cohesion.

Hence the mere economic crisis of capitalism is unlikely to promote general political disturbances and social disarray if the superstructure is a closely integrated whole; nor, as a result, can working-class consciousness flourish and expand to its proper limits. Economic crisis is a highly inflammable material, but it has to be ignited by sparks given off by friction from within the superstructure. Althusser offers no clues that might enable the political observer to detect whether or not the superstructure is out of joint. But this small oversight is understandable, perhaps, given Althusser's preoccupation with the forces of unity and cohesion at work within the superstructure of modern capitalism. The mesmerizing effects of the 'ideological state apparatuses', in particular, appear to suffer no abatement even in the depths of economic gloom. Seen through Althusserian lenses the outlook for proletarian class consciousness looks anything but rosy.

It might well be, of course, that to paint the prospects for a growth in revolutionary consciousness in the darkest colours helps, intentionally or otherwise, to prepare the way for an alternative, less troublesome solution. If, for whatever reasons, the mental and political capacities of the working class are felt to fall short of historical requirements, hope may be found in a more reliable instrument: the vanguard party. It is only a very short step from Lenin's conception of the vanguard party as the decisive agency of socialist transition to Lukacs' discovery that the party itself, rather than the proletariat, 'is the historical embodiment and the active incarnation of class consciousness'.[19] Because the proletariat is submerged in the travails of economic necessity it cannot be expected to raise itself as a class to a state of revolutionary awareness. Only the party, by virtue of the creative distance it maintains between itself and the ideologically imprisoned masses, is capable of constructing a politically coherent world-view from the inchoate sentiments that struggle for expression within the proletariat. Although not necessarily perceived as such by the workers, the party actually becomes 'the objectification of their own will'.[20] As workers gravitate towards the vanguard party they do, in this very process, attain the elusive condition of class consciousness. It is as though by embracing the party the proletariat thereby lays claim to its own true consciousness, which the party has meanwhile nurtured under its protection.

Thus, if moral endorsement of the revolutionary party is taken to be a sign of the worker's entry to a state of political grace, then for all practical purposes the problem of class consciousness is solved. The true measure of consciousness becomes the individual's readiness to bow to the will of the party, his consciousness incarnate. To be fully class conscious *and* to dissent from the will of the party would amount to a contradiction in terms; denial of the party by the proletariat would be nothing but the denial of its own political essence.

Given that class consciousness has been handed over to the vanguard party for safe keeping, an important duty falling to the party is to prevent the contamination of consciousness by workers themselves. Whereas social democracy bases itself upon the narrow and untutored aspirations of the masses, thereby elevating 'average man' to the highest political model, the vanguard party responds to the desires of the masses with a calculated coolness. Lenin warned that the party should never '*descend* to the level of the "working masses"', a descent that would, in any case, have been difficult to accomplish given his strong preference for an organization controlled by a 'dozen wise men' and the need for *'unquestioning subordination* to a single will'.[21] Likewise, Trotsky's recommendation that the vanguard party should reflect 'the leadership's organized distrust of the members', betrayed no signs of an early fascination with the merits of mass participation.[22] This organized distrust was essential to the performance of the party's instructional duties towards the working masses. Lukacs made no bones about the fact that in carrying out these duties the party was 'sometimes forced to adopt a stance opposed to that of the masses; it must show them the way by rejecting their immediate wishes'; the sad fact was that workers were often a little slow in their appreciation, so that 'only after many bitter experiences will the masses understand the correctness of the party's view'.[23]

As this suggests, the Leninist conception of the vanguard party acknowledges a certain degree of tension in the relationship between the proletariat and its organized political expression. It is at least formally conceded that the party needs to take cognizance of the sentiments and experiences of the masses in order that revolutionary theory does not become too divorced from its subject matter. This could result, however, in the party taking lessons from those who are themselves felt to be most in need of political instruction. And while there is nothing very unusual about the idea of a teacher acknowledging his occasional indebtedness to a gifted pupil, such an accommodating stance does not come naturally to a political party whose very nature, according to Lukacs, 'presupposes its possession of a correct theory'.[24] Given the strange belief that 'the consequence of a false theory would soon destroy' the party, it follows that the very existence of the party is tangible proof of its infallibility.[25] This is a belief that does not obviously promote an open-minded willingness on the part of the 'dozen wise men' to take political lessons from the not-so-wise multitudes.

The oft-proclaimed desire among western Marxists to encourage a more 'interactionist' approach between party and proletariat, within the overall framework of the vanguard model, thus appears to underestimate the difficulty of allaying the deep-seated Leninist fear of infection from the bourgeois virus, a virus that the vanguard organization was explicitly designed to counteract. Too close a contact with the masses, however desirable as an abstract principle, exposes the party to that most fatal of political diseases: reformism. The tasks of the revolutionary transition would therefore seem to require the party to maintain a healthy distance between itself and the working masses if it is not to end up in the graveyard of social democracy. Given that requirement, it seems rather unlikely that Lenin would have set much store by the claims of modern Eurocommunism to be heading for an altogether different destination.

## II

By bringing about an alteration in the relative weighting assigned to class and party in the mechanism of transition, Leninism also introduces a new set of complexities into the historical time-table. When social classes are held to be the prime movers of history the schedule is drawn up in terms of 'epochs' and 'stages of development', i.e. units of broad temporal and social span appropriate to the great transformations wrought by the action of entire classes. When, however, the vanguard party is brought to the centre of the stage, the problem of socialist transition ultimately boils down to the problem of when to seize the opportune revolutionary moment. For Leninism, historical time is measured by the second hand, with the consequence, unanticipated by Marx, that the transition to socialism could easily be missed as a result of careless timing.

This is by no means to say that Lenin adopts a posture of indifference to the classical Marxist predilection for mapping out the phases of social and economic development. On the contrary, Lenin could be regarded, more than any other Marxist, as a theorist of stages and phases occurring *within* the capitalist epoch. Because the entire period was a revolutionary one, more refined subcategories were needed for interpreting and analysing the subtle shifts and detours made by capitalism on the final stage of its journey. Moreover, the political strategy of the vanguard party had always to be determined by reference to the immediate phase through which capitalism was passing, and even short-term tactical manoeuvres could only be justified as a response to properly classified shifts in the ever-changing balance of social forces.

> 'Throughout his career, whether Lenin was examining the development of capitalism, working-class consciousness, the Party or the activities of the Soviet State, this sense of movement towards an end, the notion of *progressive and demarcated stages of advance* remained constant . . . He was, throughout, insistent upon the obligation of the theorist to judge the moment when a particular phase had exhausted its potentialities, an obligation which carried with it the task of supplying the theoretical and organisational realignments appropriate to the coming phase.'[26]

In this recent portrait by Harding, Lenin is shown to be a theorist who pays unusually careful attention to the question of 'stages' in relation to all matters of party strategy. It is a Lenin for whom political activity is subordinated to the discipline of theory, not that other, frequently-drawn Lenin who acts on purely tactical grounds and only subsequently searches for the appropriate theoretical clearance. It does indeed seem that Lenin's political recommendations are always closely bound up with his ideas about the changing constellation of social forces, the general historical situation, etc., etc., and his classificatory urge does suggest that more than lip-service is being paid to the method and doctrines of historical materialism. But to distinguish between a theory of stages on the one hand, and immediate tactical considerations on the other, would in Lenin's case be somewhat artificial given his creative abilities in discovering ever new and fleeting phases not normally visible even to the trained Marxist eye.[27]

In any case, it would seem that the very notion of stages, and the resort to periodization, was not wholly appropriate to a theorist who tended to conceive of the social order as a system of permanent flux. Capitalism in its imperialist or monopoly era was understood by Lenin as a highly volatile system in which the conjuncture of social forces was constantly and dramatically changing. Capitalism in its final phase was more than usually prone to the sudden build-up of explosive tensions and the rapid spread of disaffection; and when fundamental political realignments could occur virtually overnight, the Menshevik and social democratic formula of fixed evolutionary stages had all the appearance of an archaic dogma.

This perception of capitalism as a system of chronic turmoil and instability permeates Lenin's entire theory of the transition to socialism. His political rationale in seeking to bring down capitalism in backward Russia was that the revolution would quickly spread from there to western Europe, the appointed heartland of the new socialist order. Capitalism was likened by Lenin to an international chain comprised of weak and strong links; Russia being one of the weakest links therefore seemed the proper place at which to strike the first blow that would sever the chain. On this line of reasoning there could be nothing 'premature' or unMarxist in the policy of leading an insurrection in a backward country. The very notion of 'country' would in any case be redundant if capitalism were conceived of as a single global system comprised of various regional branches or links. Lenin occasionally makes the point that the idea of national varieties of capitalism was pertinent to the nineteenth century, when the economy of each society was still sufficiently self-contained to allow the heavy impress of local cultures upon capitalist relations. But in the twentieth century the purely national components of capitalism were far outweighed by the universal features of the system. Capitalism was now a unified world order, not a collection of distinct and separate national units; the theory of socialist transition therefore had to be brought into line with this dominant fact of the imperialist epoch.

Although the metaphor of an international chain was a useful device in Lenin's attempt to reconceptualize the problem of capitalist breakdown and revolutionary transition to conform to Russian reality, it is clear that a more appropriate metaphor would have been that of the domino theory. The Leninist assumption was not simply that the weakest link in the capitalist chain would be the first to snap; far more important was the assumption that the first capitalist state to fall would cause the others to topple. The fracture of one weak link in a chain does not cause the stronger ones to give. In effect, therefore, Lenin actually proceeded on the view that the transition to socialism in Europe could be started on its way by knocking down the least stable domino. Given Lenin's own repeated insistence that the only justification for a Russian revolution was its expected impact upon the more advanced capitalist societies, the refusal of these other dominoes to fall would negate the purpose of his entire political strategy.

It should perhaps be remembered that this commitment to the domino theory was not the product of some strange quirk on Lenin's part; belief in the contagious properties of revolution was at this time widespread both within the European working-class movement and among its opponents. Thus while Kautsky, in his condemnation of the October uprising, was perfectly correct in pointing out that the Bolsheviks 'staked everything on one card, on a general European revolution',[28] Lenin could no less correctly remind him that this expectation was 'not an infatuation of the Bolsheviks, but the *general opinion* of all Marxists'.[29]

This opinion was ultimately grounded, of course, in a highly favourable estimate of the revolutionary potential of the western working class. Retrospectively, it is bound to seem surprising that Lenin, of all people, was willing to bank so heavily on support from this quarter. On various occasions he had felt it necessary to excoriate the leading cadres of the working-class movement because of their propensity to elevate themselves into a labour aristocracy. A proletariat whose upper and most influential layers were steeped in petty bourgeois ideology, as a result of living off the imperial fat, must not have seemed the most promising candidates to take over the revolutionary torch. Moreover, after the moral collapse of the Second International on the outbreak of war, Lenin had never bothered to conceal the magnitude of his contempt for the political leadership of social democracy. The prospects of a Russian-led revolution striking a responsive chord in these burnt-out cases must surely have been judged extremely slim. The paradox is, then, knowing what he knew about the political condition of the western labour movement, how could Lenin persist so doggedly in the belief that the spread of revolution across Europe was 'beyond doubt', such that all his 'hopes for the *final* victory of socialism are founded on this certainty and on this scientific prognosis'?[30]

The answer would seem to lie in Lenin's equally firm conviction that revolutions obeyed peculiar laws of their own that superseded the ordinary rules of social life. Under conditions of routine existence the political education of the proletariat was a slow and uncertain affair. Lessons were learned by a gradual and painful process, with the ever-attendant risk that the collective experiences of one generation would not be passed on and fully absorbed by the next. But under revolutionary conditions the educative process is suddenly accelerated. 'Revolution enlightens all classes with a rapidity and thoroughness unknown in normal, peaceful times.'[31]

> 'Every revolution means a sharp turn in the lives of vast masses of people . . . And just as any turn in the life of an individual teaches him a great deal and is fraught with rich experience and great emotional stress, so also a revolution teaches a whole people many a rich and valuable lesson in a short space of time. During a revolution millions and tens of millions of people learn

in a week more than they do in a year of ordinary, somnolent life.'[32]

Lenin's idea of revolutions as 'festivals of the oppressed' is not dissimilar to Durkheim's notion of the creative powers of 'effervescence' generated by collective social action. Each suggests that under the excitation and social intensity of dramatic events individuals are liable to experience a moral transformation in which routine, taken-for-granted conceptions of the world are displaced by radically new conceptions. That is, when the 'temper, excitement and convictions of the masses must and do reveal themselves in *action*' of an extraordinary kind.[33] The impoverished consciousness of western workers was thus partly to be explained by their immersion in the routinized and deadening politics of social democracy, a politics that went out of its way not to over-excite the proletarian imagination. But once the revolutionary possibility had actually been translated into fact, and the vulnerability of capitalism had been vividly demonstrated by the Bolshevik example, workers' aspirations and ideals would quickly burst through the straitjacket imposed by the 'ordinary, somnolent life'. Because the Russian revolution would give western workers a huge psychological boost and provide them with a crash course in political education, the domino theory could not be called into question by the *prevailing* level of class consciousness. All obstacles to the spread of revolution set up by social democratic habits of mind would be swept aside by the momentum of events and by that 'revolutionary energy and revolutionary enthusiasm which can perform miracles'.[34]

Lenin's belief in the almost miraculous powers of the revolutionary spirit contrasts rather starkly with the orthodox Kautskian view of the strict limits imposed upon political action by material and social conditions. The Marxists of the Second International drew sustenance from the conviction that workers' induction into socialist ways of thought kept pace with the tempo set by the nicely maturing productive forces. Somewhat in line with Weber, they assumed the need for an 'elective affinity' between any widely acceptable system of beliefs and a socially given structure of interests and values. Any serious mis-match between the two would result in the rejection of the belief system by all save a small band of the deviant faithful. The bland, organic version of Marxism espoused by Kautsky and his colleagues was felt to be fully in tune with the general sentiments and ideals of a proletariat that had been raised in the temperate climate of liberal democracy, a climate not in the least hospitable to the propagation of Leninist principles. The same point was occasionally conceded by Lenin. He once suggested that because absolutism was a far more transparent system of oppression than bourgeois democracy, it was a

relatively simple matter to win the Russian proletariat for revolution –
'as easy as lifting a feather'.[35] The accommodating subtleties of liberal
democracy, by contrast, made this uphill work, even though the final
*consummation* of the revolution, once begun, would be far less
troublesome for workers in the west than for the Russian proletariat.

Lenin's willingness to contrast revolutionary prospects in 'the land
of Nicholas and Rasputin' with those in bourgeois societies that have
'produced a democratic culture and organization, provided it to
everybody down to the last man . . .',[36] indicates that he was not at all
insensitive to the question of elective affinities. He certainly does not
here assume that the proletariat under autocracy and under
bourgeois democracy is interchangeable, any more than he ever
regards the social class of a given country as a socially homogeneous
bloc. Hence, Carr's judgement that 'Lenin never really understood
why "reformism", which meant nothing in Russia, was a persistent
and successful rival to the teaching of revolution in western Europe' is
uncharacteristically harsh.[37] All the signs are that Lenin appreciated
the seductive powers of social democracy well enough, but assumed
nevertheless that these powers exercised greater sway under the
routine conditions of mundane life than in periods of intense social
disturbance and 'effervescence'. If Weber could suppose that consciousness of class and consciousness of status could alternate in line
with fluctuations in the economic climate; and if Durkheim could
believe that mental states could be profoundly transformed in the
heat of collective excitements; then there was nothing wildly eccentric
in Lenin's belief that reformist habits of mind could be displaced by
revolutionary sentiments in the crucible of extreme political crisis.

Indeed, it was not necessary to be a Marxist to share the presenti-
ment that European labour in this period was trembling on the brink
of a revolutionary transformation. As Carr points out, in the after-
math of the Bolshevik seizure of power there was widespread trepida-
tion among the western bourgeoisie that insurrectionary contagion
would spread across the entire continent. The sporadic eruptions of
armed revolt, and the setting up of workers' soviets, first in Hungary,
and then in Munich, appeared to justify this fear. The ringing declaration that 'The whole of Europe is filled with the spirit of revolution
. . . The whole existing order in its political, social and economic
aspects is questioned by the masses of the population from one end of
Europe to the other' came not from Lenin but from Lloyd-George.[38]
Clearly, the domino theory was not the product of a heady revolutionary optimism; and it was no small tribute to Lenin that his
enemies should, however glumly, have endorsed his own prognosis.

The fact that well-informed sections of the bourgeoisie also
appeared to believe that capitalism was in serious jeopardy, that the

dominoes *were* in fact very unstable, opens up the intriguing thought that the leaders of social democracy were almost alone in their fixed belief in the impossibility of revolution. In view of the close elective affinity between at least *their* ideals and interests, and the ideology of evolutionary socialism, they were understandably disinclined to assume that the proletarian rank and file was any less resistant than they themselves were to the appeals of a revolutionary alternative. In assuming this they were not, of course, necessarily wrong. In fact, post mortems on the failed transition to socialism in Europe frequently accept the Kautskian view that the condition of the working class was too favourable to permit the spread of revolutionary sympathies; for a proletariat cosseted by liberal democracy the Bolshevik message seemed, as Carr puts it, 'inadequate and inapplicable'.[39] Leninism is thus presented as an alien thing whose only natural habitat is absolutism and which would naturally perish in the atmosphere of liberal democracy. However, the unanswered question is: if absolutism could harbour within itself both revolutionary Bolshevism and social democratic gradualism of the Menshevik variety, why should not bourgeois democracy be similarly receptive to both philosophies? Why, in other words, are the constraints of elective affinity thought to be so much more severe in one system than in the other?

No certain pronouncement can in fact be made as to the readiness or otherwise of the western working class to follow the Russian example, for the good reason that this alternative was never squarely put to them by the leaders of social democracy. Quite the contrary, this alternative was systematically derided and dismissed from the realms of political possibility. The fact that western workers conscientiously followed the dictates of the party leadership in declining Lenin's invitation to insurrection does not therefore permit the conclusion that a profound incompatibility existed between the social condition of the proletariat on the one hand and revolutionary principles on the other. Such a conclusion could only properly be drawn if the leadership of social democracy had actually issued a call for revolutionary action that the rank and file had then proceeded to ignore. It is simply not possible to evaluate the collective state of mind of the proletariat in this volatile period as something existing quite independently of the political outlook and conduct of the mass party organization.

Lenin's guess that workers would have followed their trusted leaders to the barricades, had the call been issued, was no doubt based on a Michelsian view of the disciplined obedience of the masses. The failure of the revolution to materialize could therefore be attributed directly to the policy of the leadership itself. Lenin's charge was not merely that the leaders of social democracy had funked the revolutionary struggle, but that they had actively sought to stifle it. They had succeeded in falsifying the domino theory by intervening to prop the dominoes up. Trotsky's accusation that the extension of the revolution to Germany 'was prevented solely and exclusively by the social democrats' expressed the general Bolshevik view.[40] Interestingly, it was a view also put forward by certain of the social democrats themselves: Scheidemann felt that his party could claim most of the credit for dampening down revolutionary sympathies among the workers, so that had it not been for social democracy, 'Germany would have fallen a hopeless victim to Bolshevism'.[41] Similarly, Kautsky's immediate and disdainful reaction to the Bolshevik seizure of power made it clear that he regarded Lenin's example as one to be repudiated rather than emulated. In Kautsky's estimation it was not the battalions of capitalism but the Soviet state that presented 'the gravest menace and causes the greatest damage to the struggle of the modern working class for liberation'.[42] Social democracy could deliberately and energetically counter the revolutionary impulse, fortified by the conviction that in so doing it was defending, not betraying, the best interests of the working class.

It would seem from this that Lenin's great error was to underestimate the determination of the social democratic leadership to work actively for the cancellation of the 'festival of the oppressed', instead of being satisfied with the role of helpless onlookers. Lenin's faith in the preparedness and capacity of the proletariat to 'push aside such "leaders" . . . to rise in revolt *in spite of* them, *without* them, and march over their heads *towards revolution'*, was a remarkable departure for a theorist not usually given to singing the praises of spontaneous class action or the efficacy of leaderless revolt.[43]

This mistaken appraisal of social democracy was perhaps tied up with his similar failure to grasp the true significance of Kautsky's doctrines until very late in the day. It is noticeable that almost all Lenin's references to Kautsky prior to 1914 are extremely laudatory, suggesting that he never felt much inclined to question Kautsky's reputation as the 'Marxist Pope'. Because Kautsky's encyclicals on all matters of theory and strategy were extremely influential in shaping the general outlook of social democracy, Lenin's singular lapse in believing Kautsky to be a Marxist of the same school as himself carried serious consequences. To say the least, it was not the best augury for a realistic assessment of the political temper of the European working-class movement. Not until the outbreak of war, and the disintegration of the Second International, did the true nature of Kautsky's Marxism dawn upon Lenin, though all the signs were evident long before.

Part of the reason for Lenin's strange misjudgement was that

Kautsky was extremely adept at manipulating the language and concepts of revolutionary Marxism in advocating a policy of parliamentary socialism. In addition, Kautsky's polemics against Bernstein's brand of revisionism, and his own regular insistence on the need for 'social revolution', could superficially be construed as a line of thought having more in common with a Bolshevik than a Menshevik cast of mind. In defending the need for social revolution Kautsky was aligning himself against that trend in the party that saw the transition to socialism as a tranquil and barely perceptible change in economic and social relationships.[44] Wholesale revisionism was objected to by Kautsky because it proposed that the bulk of existing institutions could simply be refashioned to meet new needs, instead of being superseded by institutions of completely different design. Moreover, the revisionists' erroneous belief that the capitalist class could quietly be expropriated had the unfortunate consequence of lulling the working class into a false sense of political security instead of preparing it for the intense class conflicts that lay ahead. Kautsky, not unlike Lenin, held that labour could only overcome the might of capital by way of a bitterly contested struggle, and that final victory could not be secured until the working class had captured the power of the state. 'The social revolution for which we are striving can only be achieved by means of a political revolution, by means of the conquest of political power by the militant proletariat.'[45] It was this type of language that put Lenin off his guard and caused him to back Kautsky in the latter's polemics against genuine revolutionaries such as Rosa Luxemburg.[46] This was Kautsky the true Marxist, before he turned 'renegade'.

However handy as a face-saving formula, Lenin's identification of two Kautskys – an early revolutionary one, and a later reformist one – does not bear close scrutiny. Kautsky's theoretical position was in fact remarkably consistent. As already suggested, the misconception arises largely because of his facility in exploiting the ambiguities in Marxist terminology. His writings are punctuated with references to 'class struggle', the 'fighting proletariat', the 'capture of state power', the coming 'political revolution', and similar trigger phrases drawn from the repertoire of revolutionary Marxism. But it is quite clear throughout that the vocabulary of conflict and struggle is being employed in its strictly *non-violent* usage. The class battles and political confrontations envisaged by Kautsky were of an institutional and parliamentary, not a physical, kind. Nothing was more foreign to his version of Marxism than the idea of an armed proletariat storming its way to socialism. His definition of a revolutionary as one 'whose aim is that a hitherto oppressed class should conquer the power of the State', allowed him to include himself in Leninist company.[47] But by conquering the power of the state he did not mean, as Lenin did, taking it by force; he meant winning key positions one by one through parliamentary and other legal means – that is, by dint of 'economic, legislative and moral pressure'.[48] The revolution, for Kautsky, took the form of an irreversible takeover by the working class of all positions of social and economic power culminating, despite spirited constitutional resistance by the bourgeoisie, in the bloodless triumph of labour over capital. The overwhelming preponderance of the working class, and the formidable power of its organizations, made the resort to violence quite unnecessary.

These arguments were lucidly presented by Kautsky in *The Road to Power* in 1909, though they had been deployed much earlier in his newspaper articles. The passages that ought to have given Lenin greatest pause were not only those that eschewed the use of revolutionary force, but those that drew a pointed distinction between a revolutionary party and a 'revolution-making' party:

> 'Social democracy is a revolutionary party, but not a revolution-making party. We know that our objective can only be reached through revolution. But we also know that it is no more in our power to make this revolution than it is in the power of our enemies to prevent it. We have no wish either to stir up revolution or to prepare the ground for one.'[49]

Kautsky could hardly have made it plainer that his understanding of Marxism was completely at variance with Lenin's on all fundamental points, including the very meaning of revolution. As Nettl observes, 'The whole concept of revolution, indeed the very use of the word by Kautsky, proved to be meaningless; it had only to come into contact with a real revolutionary situation to break down into its constituent syllables, so many daring sounds without real meaning'.[50]

It can only be a matter for wonder that Lenin could have been so taken aback at Kautsky's censorious reaction to the Bolshevik seizure of power when such a response was so plainly foreshadowed in practically all of Kautsky's dicta on the transition to socialism. Lenin's hopelessly defective reading of Kautsky's Marxism must have contributed to his underestimation of the counter-revolutionary potential of German social democracy, the movement that Lenin had banked on above all others to consummate the European revolution. This grave error of judgement helped to ensure the falsification of the domino theory and so, ironically, confirmed the aptness of Lenin's own unhappy metaphor of a chain being severed at its one weakest link.

# III

The failure of the European socialist revolution raised in a particularly acute form the question of political leadership in the transitionary process. No matter how propitious the economic and social circumstances, faulty or corrupt leadership could apparently cause the 'locomotives of history' to become derailed. The urgent need, therefore, was to raise the quality of working-class leadership to the level of the Russian model, a task the Bolsheviks undertook by setting up the Third International. This organization was designed to loosen the social-democratic grip on the western proletariat by cultivating a hardier revolutionary breed trained and supervised by the proven specialists in the field. As a result, what was thought of as the 'leadership problem' was not so much resolved as restated. The trouble now was not so much a lack of revolutionary will, as it had been in the case of the social democrats, as lack of political competence in reading the arcane signs of a 'revolutionary situation'.

The difficulty arose from the fact that Leninism decreed that the successful overthrow of capitalism hinged to a very large degree upon the actual timing of the operation. Revolutionary leadership therefore called for special skill in diagnosing the ever-changing balance of class and political forces in order to determine the exact moment when the insurrectionary blow should be struck. The need was for leaders who possessed what Rosa Luxemburg called 'the scrutinizing eye, trained to decipher the historical dialectic of revolution. . .'.[51] No one pursued this point more tirelessly than Trotsky; his conviction that 'in our epoch of abrupt turns the greatest difficulty for a revolutionary leadership lies in being able to feel the pulse of the political situation at the proper moment, so as to catch the abrupt contingency and to turn the helm in due time', was a conviction that grew stronger over the years.[52] Trotsky, like Lenin, reckoned revolutionary time in very fine units, so that he felt it more than usually incumbent upon party leaders to develop that special sixth sense that was needed to 'catch the abrupt contingency'. Failure to pinpoint correctly the fleeting revolutionary moment would be punished by history's cruellest possible retribution:

> 'To rise in arms, to overwhelm the enemy, to seize power, may be possible today, but tomorrow may be impossible. But to seize power is to change the course of history. Is it really true that such a historic event can hinge upon an interval of 24 hours? Yes, it can. . . To lose several weeks, several days, and sometimes even

a single day is tantamount under certain conditions to the surrender of the revolution. . .[53]

If, as it seems from this, the transition to socialism hangs very much in the balance, and is settled finally by the delicacy of the party's sense of timing, then responsibilities of awesome magnitude are placed on the shoulders of the vanguard leadership. It is small wonder that Trotsky spent such a large part of his life in bitter lamentation that this leadership was nowhere fit to discharge such responsibilities. Almost wherever he turned his gaze Trotsky could see golden revolutionary opportunities being frittered away because of the political ineptitude of party cadres. His diagnosis of the failure of the German insurrection in 1923 as a classic case of a 'mature revolutionary situation without a revolutionary party of due stature and without correct leadership', came to be applied quite liberally to a growing list of societies and periods.[54] This was especially so when the iniquities of social democracy became in his mind compounded with the incompetence and treachery of the Third International in the Stalin period.

'In the German revolution of 1918, in the Hungarian revolution of 1919, in the September movement of the Italian proletariat in 1920, in the English general strike of 1926, in the Vienna uprising of 1927, and in the Chinese revolution of 1925–27 – everywhere, one and the same political contradiction of the entire past decade . . . was manifested. [Namely] the subjective factor, that is, a revolutionary mass party, was lacking or else this party lacked a farsighted and intrepid leadership.'[55]

Trotsky's infatuation with the leadership problem marked what could perhaps be seen as the culmination of a tendency within Marxism towards the progressive narrowing down of the social basis of revolutionary agency. If Leninism signifies a shift away from Marx's emphasis on social class to a greater emphasis on the role of party, Trotskyism signifies a further shift from the role of party to the role of leader. A fairly unconvincing case might just about be made out for the proposition that class, party, and leader were regarded by all three theorists as essential ingredients in the transition to socialism. But it would call upon immense resources of textual inventiveness to show that the political recipes of Marx, Lenin, and Trotsky each combined these different ingredients in similar measure.

The strength of the leadership ingredient in Trotsky's own special blend is well shown in his speculation upon the likely fate of the Russian revolution in the absence of Lenin. Considering the wealth of Marxist talent in the Bolshevik party at the time, it might reasonably have been supposed that had Lenin not been at hand to take personal charge of things, some other figure would have stepped forward, in accordance with the well-known formula that 'events call forth the man'. In Trotsky's judgement, however, this would not have happened because there was only *one* possible man – Lenin – capable of setting the revolution in motion. However well-versed in the Marxist arts Bukharin, Zinoviev, Kamenev, Stalin, and the rest might have been, '*not a single* one of them showed himself capable of applying independently the theoretical and practical experiences of the party at a most important and most critical historical moment'.[56] Trotsky acknowledged that he himself, in the absence of Lenin, would have been unable to direct the party on to its insurrectionary course, though Lenin would most likely have succeeded without the assistance of Trotsky. 'If neither Lenin nor I had been present in Petersburg, there would have been no October Revolution: the leadership of the Bolshevik Party would have prevented it from occurring.'[57]

The rather startling implication of this is that the path from capitalism to socialism can be traversed only under the guidance of a once-in-a-lifetime political superman. And, as Trotsky ruefully reminds us, 'not every party will have its Lenin. . .'.[58] The elaborate Marxist choreography of social forces and class conjunctures, danced by a cast of millions, cannot actually be staged in the absence of the leading virtuoso. Historical materialism and the laws of social motion are now held in abeyance, neutralized by the chaotic forces of historical accident and contingency. No sealed train = no Lenin = no socialist revolution. In the light of his own account of the touch-and-go nature of the event, Trotsky's claim to have 'foretold the inevitability of the October Revolution thirteen years before it took place', rather seems to blur the distinction between Marxist science and clairvoyance.[59]

What, indeed, is to be made of this science as a source of special insight and understanding not accessible to the bourgeois mind when even its most illustrious exponents are deemed incompetent to apply it? It is a novel type of scientific knowledge that requires for its successful application the combination of superhuman gifts and freakish circumstances. Not surprisingly, with the passing of Lenin, Trotsky could conclude: 'There is now no one except me to carry out the mission of arming a new generation with the revolutionary method . . .'[60] It is hard to imagine Trotsky dissenting from the thought that the secret of that method accompanied him to the grave.

## IV

The more prominent the place given to factors of happenstance and contingency, the smaller the scope for the pretensions of grand theory. The presentation of history as a chapter of accidents is a standpoint commonly put forward in direct opposition to Marxist or sociological attempts to discern some pattern and regularity in the apparant randomness of events. When Marxism is injected with a heavy dose of contingency the outcome is bound to be lethal for those variants that seek to provide a general theory of transition. History becomes, moreover, if not exactly open-ended, at least open to the very real possibility that the transition to socialism might never occur, that the bourgeois stage of development might be followed by something quite unlike a workers' state. From Trotsky, and more especially from Lukacs and Luxemburg, onwards, Marxism confronts for the first time in any systematic way the daunting thought of a possible future without socialism.

This readiness to think the hitherto unthinkable did not spring from revisionist beliefs in the regenerative powers of capitalism; rather the reverse. Luxemburg's celebrated doctrine that 'the collapse of capitalism follows inevitably, as an objective historical necessity' required not the slightest modification.[61] The reason is that although bourgeois society could not avoid the fate that Marx had predicted for it, it could quite easily be followed not by a new socialist order but by what Lukacs and Luxemburg called a 'new barbarism' nowhere envisaged by Marx. Phoenix would still rise from the smouldering ashes of bourgeois democracy, but possibly in the monstrous form of military dictatorship or fascism. The introduction of the formula 'socialism or barbarism' drove home the point that socialism was not historically privileged, and that if the dark alternative was to be avoided political action of the most resolute kind was called for.[62]

This formula could be said to have resolved an apparent paradox in Marxist theory: namely, the combination of a doctrine of inevitable capitalist collapse with a rallying call to political action to bring this end about. Pronouncements to the effect that political action was necessary to accelerate the inevitable, to nudge history along, skated over rather than resolved the paradox. The Lukacs-Luxemburg formula, on the other hand, managed to synthesize the seemingly irreconcilable elements of agency and determinism. It was precisely on account of the fact that capitalism *was* set irretrievably on its doom-laden course that strenuous social intervention was needed to settle the sharply contested issue of the political *succession*. The unwarranted optimism of Kautskian social democracy encouraged a dangerous fatalism that might allow barbarism to triumph by default. The recognition of a clear political either/or, following the collapse of bourgeois democracy, meant that the call to action could be reconciled with determinist convictions, somewhat akin to the Calvinist attempt to square the doctrine of predestination with the injunction to perform good works.

The 'socialism or barbarism' thesis was an interesting innovation in historical materialism in that the nature of the system earmarked to follow the bourgeois stage of development was now indicated by a question mark. Whereas the passage from feudalism to absolutism, and from absolutism to capitalism, allowed of no exceptions or alternatives, the passage from capitalism led to more than one possible destination. To parody Marx, if the embryo of the new order matures in the womb of the old, then bourgeois society appears to be pregnant with non-identical twins, only one of which could be a live birth.

Events in various parts of Europe in the inter-war period appeared to justify Lukacs' and Luxemburg's worst forebodings, and in so doing raised another awkward problem: how to account for the transition from bourgeois democracy to fascism. Starting from the assumption that the capitalist system in general was in a state of severe crisis, how was it to be explained that some capitalist societies developed in the direction of fascism while others held fast to bourgeois democracy? What common features could be discerned in the make-up of Italian, German, Spanish, Portuguese, and Japanese society that were conducive to a 'fascist solution', and which were absent in Britain, France, Scandinavia, and the United States?

It is when this type of problem is addressed that a more than usually wide discrepancy appears between the confident theoretical claims of Marxism and its actual explanatory performance. The standard opening gambit is to accentuate the generic, universal features of capitalism as the main elements of the explanatory model, i.e. those features that are taken to be the defining characteristics of the system and which are therefore present in some combination or other in all capitalist societies. At the same time, recognition is given to the fact that each society is historically and culturally unique, so that each society will combine the basic features of the system in its own special way. This idea is enshrined in the 'law of uneven development', which postulates that the various institutions of capitalism evolve at a different pace and in a somewhat different manner. The problem for Marxism is how to strike a proper balance between the generalizing scope of its global model and the particularizing slant that pays due homage to local variety and distinctiveness. No explanation is deemed possible that does not directly engage with the facts of the purely national context; at the same time, however, if these national factors are weighted too heavily the explanation would be couched in terms of cultural peculiarities and traditions, and unique historical experiences, that are not the essential ingredients of a capitalist system as defined by the general model.

Thus, in seeking to account for the vulnerability of certain bourgeois societies to fascism and allied forms of barbarism, Marxist theory attempts to integrate the variety of specific causes into some general global explanation. In at least one application of the theory, the notion of an 'imperialist stage' is felt to provide the necessary theoretical focus for examining each national variant of fascism:

> 'Fascism in effect belongs to the imperialist *stage* of capitalism. The point is therefore to try to elucidate certain general characteristics of the stage, and their impact on fascism. The primary causes of fascism are not the factors often seen as its basic *sine qua non*, such as the particular economic crises Germany and Italy were caught in when fascism was establishing itself, the national peculiarities of the two countries, the consequences of the First World War, etc. These factors are important only in relation to the stage of imperialism, as elements *of one of the possible conjunctures* of this stage.'[63]

Without the international antagonism arising from the imperialist crisis, the national stresses and strains so conscientiously documented by bourgeois writers would not lead to the kind of breakdown that prepares the way for fascism. The global crisis of capitalism in the imperialist stage creates a general disposition to a fascist solution in *all* capitalist societies, which is then triggered off in a certain few. But the fact that the accumulation of tensions and contradictions is politically manageable in some capitalist societies but not in others must also be accounted for by recourse to some general proposition if the descent to bourgeois particularism is to be avoided. The assumption must be that Italy, Germany, Spain, etc. combined the elements of the capitalist matrix in such a way as to render them especially vulnerable to the external pressures emanating from the global crisis. What, then, is the nature of the fatal flaw running through these societies that distinguishes them from the rest?

Trotsky, true to form, proposed that the answer was to be found in the quality of working-class leadership. He saw the emergence of a fascist movement as the most palpable sign of a revolutionary situation; consequently, the failure of the proletariat to rise to the occasion would almost certainly leave the way clear for the fascist alternative. Whether or not any particular bourgeois society succumbed to the

temptation of fascism would, in other words, be decided by the
political response of the working-class movement. Trotsky's position
is summed up in an 'historical law' that stated that 'fascism was able
to conquer. only in those countries where the conservative labour
parties prevented the proletariat from utilizing the revolutionary
situation and seizing power'.[64]

This freshly-minted Marxist law leads to the rather unexpected
conclusion that bourgeois societies that spurned fascism must either
have been blessed with sound working-class leadership or were not
potential candidates for socialist revolution – the two conditions that
Trotsky usually regards as barely conceivable. It seems improbable, to
say the very least, that he intended such a handsome tribute to the
working-class leadership of so many western countries. Trotsky's
'law', in fact, reveals the obvious defect in the 'socialism or barbarism'
thesis: the neglect of a third alternative in the continued existence of
bourgeois society itself. Since the question is stated incorrectly in the
first place it is not surprising that the answer should be so seriously
awry.

Only the most faithful devotees of Parisian Marxism would be
likely to feel that the answer offered by Poulantzas is much of an
improvement. Adopting Lenin's ill-starred concept, he suggests that
fascism triumphed in those countries that were the weakest links in
the capitalist chain. These links gave way under the extreme tension
that the entire international chain was subjected to; and the fact that it
was the Italian and German links that gave way was due to their
internal structural weaknesses. In the case of Italy, this was to do with
the contradictions set up between an industrializing north and a
backward, agricultural south; in the German case, it arose from the
country's late entry on to the imperialist stage.[65] France, Britain, and
the United States were also 'affected by the transition to monopoly
capitalism and by "economic crises". But they do not have the
accumulation of contradictions which typify Germany and Italy'.[66]
For any society known to have embraced fascism Poulantzas is ready
to disclose that it was wracked by contradictions sufficiently intense
to qualify it for membership in the family of weak links. It therefore
comes as no surprise to be told that, after Italy and Germany, 'Spain
in its turn became the nodal point of imperialist contradictions in
Europe'.[67] Poulantzas' theory is resoundingly confirmed by the fact
that none of the societies whose internal tensions were politically
manageable took the route to fascism; none of the strong links
snapped under tension, while all the weak ones did. This revealing
exercise in the comparative method shows the same order of Marxist
scientific rigour as that shown by Althusser in his theory of socialist
transition.

For Althusser, the transition to socialism also occurs only when inner contradictions have built up to an explosive pitch. Why this process occurs in some bourgeois societies but not in others depends on the actual conditions prevailing at any given time and in any given place.[68] On the face of it this would seem to be a highly empirical approach, leading to different explanations for each successful socialist revolution. However, Althusser is at pains to point out that the notion of appropriate 'conditions' is 'essential to Marxism precisely because it is not an empirical concept: a statement about what exists. On the contrary, it is a *theoretical* concept. . . '.[69] Armed with this theoretical device, Althusser is then able to explain that socialist revolution 'could only break out . . . in Russia, in China, in Cuba, in 1917, in 1949, in 1958, and not elsewhere; and not in another "situation". . .'.[70] Thus, remarkably, the transition to socialism nowhere occurred where the conditions for it were not properly ripe, any more than had the transition to barbarism.

Since accumulated contradictions sometimes prepare the ground for fascism and sometimes for socialism, it would be of more than passing interest to know in what way the contradictions preceding the one differed from the contradictions preceding the other. Poulantzas does seem to recognize the problem:

'. . . although the revolution was made in the weakest link in the chain (Russia), fascism arose in the next two links, i.e., those which were, relatively speaking, the weakest in Europe at the time. In no sense do I mean that fascism was fated to happen there, any more than the Bolshevik Revolution was fated to occur in the weakest link. I simply mean that in the particular *conjunctures* of class struggle in these countries, which for a whole series of reasons led to such different results, their position in the imperialist chain was of crucial importance.'[71]

Not even a few of the 'whole series of reasons' that lay behind the transformation of one weak link into fascism, another into socialism, are thought to be worth mentioning. To do so might after all reveal the decisive importance of those purely national features and local circumstances that play such havoc with systemic models. Even worse, a proper comparison of the structure of weak and strong links might easily end up by doing away altogether with the cherished notion of an imperial chain.

The metaphor of embryos maturing in wombs, with which the discussion started off, seems to have given way to the less homely one of chains under tension and weak links snapping. It would be tempting to ask whether this new play on metaphor also counts as explanation, or is simply one more contribution to the Marxist science of predicting the past; but perhaps that would be to reveal another symptom of that strange inability to think outside the confines of a bourgeois problematic.

# Notes

1 Avineri 1968:174 ff.
2 Marx 1959:428.
3 Marx 1959:429.
4 Marx 1959:431.
5 Marx 1959:431.
6 'According to Marx, the recourse to political power can never do more than realize potentialities already existing within the socio-economic structure. Political power, according to Marx, can never create anything *ex nihilo*. . . Political power may be crucial for the realization of potentialities, but it does not create the new structures realized . . . it can never be the prime mover.' Avineri 1968:181.
7 Kautsky 1922:181–82.
8 Bernstein 1909:163.
9 Kautsky 1902:42 and 43.
10 Lukacs 1971:282.
11 Lenin 1950:Vol. I, part II 'Two Tactics of Social-Democracy in the Democratic Revolution'. Lenin felt that the bourgeoisie preferred an incomplete revolution because it would need to draw on support from autocratic powers in its ensuing struggle against the revolutionary proletariat. An 1848-style revolution was therefore preferable to a 1789, since the latter might unleash popular revolutionary forces that the bourgeoisie would be unable to restrain.
12 Lukacs 1971:279 and 284. Thus in Rosa Luxemburg's statement that 'The relations of production in capitalist society become increasingly socialist but its political and legal arrangements erect an ever loftier wall between capitalist and socialist society', Lukacs detects the 'seeds of a belief that the Revolution was needed only to remove the "political" obstacles from the path of economic developments'. Lukacs 1971:277. Luxemburg's theory of 'spontaneism', with its implied opposition to Leninist organizational principles, is traced back to this 'error'.
13 Lukacs 1971:283.
14 'Classes that successfully carried out revolutions in earlier societies had their task made easier *subjectively* by this very fact of the discrepancy between their own class consciousness and the objective economic set-up, i.e., by their very unawareness of their own function in the process of change. They had only to use the power at their disposal to enforce their *immediate* interests while the social import of their actions was hidden from them and left to the "ruse of reason" of the course of events.' By contrast, 'in the centre of proletarian class consciousness we discover an antagonism between momentary and ultimate goal.' Lukacs 1971:71 and 73.
15 Lukacs 1971:65.
16 Lukacs 1971:310.

17 Lukacs 1971:305.
18 Althusser 1969; and 1971.
19 Lukacs 1971:42.
20 Lukacs 1971:42.
21 Lenin 1950:Vol. I, part I 343 and 333; Vol. II, part I 482.
22 Cited in Deutscher 1954:76.
23 Lukacs 1971:329.
24 Lukacs 1971:327.
25 Lukacs 1971:327.
26 Harding 1977:Vol. I 102.
27 In 1902, when his party was in only its eighteenth year, Lenin felt it already had a 'history' that could be 'distinctly divided into three periods', the first ten years being the period of 'foetal development'; the next four years marking 'the period of its childhood and adolescence'; and the last four years being the 'period of disunity, dissolution and vacillation'. Lenin 1950:Vol. I, part I 396 and 397. Again in 1910, surveying the political scene over the past six years, he could 'at once discern two three-year periods into which this six-year period falls'. The first period, ending with the summer of 1907, was 'distinguished by rapid changes in the fundamental features of the state system . . .'. The second period, ending with the summer of 1910, was distinguished by 'an evolution so slow that it almost amounted to stagnation. There were no changes at all noticeable in the state system'. Lenin 1950:Vol. I, part II 202.

As 1917 approaches his periodization becomes ever more refined, as when the 'July days' (3rd and 4th) are sharply counterposed to the 'September days'. During the former, 'the objective conditions for the victory of the insurrection did not exist', whereas during the latter period, 'all the objective conditions . . . for a successful insurrection' were suddenly visible. Lenin 1972:580 and 581. With even more exactitude, the period justifying the slogan 'all power to the Soviets' was pinpointed as that lasting from February 27 to July 4. The period immediately following July 4 was classified as one in which the 'objective situation underwent a drastic change', rendering the same slogan 'absolutely impossible', until the commencement of a new period on October 8 when it once again became wholly correct. Lenin 1950:Vol. II, part I 88, 89 and 186.
28 Cited in Lenin 1950:Vol. II, part II 100.
29 Lenin 1950:102.
30 Lenin 1950:Vol. II, part I 387.
31 Lenin 1950:Vol. II, part I 106.
32 Lenin 1950:Vol. II, part I 97.
33 Lenin 1950:Vol. I, part II 72. Durkheim suggests that under the influence of 'effervescent social environments' the individual feels himself 'dominated and carried away by some sort of an external power which makes him think and act differently than in normal times . . . everything is just as though he really were transported into a special world, entirely different from the one where he ordinarily lives, and into an environment filled with exceptionally intense forces that take hold of him and metamorphose him.' Durkheim 1964b:218.
34 Lenin 1950:108.
35 Lenin 1950:Vol. II, part I 429.
36 Lenin 1950:Vol. II, part I 429.
37 Carr 1966:185.
38 Cited in Carr 1966:134–35.

39 Carr 1966:186. Sturmthal also phrased his guess in the form of a factual statement that 'Most German workers refused to risk a war against what they considered hopeless odds for the sake of a proletarian revolution . . .'. Sturmthal, 1944:52.
40 Trotsky 1937:30.
41 Scheidemann 1929:645.
42 Kautsky 1946:142. This judgement was made in 1937, though offered as confirmation of his earlier prediction about the development and character of Leninist Russia.
43 Lenin 1950:Vol. II, part II 105.
44 Kautsky 1909; and 1903.
45 Kautsky 1909:53.
46 Nettl 1969:292.
47 Kautsky 1902:3.
48 Kautsky 1909:53.
49 Kautsky 1909:53.
50 Nettl 1969:290.
51 Luxemburg (ed. Davis) 1976:93.
52 Trotsky 1970:91.
53 Trotsky 1971:47.
54 Trotsky 1972:11.
55 Trotsky 1970:85.
56 Trotsky 1962:2.
57 Trotsky 1976:46.
58 Trotsky 1971:38.
59 Trotsky 1962:27.
60 Trotsky 1976:47.
61 Luxemburg 1951:417.
62 For a full discussion of this point see Geras 1976.
63 Poulantzas 1974:17.
64 Trotsky 1975:468.
65 Poulantzas 1974:Chapter 2.
66 Poulantzas 1974:34.
67 Poulantzas 1974:35.
68 Althusser 1969: 'Contradiction and Overdetermination'.
69 Althusser 1969:207.
70 Althusser 1969:207.
71 Poulantzas 1974:24.

# 9

# The dictatorship
# of the proletariat
# and social democracy

The great promise contained within the heart of Marxism is not merely that of a classless future, but of a society in which the highest aspirations for liberty will find fulfilment. Marxism does not differ from other and earlier traditions of socialist thought in the importance it attaches to the combined package of equality and freedom, nor in the conviction that one hardly makes sense without the other. The socialist critique of the liberal theory of freedom revolves around the argument that formal rights and liberties enshrined in bourgeois law are purely notional in a class-stratified society. Great disparities in wealth and opportunity ensure that only a favoured few are able to activate and realize the rights supposedly available to all. Bourgeois liberty, in a well-known formulation, is the freedom of the unemployed to dine at the Ritz or the freedom of every ghetto child to enter university. The very existence of social classes is taken to be a diminution of, or restriction upon, personal liberty by virtue of the commanding powers conferred upon those of property and wealth over the rest of the community. The unequal distribution of liberty follows as a natural consequence of the unequal distribution of power embodied in class society.

The Marxist case for the classless society is that social equality is not only a valuable end in itself, but also the precondition for a genuinely free society. Socialism transforms nominal or formal liberties into real or substantive liberties by providing all citizens with the material and social wherewithal for utilizing their legal rights to the full. In Lenin's illustration, the difference between rights of assembly under bourgeois democracy and under proletarian democracy was that under the latter the palaces and mansions of the dispossesed class would be made over to workers as places to *assemble in*. Similarly, the freedom of the press would be given content under socialism because the printing presses would be removed from the monopoly of press barons and handed over to workers' committees.[1] The point being made by Lenin's polemic is that the dissolution of bourgeois democracy – the 'dictatorship of the bourgeoisie' – results in the expansion of practical freedom well beyond the limits envisaged in liberal theory.

The traditional argument for the inseparability of equality and liberty has undergone something of a revival in current Marxist debate, provoked in no small part by the unspectacular record of socialist states in actually pushing forward the frontiers of freedom. The sensitivity to this matter on the part of Eurocommunists, in particular, is not of course unconnected to the fact that the western working class, to whom their message is directed, is in a position to draw some rough comparisons between the conditions of liberty prevailing in European bourgeois and socialist states. Eurocommunism acknowledges that a socialist society in western Europe would call for the active endorsement of a working class whose expectations in the field of civil and political liberties had been shaped by the relatively high standards set by bourgeois democracy. Almost without exception, the societies in which capitalism has been displaced by socialism had no prior tradition of established civil liberties and citizenship rights; consequently, the absence of such liberties under the new dispensation would hardly be perceived by the working class as a novel and worrisome deprivation. In large parts of western Europe, by contrast, the working-class movement has come to regard the extension of citizenship and civil rights as one of its most impressive political monuments. And it is by no means certain, to put it mildly, that the material and social gains offered by a socialist society would be regarded as acceptable compensation for any corresponding loss or diminution of existing liberties. The strategists of Eurocommunism are probably correct in their calculation that popular legitimacy could only be won for western socialism if the claims of liberty were treated no less seriously than the claims of equality.

Now the political theory of liberty in the classless society or in the transitional socialist state is not to be found ready made in classical Marxism and its offshoots. Nor for that matter have latter-day Marxists given it the prominent place it might be thought to deserve in a programme ostensibly designed with human emancipation in mind. Despite the avowed responsiveness of Marxism to the lessons of history, there is still no general schema of a socialist political system that indicates how power should be distributed, how conflicting interests should be represented and resolved, how abuses to socialist legality should be checked, and so on. There are no principles or guidelines of even the most general kind pertaining to the conduct of political life under the dictatorship of the proletariat, nor any attempt to systematize Lenin's own scrappy remarks on the subject. Miliband's judgement that the exercise of power under proletarian dictatorship is the 'Achilles' heel of Marxism' is in no obvious danger of becoming outdated by current theory or practice.[2]

This is all the more surprising in that few Marxists today suppose that classes and class conflict would suffer immediate decline following the socialization of property and the expropriation of the bourgeoisie. It is well understood that conflicting claims and interests stemming from the division of labour are quite capable of outliving changes in the legal status of productive property, so that some social and political mechanisms would be required for resolving these antagonisms. Within a western context, in particular, difficulties could be expected in the integration of professional and managerial elites into a system founded on the assumption of proletarian hegemony. Although the skills and aptitudes of the former middle classes would presumably be essential to the success of the new system, all the precedents suggest that the political allegiance of these white-collar groups would be less than wholehearted. As the architects of the first proletarian dictatorship discovered, the services of white-collar elites could only be secured under the promise of concessionary privileges that were in direct violation of egalitarian ideals.[3] In any conceivable western version of a proletarian state the problem of white-collar or elite incorporation would loom larger rather than smaller, given the proportionate size of these groups in the working population. Consequently, the need for representative bodies to speak for the interests of this 'honorary proletariat' would be that much greater.

At the same time, this matter of representation has never really been Marxism's strong suit. Classical Marxism fostered the comforting belief that antagonistic interests were the by-product of a particular mode of appropriation, and that once this noxious element had been removed from human affairs, the way would be clear for a more harmonious and accommodating political mood. It was as if the model for socialist society were to be drawn from sketches supplied by Durkheim or Parsons rather than by Marx himself. In the post-alienation society individuals would apparently be too absorbed in the fascinating arts of self-realization to bother unduly with anything as squalid and divisive as the pursuit of material interest. The rationale for a one-party monopoly of political life is traceable to this belief that with the elimination of property the worst of human passions could be calmed down to an extent that would render obsolete the complex political machinery of conflict resolution. Such machinery is thought to be necessary for bourgeois society precisely because this type of society knows only a condition of rancour and civil strife. In that explosive condition where the few seek to dominate the many, safety-valves must be numerous and sophisticated.

Lenin's own artist's impression of the proletarian state highlights the contrast between a cumbersome and elaborate battery of constitutional bodies and formal rules required by an exploitative system, and the sheer simplicity of government by workers' decree. In his total unconcern for the formalities of legislation and administration Lenin conveys the impression that governing a socialist state is about on a par with running a branch office of the Thames Valley Water Board.[4] He appears, in fact, to have taken very seriously Saint-Simon's famous and absurd distinction between a society founded on the 'governance of men' and one founded on the 'administration of things'. Marxists have yet to reveal the secret of how 'things' are to be administered without the need to cajole, placate, and coerce 'men'. But the very fact that it is thought to be both desirable and possible to separate the two tasks gives useful advance warning of how ill-suited Marxism is as a guide to the practical realities of government in a socialist state.

## II

Part of the reason why proletarian dictatorship was felt to require only the flimsiest administrative apparatus was that with the majority class in control for the first time the load could be spread thinly among all properly accredited citizens. The baroque edifice of parliament, political parties, executive and judicial bodies was an historically specific and limited form of democracy answering to a particular set of class needs; it was not a universally valid form applicable to all state systems, least of all socialist ones. In Rosa Luxemburg's view the parliamentary variant of democracy was set up by the bourgeoisie principally as a vehicle in its struggle against absolutist regimes, so that once bourgeois authority had become decently established parliament and its supporting institutions would serve no further purpose.[5] It could certainly not be taken over and transformed by the proletariat to serve its own very different ends. For Marxists there is something in the very nature of the parliamentary form that makes it an unsuitable instrument for proletarian rule, even when completely in the hands of the workers' own representatives.

Marx's own comments on 'parliamentary cretinism' served to set the tone for all subsequent assessments of representative democracy by his followers. If bourgeois democracy set far too great a store by what Lukacs called the 'cretinism of legality', then it seemed to Lenin only proper that the dictatorship of the proletariat should be a system of rule 'unrestricted by any laws'.[6] Discredited democratic ways could be made all the more dispensable by the introduction of a superior institution in the shape of the soviet. Rather in the manner proposed by Durkheim in respect of professional associations, the system of soviets was intended to shift the electoral basis of politics from territorial to occupational units. But whereas Durkheim felt that professional and trade associations should themselves provide the source of moral and political identity, Lenin felt that industrial groupings that cut across these parochial loyalties would be more appropriate units for the articulation of class power. Significantly, however, neither Durkheim nor Lenin go beyond the technical matter of representation to raise the more fundamental question of the rights and forms of organized *opposition*. A representative system founded upon soviets or upon professional associations, as an alternative to political parties, invokes a model of the distribution of power not unlike that of pluralism. According to this model, multiple-interest groups do not coalesce into two broadly defined class groupings, each united around a set of core values and purposes. Rather, each specific interest group is engaged in an unstable pattern of alliances, trade-offs, and bargains with all other groups. Because interests do not crystallize permanently around a single line of cleavage, the conventional distinction between government and opposition loses much of its force. Individual soviets or individual professional associations presumably would bargain for their members' interests on an *ad hoc* basis, in the standard manner of veto groups. A system of political brokerage would replace the static parliamentary form of permanent parties espousing different philosophies and programmes. Political parties only flourish in a house divided against itself; professional associations and soviets are thus more fitting to a society founded on common moral sentiments. Marxism again finds Durkheimian theory much to its taste, *after* the revolution.

Certainly the notion of a 'loyal opposition' is one that is not easily squared with the stern imperatives of proletarian dictatorship. Lenin held that ' "opposition" is a concept that belongs to the peaceful and only to the parliamentary struggle, i.e. a concept that corresponds to a non-revolutionary situation . . . to an *absence of revolution*'.[7] But since a proletarian dictatorship, almost by definition, presupposes a condition of potential or actual civil war the case for an opposition can never be sustained. When society is divided into 'two armed camps', to press for the right of opposition would be akin to demanding parliamentary procedures in the trenches.

It is on these grounds that the workers' state has never felt able to tolerate peasant and proletarian parties other than the Leninist vanguard. On the face of it, it might seem reasonable to suppose that a socialist society could operate with at least two parties in competition for political power, as a means of providing some check against the abuse of office by a single political clique or leader. Reflecting upon the degeneration of the Russian revolution, Trotsky concluded that it was 'absolutely indisputable that the domination of a single party served as the juridical point of departure for the Stalinist totalitarian system'.[8] Under a genuine workers' dictatorship, therefore, it was essential to have two or more independent political parties that differed only programatically and not in their commitment to the defence of the revolution. An analogy might be pressed with the American party system in which Republicans and Democrats compete for power within the framework of a capitalist system that each endorses unreservedly. If bourgeois society can run successfully along the lines of a two-party system in which the main contestants are divided ideologically only on matters of nuance, then could not socialist society follow suit?

The reason why the answer to this question cannot be a straightforward yes is that a newly constituted proletarian state is essentially a siege society. It is a type of system that only comes into being in the teeth of concerted resistance, internal and external, and which at once finds itself in a less than friendly political environment. Perhaps the most telling difference between bourgeois and socialist revolutions is that, in their opposition to the revolutionary bourgeoisie, the absolutist regimes acted almost wholly within the boundaries of their own national territory; absolute monarchies were not constituent parts of a single international economic and political order to anything like the same extent as capitalist regimes. Consequently, bourgeois threats to royal and aristocratic power had to be countered largely by loyalist forces within the nation. By contrast, any attempt to topple the bourgeoisie from its perch in any one nation-state is likely to provoke a concerted reaction by other capitalist powers. Socialism thus begins its life as a society under siege.

In a siege society, internal class relations and political divisions have exceptionally sharp edges. The indigenous bourgeoisie is at once cast in the role of a potential fifth column; real and imaginary enemies abound. Under these tense circumstances there is a tendency for the governing party to construe the smallest degree of opposition from other parties as a sign of political defection from the new system. When the only legally permitted parties are those committed to the defence of the revolution, opponents of the regime will be inclined to gravitate towards the main opposition party *faute de mieux*. This party then becomes politically tainted by such association, so that official doubts can then be cast upon the genuineness of its support for socialism, and hence upon its very legality.[9] The first law of the siege society is that *all* other parties, whatever their avowed intentions, contain within themselves the seeds of counter-revolution. The fate of workers' and peasants' parties in the young Soviet state is a fate that awaits all parties that seek to play the role of loyal opposition in a socialist society under siege. The line between treasonable activites and a legitimate 'workers' opposition' or 'left opposition' is much easier to discern in the orderly world of Marxist theory than in the unavoidable chaos of a proletarian dictatorship.

The fact that capitalism's writ no longer runs unchallenged throughout the world, but only in diminishing areas of it, by no means alleviates the pressure on a siege society. Indeed, the first western socialist society could expect to find itself under particularly severe external constraints. It is precisely because a large slice of the world has become labelled as the socialist camp that any move in the direction of this camp by a western state would be regarded by other bourgeois states as an unacceptable political defection. It would be interpreted by the western powers not merely as a defeat in the ideological struggle between democracy and communism but, more seriously, as a direct military threat. The manichaen division of the industrialized world into opposing military blocs is an additional complicating factor in the transition to socialism, and one that raises difficulties not experienced by the working-class movement in the inter-war period. The first western state to declare a proletarian dictatorship could expect to become the siege society *par excellence*. The prospects for anything approaching an open socialist society, with legal parties and rights of opposition, must be judged against this unpromising background.

# III

If the labour movement in a proletarian democracy finds that its political wing has become severely clipped, it is also likely to find that its industrial wing is unable to compensate for this through its own energetic efforts on behalf of the working class. In many respects, the role allotted to trade unions under socialist regimes reflects the ambivalent stance that Marxists have always adopted towards these bodies in capitalist society. On the one hand, unions are considered to be a useful training ground for workers in the coming struggle for power; on the other hand, they are charged with lowering or displacing working-class consciousness through the promotion of purely 'economistic' strategies. Paradoxically, in striving for the incorporation of workers into the trade union movement Marxists contribute to that very process by which potentially revolutionary material is fashioned into conservative designs. (This paradox can, however, immediately be resolved by driving a conceptual wedge between the rank and file membership and the 'bureaucracy'; with the surgical removal of the latter, workers' organizations would be free to act more in accordance with the expectations of revolutionary theory.)

The question facing the proletarian dictatorship is: could these same organizations, created to defend workers against capitalist exploitation, be carried over into a new order set up as the very antithesis of exploitation? The dictatorship's answer is an unequivocal yes – and no. Unions cannot in practice be accorded the same rights under socialism that they have traditionally enjoyed in modern bourgeois regimes, since these rights are not compatible with egalitarian aims. Because industrial bargaining power is unevenly distributed among trade unions, the right to use this power in furtherance of wage and other demands would give rise to inequalities between stronger and weaker groups. Whereas under capitalism unions can be encouraged to use their industrial muscle to the full, under socialism the Durkheimian philosophy of self-restraint becomes immediately respectable. When the national product is divided not principally between capital and labour, but between different categories of labour, different moral rules of distribution apply. Under the dictatorship of the proletariat, powerful groups of workers really cannot be permitted to 'hold the country to ransom'. What possible place could there in fact be in the new society for organizations that, in their aggressively competitive and divisive behaviour, so plainly reveal their bourgeois origins?

If, in the best interests of socialism, trade unions are to be denied their traditional bargaining rights, they are not simply to be dumped in the junkyard of history. In practice, their duties become redefined by the dictatorship to allow them to continue in the service of the working class, albeit in somewhat novel ways. Trotsky's imagination was especially exercised with this problem. The founder of the Red Army was also a forceful advocate of the 'militarization of labour', believing that factories needed to be run along regimental lines and with military discipline.[10] Trade unions were thus to become part of an army-style command structure, with workers as front-line troops. Trotsky decreed that under the dictatorship trade unions had to be transformed into an 'apparatus of revolutionary repression against undisciplined, anarchical, parasitic elements in the working class'.[11] The full weight of this repressive apparatus was to descend on workers who were resistant to the dictates of management and who still harboured petty-bourgeois yearnings for 'workers' control'. As Lenin reminded the trade union leadership, since they were now 'participants in the exercise of state power' they could not 'refuse to share in the work of coercion'.[12] With the transition from capitalism to socialism the trade unions appear to exchange their place in the ideological state apparatus for one in the coercive state apparatus.

The fact that, under the dictatorship, the 'superintendence of labour' is to be carried out by the combined forces of management and unions might suggest that the latter are performing the 'global functions of capital' with a vengeance. Trotsky, however, ridiculed all attempts to point up apparent similarities in the subordination of labour under capitalism and under socialism as 'shallow liberal analogies'.[13] The relevant question for him, as for any Marxist, was: for what *ultimate purpose* were workers being subjected to the discipline of the barracks? Marxism appraises the meaning and significance of social facts not as isolated phenomena but in relation to their place in the total moral configuration of which they form part. So although at first blush it might seem as if the treatment of workers under the dictatorship of the proletariat was at least as harsh as their treatment under capitalism, the fact that the overall political contexts were altogether different meant that apparently similar factual conditions had entirely different moral connotations. As against the bourgeois conception of a universally valid morality, Marxism asserts the politically contingent nature of morality.[14] Whereas it would be necessary to condemn the use of disciplinary powers over labour in capitalist society, the condemnation of labour discipline under socialism could not be justified since it is not used in the service of an exploitative system.

> 'The whole question is: who applies the principle of compulsion, over whom, and for what purpose? What State, what class, in what conditions, by what methods?'[15]

As Trotsky's question here implies, the massacre of the Kronstadt workers cannot be equated with the massacres at St Petersburg or Peterloo since the system of class relations under the proletarian dictatorship was entirely different from that of absolutist Russia and bourgeois England. To shoot down workers in the defence of capitalism is a qualitatively different act from shooting down workers in the name of socialism. To put the two acts on a par is to display a sad inability to think dialectically.

# IV

The Marxist claim that the dictatorship of the proletariat is a higher form of democracy than anything offered by bourgeois society could be advanced on grounds quite unrelated to the matter of formal political rights and representation. It could be argued that the true measure of democracy is to be found not in the nature of the decision-making process but in the distributive outcome that this process yields. The charge against bourgeois democracy would be that despite the jealously guarded rights of groups and individuals to press their claims upon employers and the state, the division between rich and poor stubbornly persists. To allow the appellation 'democratic' to a system whose end product is the enrichment of a few and the impoverishment of many is to empty the term of all meaning. It is a political usage that betrays a greater regard for the legal procedures by which social assets are divided and distributed than for the actual pattern of allocation.

In contrast to this procedural fetishism the dictatorship of the proletariat seeks to be judged on the principle 'who gets what?'. A social system that discriminates consistently in favour of the majority class and against the once-privileged minority has, on this reckoning, a stronger claim to the democratic title than any bourgeois society, however 'free'. The dictatorship of the proletariat is, in Lenin's phrase, 'democracy for the poor'.[16] As this suggests, it is not the case that under the dictatorship the poor will cease to be with us, but rather that the rich will. Where there are no rich the poor may remain, but poverty may not. Poverty is a condition brought about not so much by a low level of material subsistence as by the flaunted wealth of a favoured few. In removing privilege and wealth the dictatorship removes the humiliating sting of poverty, and creates a society of dignified and equal poor. In response to the predictable bourgeois sneer that socialism is a system of levelling-down, in contrast to the liberal ideal of levelling-up, the dictatorship replies: levelling-down is the only kind of levelling that is socially and economically feasible, given finite resources. To suggest that everyone, with sufficient drive and application, could enjoy a place in the sun on millionaire's row, or even in the leafy suburbs, is typical of the deception that liberals practise on themselves and on others. Levelling-up is the doctrine of those who are in fact alarmed at the very prospect of equality; it is the friend of privilege masquerading as its foe.

The liberal rejoinder to all this is to pose a question of its own: namely, which of the following notional alternatives would workers actually prefer – a small cake divided into equally thin slices, or a large cake divided into slices of varying size, the great majority of which are bigger than the slices of the smaller cake? The liberal expectation is that more personal satisfaction is to be got from a larger than a smaller share, irrespective of how much *others* get. Moreover, the fact that some receive a much larger share than average would not cause general resentment once it were properly understood that the steady and continuous increase in the size of the cake as a whole was dependent upon this fact. To reduce the size of the bigger slices is to weaken the resolve of those responsible for finding ever new ways of enlarging the cake to the benefit of all.

The liberal justification for unequal shares rests squarely on this view that by identifying and rewarding generously a wealth-creating few the material well-being of everyone is enhanced. In its most recent and systematic formulation the thesis holds that an increase in the share accruing to the best rewarded is justifiable if, and only if, it results in an enlargement of the share going to the least rewarded. [17] On the basis of this principle the relationship of the few to the many cannot be one of exploitation since each party to the relationship stands to benefit. False consciousness from a liberal perspective would thus manifest itself in the peculiar tendency for workers to construe the rewards accruing to capital as a species of theft instead of the very source of their own material well-being. In illustration of the point, western workers are invited to compare their lot with that of their counterparts in eastern Europe. The expropriation there of an entrepreneurial class and the replacement of market 'anarchy' by central planning and egalitarianism have resulted, so the story goes, not in the anticipated dawn of abundance but a bleak land of slowly-moving bread queues and cardboard shoes.

This is a line of attack that, accurate or otherwise, would not necessarily be regarded by Marxists as especially devastating, since the virtues of the classless society are felt by many to lie more in the sphere of spiritual enrichment than in the accumulation of worldly things. The Founder's contempt for 'commodity fetishism' offered more than a hint from the outset that the good society was not to be measured solely by its display of cream buns and outboard motors. His self-parody of a society of part-time hunters, fishermen, and critics was intended to highlight a recurring theme that the fascination with possessions was an unwelcome distraction from the serious business of living life constructively. Even if, against all expectation, capitalism were to outpace socialism in the production of things, it could not compete on the territory that really mattered – the restoration of the individual's lost internal unity.

Capitalism's obsessive concern with ever-increasing output seemed to give the clearest indication that material satisfaction was all it had to offer; if it failed in this primitive endeavour there was little else left to hold the system together. The belief that capitalism could not go on indefinitely meeting ever-higher material expectations contained the moral for socialism that the foundations of the new order should not be laid in the shifting sands of consumer wants. An economic environment fraught with great uncertainties, anxieties and social dislocation was in any case too high a price to pay for the tawdry benefits of a consumer society. Better a society that gives full protection to the traditional victims of market rationality than one in which the threat of the dole queue hangs like a suspended sentence over every worker. If the demand for economic efficiency is necessarily at odds with the demand for personal economic security, better a society that gives first priority to the latter, cardboard shoes and all. And if this high regard for personal economic security, as the bedrock of all moral enrichment, should entail restrictions on the rights and liberties of individuals, so be it. Bourgeois society, it is conceded, is a society of many freedoms and the greatest of these is the freedom to treat labour as a mere commodity. All other bourgeois rights and liberties are not only directly contingent upon this one inalienable right of capital, they are diminished by it too. Thus speaks the dictatorship.

# V

These two contending philosophies could be regarded in some not completely abstract sense as being in competition for the allegiance of the western working class. But although liberalism and Marxism mark out the two important poles of ideological contention in the west, the schism within the working-class movement is expressed by these doctrines not in their pure or classical form but in their contemporary application in imperfect societies. That is to say, the ideological struggle throughout much of the post-war period has, in practice, been between Marxism as represented by the Soviet achievement and liberalism as represented by social democracy. Within the context of working-class politics it is the social-democratic adaptation of liberal theory, not the pristine bourgeois version, against which contemporary Marxism is required to measure itself. Or, as social democracy itself might choose to express it, the relevant comparison is now between socialism Scandinavian style and socialism east European style.

One good reason for regarding social democracy as a natural extension and adaptation of liberalism is that it seeks to preserve, in attentuated form, two of the main props of bourgeois society – private property and market relations. Within this accepted framework it strives at the same time to bring the opposing forces of capital and labour into some kind of uneven and always unsteady equilibrium. Social democracy, unlike classical bourgeois liberalism, does not hold that the relationship between capital and labour is one of equally beneficial exchange. The relationship is not, and cannot become, one of simple harmony and reciprocity. It is accepted that the exclusionary powers of capital are always greater than the usurpationary powers of labour, and that as a consequence irresolvable tensions between the two are bound to persist. The unstated ideal is not to reverse this power relationship but to tilt it, by legislative means, as far as possible to labour's advantage until capital is *only just* the dominant partner. With this in mind, organized labour becomes an 'estate of the realm' via the incorporation of its leaders into the governing bodies of the state – the final stage of that arduous journey from Tolpuddle to Whitehall. But since capital would lose its *raison d'être* if its powers were completely negated by the countervailing powers of labour, an unsteady equilibrium has to be struck at some notional level just below the point of balance.

Thus, even under 'full' social democracy exploitation would persist, even if to a controlled and limited degree. This notion of degrees of exploitation is quite foreign to Marxist theory. For Marxists, a relationship is exploitative or it is not; there is no half-way house. If the dominion of capital over labour were to be presented as anything other than absolute it would imply that the power relationship between classes under capitalism was also a matter of degree. It might easily lead to the view that the proletariat could gain some small modicum of power at the expense of the bourgeoisie as a result of political action at the national or state level. Hence it is important to scotch any idea that workers in a capitalist society could ever

'hold *the least scrap of state power*, as if State power could be divided up into a number of different local or individual powers, shared out between the classes in proportion to their political strength, and thus cease to be *absolutely* in the hands of the ruling class.'[18]

As Balibar here implies, class hegemony, like exploitation, is an all or nothing affair: either total domination or complete emancipation, with no intermediate stages. Any idea that labour's lot today is an improvement over that described by Engels in *The Condition of the Working Class in England* is therefore purely illusory.

Because social democracy is quite able to conceive of a possible diminution in the extent of capital's supremacy over labour, it can also hope for some lowering of the temperature of class conflict. Classes and class antagonisms are accepted as depressingly unavoidable, though not especially horrendous, features of an open society. The aim is not to eradicate class conflict but to ritualize it. Marxist theory presents this conflict as the surface expression of deeper contradictions that are not resolvable within a propertied society. Such contradictions are not merely irresolvable, they are cumulative in nature, building up to an explosive pitch at some unknowable future point. Social democracy, by contrast, conceives of class conflict simply as a form of social tension that, although more or less permanent, is in theory manageable. The concept of tension, unlike that of contradiction, does not imply a fatal flaw at the centre of the system that must lead to its eventual collapse. The troubled relationship between capital and labour, rather like the average marriage, goes through its periodic crises and disturbances without necessarily ending in dissolution. Whereas Marxism recommends divorce as the only solution, social democracy bends all its efforts towards marriage guidance. One step in this direction is the attempt to make the notion of class a bit more palatable by dismantling those forms of closure that foster the self-reproduction of classes along kinship lines and replacing them by purely meritocratic forms of closure. In this strong preference for individualist over collectivist patterns of exclusion, social democrats could be regarded as liberals who really mean it.

Social democracy asks: given the flawed and imperfectible human material we have to work with, what is the least disagreeable social system we could create? Marxism operates with the concept of the good society, social democracy with the concept of the not-as-bad-as-it-might-be society. Underlying this is social democracy's implicit rejection of the doctrine of alienation and the associated belief that, by determined political engineering, it would be possible to pluck out the maggot in the soul. The Marxist belief in the possibility of ultimate human renewal means that any system falling short of this lofty attainment can never quite be accepted as truly socialist; at best it is 'socialism' in heavily sardonic inverted commas, at worst a political deformity with easily recognizable capitalist features.

Although social democracy harbours no great hopes for the political redemption of mankind, neither does it endorse the conservative doctrine of the unchangability of human nature. Social democracy assumes that moral conduct is conditioned by environmental factors and that improvements in human circumstances do bring about corresponding improvements in social behaviour. But it holds, too, that there are definite limits to what could, or indeed should, be accomplished by way of human remoulding. Even under the best and brightest conditions of life, anti-social and deviant behaviour could be expected to erupt in some shape or form. And this is to be understood not as a residual legacy or throwback from a less agreeable past, but as a manifestation of that small inner core of human individuality that is thankfully resistant to all the blandishments of moral entrepreneurs and social engineers. Social democracy thus aims to administer first aid to the psychic and social injuries caused by human existence, not to effect a permanent cure. Those sharp pains diagnosed by Marxism as alienation are believed to have no remedy this side of the grave.

It has already been suggested that social democracy's affinity with liberalism, and its corresponding distance from Marxism, is most clearly shown in its toleration for the exclusionary rights of private property. The commitment to a mixed economy is not solely, or even principally, made on the grounds of efficiency; rather, the belief is that multiple forms of ownership bring about a politically desirable fragmentation and dispersal of power. Where all economic power is controlled from a single source, as under state socialism, individuals and groups are thought to have no room for independent political manoeuvre. The complete monopolization of productive forces by the state always spells the end of political and civil liberties. So however lacking in enthusiasm for the rights of property *per se*, social democracy nevertheless feels these rights to be worth preserving for their beneficial side effects. The calculus seems to be that some degree of subordination of labour to capital, though falling far short of the latter's hegemony, is a price worth paying by the working class for the preservation of hard-won civil liberties. Because social democracy regards these liberties not as a worthless offering from the bourgeoisie, but as the brightest jewels in the crown of the labour movement, it is unwilling to trade them in for other presumed benefits in kind. And in response to the western Marxist claim that, under the authorized version of socialism, full political and civil liberties would still be preserved in the absence of private property, the social democrat gives a wry smile and points in an easterly direction. On all matters pertaining to liberty, the smile says, Marxists would do well to maintain an embarrassed silence.

For its part, however, social democracy would do well to ponder a little more closely the relationship between property and liberty. In particular, it should not be assumed that because liberal democracy and private property have often happily co-existed in the west, property is in some sense a guarantor of an open society. Western and other regimes have also successfully combined private property with very different political arrangements, including fascism and military dictatorship. Indeed, the frequency with which the men on horseback have been called in to shore up crumbling bourgeois regimes plainly indicates that whenever a propertied class has faced a choice between loss of liberty and loss of property it has not usually been paralysed by indecision. On any historical reckoning, the combination of private property and political despotism has been the normal pattern. The co-existence of liberty and property in bourgeois democracies is more in the way of being a freak occurrence than the spontaneous pairing of complementary institutions. Private property, unlike Professor Hayek, is indifferent to the 'constitution of liberty'. If state socialism finds civil and political liberties a burden too heavy to bear, this must be for reasons other than the absence of property's supporting role.

Social democracy needs to look no further than to its own history to observe the consequences of a faulty appreciation of the political significance of property. The German party in the inter-war period shared Kautsky's fatal belief that the ownership class was just as devoted as was social democracy to the principles of legality and order, and would therefore not resort to unconstitutional means to defend itself against the encroachments of the labour movement. It certainly did not occur to the leadership of the movement that the fear of dispossession could be so intense as to make barbarism the preferred alternative. Although modern social democracy does not aspire to the complete expropriation of private property, its strategy of gradually gnawing away at the foundations of the institution could also meet at some point with unexpected resistance. The closer the prospect of dispossession looms the more obvious it seems to those under threat that democracy has finally 'failed', and that a more muscular replacement is called for.

In so far as the lines of connection between property and liberty can so easily become frayed, the case for retaining property rights as a check upon the abuse of power loses its persuasiveness. Moreover, the classical liberal thesis on the separation of powers, as set out by Tocqueville and Durkheim, requires only that a multiplicity of independent bodies and institutions be allowed to flourish in the intermediate levels between family and state. It is not essential to the thesis that property should be one of these institutions. In Durkheim's formulation, professional and trade associations are singled out as the bodies capable of bearing most of the weight of this intermediate structure known as civil society.[19] If a large measure of autonomy is granted to various groups in the middle layers of society, then the desired fragmentation and dispersal of power could be achieved without reliance upon private property. Not only does property not guarantee liberty when it does exist, but its absence need not necessarily result in the monopolization of power, even on the reckoning of liberal theory.

Now it could perhaps be argued that the separation of powers and the maintenance of distance between state and civil society, are themselves dependent upon the fulfilment of a prior condition: namely, the existence of independent political parties. It might well be that only under a system in which the party of government was willing to be elected out of office and replaced by its opponents could the separation of powers be anything more than a constitutional fiction. If an open or competitive party system is the bedrock on which the house of liberty must be built, then a weak case for private property might just about be made on the grounds that the only genuine opposition to the party of labour would be from the party of capital and its traditional supporters. At any rate, social democracy does appear to operate on the peculiar assumption that a private ownership class is needed to furnish the material basis of its own potential displacement. Whereas the dictatorship of the proletariat recommends a final solution to the problem of private property and the bourgeoisie, social democracy implicitly defends both in the name of a higher political ideal. It is rather as if social democracy were to fear the worst of itself if left with untrammelled power and permanent office. On this line of reasoning, the working class would have something to gain from the preservation of private ownership – not because it opens up a separate source of power from that of the state, but because without it bourgeois parties would have no life, the electoral system would atrophy, and the fragile structure of civil society would at once be in jeopardy. Rosa Luxemburg prophesied that: 'Without general elections, without unrestricted freedom of press and assembly, without a free struggle of opinion, life dies out in every public institution, becomes a mere semblance of life, in which only the bureaucracy remains as the active element.'[20] If the final choice is between the rule of property and the rule of the bureaucracy, then perhaps the working class would do well to opt for the former; property after all gives rise to nothing more disabling than alienation, whereas the torments inflicted by the bureaucracy are likely to be of a more corporeal kind. So says social democracy.

## VI

Contemporary western Marxism understandably denies that any such stark choice has to be made between the twin evils of property and bureaucratic domination. Social democracy and state socialism are each regarded as failed varieties of socialism having little affinity with the model workers' state embalmed in western revolutionary literature. This is that well-known state in which the proletariat is free from the despotism of either capital or the central committee, in which the forcible suppression of the enemies of the state goes hand in hand with the respect for civil liberties and the rule of law, in which centralized planning is neatly reconciled with workers' control of industry by factor committees, in which independent trade unions co-operate in the erosion of traditional differentials, in which a workers' opposition enjoys full legal and political rights, and in which those in high places are every ready to be recalled to the ranks. Measured against this version of socialism, east European or Scandinavian varieties are almost bound to seem equally depressing.

This third or 'genuine' version of socialism is one that allegedly falls outside the limited conceptual range of bourgeois thought.

> 'Bourgeois ideology can imagine . . . two forms of the exercise of State power: the democratic form (parliamentary institutions, multi-party system, freedom of speech and assembly, etc.) and the dictatorial form (single party system, fusion of party and state, refusal to tolerate opposition, and so on) . . . *What it cannot imagine* is a State of the kind portrayed by Lenin, a genuinely proletarian State, a State whose function is to exercise power *only and precisely* in order to prepare the conditions for its own disappearance . . . bourgeois ideology cannot imagine such a thing.'[21]

Marxists, being of more vivid imagination, can easily picture such a society, even while acknowledging that its translation from the mental to the material world does appear to have run into a few snags. Not the least important reason for these difficulties is, of course, to do with the political method by which the translation is typically carried out. The complete dismemberment of bourgeois society has only occurred under the leadership of a Leninist party – an organization that is not altogether attuned to the idea of sharing power with other political bodies, including soviets, in the manner required by the model of a democratic workers' state. The social character of the new order is stamped from the very outset by the imprint of the political organization largely responsible for orchestrating the forces of revolution. This is why Lenin's organizational handbook *What is to be done?* proves to be a much more reliable guide to the future character of Soviet society than the optimistic sketch contained in *State and Revolution*. To suppose that the libertarian workers' democracy outlined in the latter document could be attained by way of the authoritarian instrument recommended in the former is to believe in the almost complete dissociation between political ends and means.

Assuming that there is no parliamentary route to the third and so far unrealized version of socialism, the only alternative is the revolutionary route under the guidance of a Leninist party. The proponents of the new model socialism must therefore pin all their hopes for proletarian democracy on the willingness of the revolutionary leadership to relinquish its 'emergency powers' after the class enemy has been put down. In other words, the expectation must be that 'western' Leninism would not follow the example set by all previous vanguard parties that have captured state power. However, Marxists have not yet addressed themselves to the intriguing question as to precisely why revolution in the west could be expected to depart from the well-established pattern elsewhere by ushering in Leninism with a human face.

The realization of a fundamentally new type of socialism cannot of course be declared beyond the bounds of possibility, even though it is a species that has nowhere survived outside the protected environment of Marxist theory. But the likelihood of any such third model coming into being is not enhanced by the fact that there are only two broad political strategies available as means to this end – parliamentary and revolutionary. On all the now considerable evidence, the former leads no further than social democracy and the latter to some variety of state socialism. It is not as if parliamentary and revolutionary strategies were simply end points on a political continuum between which were to be found various hybrid forms leading to various socialist outcomes. The commitment to a constitutional route cannot be dovetailed into a programme based on the violent seizure of the state, nor vice versa. They represent stark either/or choices, excluding any third way. And since the political means by which power is attained indelibly marks the end result, the range of outcomes is as narrow as the choice of strategies. This is not to say that state socialist regimes display no significant variations, nor that social democracies are interchangeable; but it is to say that the central and defining characteristics of these two general types are largely formed by the manner of their political inception.

It should follow from this that once Marxist parties abandon insurrectionary programmes in favour of the parliamentary road they point themselves towards a political destination at which social democracy long ago arrived. The advocates of Eurocommunism seek to disprove this thesis by suggesting that the constitutional route does lead to a form of socialism that is true to the spirit of Leninism without reproducing what Althusser has called 'the "grey" variety built on force or even repression'.[22] Moreover, however colourful and easy-going the new variety is thought likely to be, any family resemblance between it and social democracy is vehemently denied. According to Carrillo,

'. . . *there cannot be any confusion* between "Eurocommunism" and social democracy in the ideological sphere . . . What is commonly called Eurocommunism proposes to *transform* capitalist society not to *administer* it, to work out a socialist alternative to the system of state monopoly capitalism, not to integrate in it and become one of its governmental variants.'[23]

This transformation is to be achieved not through the dictatorship of the proletariat but by way of a socialist regime that will respect the rights of private property and bourgeois opposition parties. The aim is not to extinguish capital but only to remove its hegemony over labour. Furthermore, the traditional Marxist disdain for the institutions of bourgeois democracy suddenly gives way to a more appreciative stance. Carrillo, having belatedly discovered that Lenin was somewhat prone to 'underestimate and belittle the generic concept of democracy', is clearly keen to make amends:[24]

'the political system established in Western Europe, based on representative political institutions – parliament, political and philosophical pluralism, the theory of the separation of powers, decentralization, human rights, etc. – . . . is in essentials valid and it will be still more effective with a socialist, and not a capitalist, economic foundation.'[25]

The obvious and embarrassing parallels between this conception and that of social democracy renders it necessary for Eurocommunism to give renewed endorsement to the Leninist anathema placed upon the founding fathers of revisionism. To revive the ancient denunciations of Kautsky and Bernstein is perhaps one way of allaying suspicion that the political ideas of renegades and revisionists have been plagiarized by the exponents of Eurocommunism.[26] Parliamentary Marxism is somehow able to see a world of difference between the recent claim that socialism can be attained 'without breaking the rules of democracy' but by 'changing the content of traditional democratic institutions, complementing them with new forms which expand and establish democracy still more firmly',[27] and Bernstein's much-derided claim that because of their flexibility bourgeois institutions 'do not need to be destroyed, but only to be further developed'.[28] It is, in fact, difficult to see what objections the early theorists of social democracy would be able to raise against the Eurocommunist programme – other than in Kautsky's case, perhaps, the marked absence of any reference to 'revolution'.

The early social democrats would have been especially approving of the Eurocommunists' renunciation of Lenin's teachings on the art of armed struggle and the constructive uses of 'red terror'. Lenin placed much emphasis on the need to arm the proletariat and instruct it in the techniques of street fighting and urban guerilla warfare. One of Trotsky's great complaints against Rosa Luxemburg was that her theory of the mass strike fudged the crucial issue of armed revolt. In his view, the seizure of power would come about not by means of the general strike itself but through 'the armed insurrection on the basis of the general strike'.[29] Proletarian power came, ultimately, not from its collective social and political strength, but through the barrel of a gun. Hence Lenin's stern admonition that 'an oppressed class which does not strive to learn to use arms, to acquire arms, only deserves to be treated like slaves'.[30]

This call to arms was closely bound up with Lenin's strategic conception of 'dual power'. The extinction of the bourgeois state was to be preceded by the emergence within it of an autonomous political force that could successfully challenge the jurisdiction of government and its allied institutions. This alternative power structure, embodied above all in the soviets, was to become a kind of state within the state in so far as it sought to enforce its own political and moral authority by resort to the ultimate sanction. As a political strategy, the setting up of a dual power is at considerable variance with the 'salami tactics' recommended by both Kautsky and the Eurocommunists. These tactics call for the piecemeal absorption of existing state bodies by the working-class movement exercising its constitutional powers. The bourgeois state is not so much destroyed as gradually whittled away; consequently, the need for a workers' militia is less apparent. The conflict issuing from dual power, on the other hand, can only be settled by a violent showdown between the bourgeois state and its potential usurper. The military proficiency of the proletariat would therefore be of decisive importance to the outcome.

The distaste expressed by the early social democrats for this idea that the class struggle was to be decided by a contest of arms arose partly from the conviction that in such a contest the proletariat would be on the losing side. Kautsky pointed out that the technical innovations of advanced capitalism were being applied to the tools of violence; the sophisticated weaponry at the disposal of the state made dangerous nonsense of those romantic ideas of workers manning the barricades. Moreover, the professionalization of the standing army meant that it was no longer realistic to rely upon the mass defection of the ranks to the side of the proletariat.[31] Soldiers were no longer simply 'peasants and workers in uniform'. Kautsky felt that armed insurrection could only be successful in under-developed societies in which the capital city was the only centre of mass population, as in the case of many absolutist states. By seizing a few strategic positions the entire apparatus of power could be taken over by armed men. In developed capitalist societies, on the other hand, the population was typically dispersed throughout many metropolitan centres, linked by good communications, so that the system could not be paralysed for long by the seizure of a few key buildings or the erection of street barricades.[32] Kautsky's implied question is: what exactly would workers have to seize in order to take over the modern state? Where precisely is the Winter Palace?

These doubts and misgivings about the efficacy and likely outcome of an armed proletarian uprising had earlier been voiced by Engels in his last major pronouncement on the strategy of class struggle. In an essay that could stand as the charter for Eurocommunism, Engels drew a pointed contrast between 'the old-style, street fighting with barricades', typical of the 1848 rebellions, and the more promising line of attack opened up by the extension of the franchise.[33] Echoing the theme of Marx's Amsterdam address, Engels argued that as a result of electoral reforms, the franchise had become 'transformed . . . from a means of deception, which it was before, into an instrument of emancipation'.[34] Not even Kautsky could match Engels' euphoria over the unimpeded progress of social democracy throughout western Europe as the citadels of capital appeared to crumble beneath the weight of the organized labour movement. Engels felt that German social democracy, in particular, would within a very few years be 'the decisive power in the land, before which all other powers will have to bow. . .'.[35]

Engels was not merely unenthusiastic about the use of arms by the proletariat; he believed that an armed uprising would play directly into the hands of their far better equipped opponents. Why else, he enquired, should these class enemies 'so earnestly implore us to play for once the part of cannon fodder?'[36] The only thing that could now halt the progress of the working class was that type of violent confrontation with the state that Lenin was later to declare mandatory. With the organizational and electoral power of the working class growing boundlessly, Engels warned the movement explicitly against all temptation 'to fritter away this daily increasing shock force in vanguard skirmishes. . .'.[37]

There is much here to give comfort to the latter-day advocates of parliamentary Marxism, especially if they are able to erase all memory of the fact that these same arguments brought similar relief to Kautsky and his colleagues more than half a century earlier. Ironically, the same doctrinal authority on which early social democracy took its stand is now appealed to by the proclaimed opponents of social democracy. The attraction for Eurocommunists of Engels' own embellishments upon the Amsterdam address is understandable enough; it provides the clearest legitimation for an alternative to Leninism to issue from a totally unimpeachable source. But in counterposing Engels to Lenin, parliamentary Marxism is not exactly in the best position from which to preach the apostasy of the erstwhile Marxist Pope and his followers. In so far as Eurocommunism continues to invoke the name and ideals of Lenin, while heading down the peaceful road to socialism, it is bound to seem to incorrigible revolutionaries that the spirit of Kautsky lives on. However this may be, the case for a third version of socialism can hardly be said to draw strength from the Eurocommunist example. If social democrats are liberals who really mean it, Eurocommunists seem well on the way to becoming social democrats who really mean it.

# VII

Western Marxists who maintain faith in Leninist principles and practice are also more likely to have their sights set on some as yet unattained model of socialism than on any of the existing state varieties. However, the political and institutional forms proposed for the new dispensation are never revealed in any more detail than they were in Lenin's own shadowy prototype. Now, as then, the task of seeing away with the existing order is apparently too absorbing to permit much time for reflection upon the character and quality of its replacement. The new system is characterized in effect only in terms of what it will *not* be; it will not be Eurocommunism's liberal democracy for the working man, nor of course will it be that bureaucratic travesty of proletarian dictatorship that everywhere sullies the good name of Marxism. Those who crave more positive clues about the intended political format of the new order can always be reminded of the fact that Marxism has never gone in for blueprints. New social and political formations, we are told, emerge in response to concrete historical imperatives and unforeseen contingencies. The curious, in other words, will have to wait and see.

Now, it could well be that those expected to bear the main brunt of the insurrectionary effort might require something more solid than this to go on. Given what they now know about Marxist societies-without-blueprints built elsewhere, it should come as no great surprise if western workers were to show some scepticism about the reliability of this architectural procedure. It is not, after all, as if the unflattering image of existing socialist states is a malicious fabrication of the bourgeois mind. Western Marxists of many breeds and dispositions have been just as disparaging of state socialism as any mere liberal. With social democrats, conservatives, anarchists, and Marxists of different hue all chanting their own version of the same refrain, the western working class could easily be forgiven for concluding that something must be very badly wrong with state socialism after all. They might also reasonably wonder why, if all known versions of Marxist society are so seriously flawed, and their revolutions always betrayed, the result next time should be any different.

Latter-day Leninists continue to maintain that a new, western brand of socialism is perfectly conceivable and is not made any less so by repeated failures elsewhere. In any case, things might have worked out very differently the first time round if only conditions in Russia had been less harsh, if only the revolution had spread across Europe, if only Lenin had not died prematurely, if only Trotsky had succeeded him instead of Stalin, and if only the bureaucracy had been nipped in the bud. A genuine workers' state is perfectly attainable, provided it is not expected to cope with any unforeseen difficulties.

Naturally the realization of a model Marxist state cannot be dismissed as logically unsound or empirically impossible. Such a society has as much warrant to a conceptual life as the idea of a society without sin or wickedness. Because sin is everywhere rampant now does not clinch the argument for the sheer impossibility of a redeemed society. As with real socialism, there is always the future prospect. In the case of real socialism, however, the snag is that those assigned the burdensome and hazardous task of making it come about are much more likely to be impressed by what is *empirically probable* than by what is merely *theoretically possible*. If it is assumed that workers are mentally capable of weighing up the political costs and benefits of alternative forms of action, then it should not occasion great wonder if their preference was for social democracy (including the Eurocommunist variant) with all its well-known imperfections, rather than for the uncertainties of the high-risk alternative offered by Leninism. Only if it were patently and unambiguously the case that the forcible overthrow of bourgeois regimes elsewhere had usually resulted in the reclamation of the proletariat would a social-democratic commitment on the part of western workers seem especially odd. But, as things stand, Marxists are all alone in their puzzlement at this phenomenon and in their busy search for its causes among the ideological state apparatuses.

# VIII

This being said, it would nevertheless take a good deal of ingenuity on the part of even the most unswerving supporters of social democracy to present this movement as anything but uninspired. Social democracy in the inter-war period was by any standards an inglorious affair, particularly on those occasions when the party was suddenly thrust into the unaccustomed role of government. The debacle of Weimar and the capitulation to fascism by the leading party of social democracy were stigmata borne by the entire movement, even though the German case was not wholly typical. In the modern period, social democracy has become transformed into one of the natural parties of government while presiding over the kind of society that would not meet even Kautsky's minimal definition of socialism. Indeed, it could be said that the very electoral successes of the movement have increased the political distance between the modern parties and their early predecessors. Modern social democracy often has some difficulty in distinguishing itself ideologically from liberalism and conservatism, a distinction that was always perfectly apparent in the Kautskian heyday.

Marxist critics are able to point out, quite correctly, that post-war social-democratic governments have not been conspicuously successful in pushing through even their modest reform programmes; the eradication of poverty, the redistribution of wealth and income, and the creation of equal opportunities all seem to elude the social-democratic touch. The explanation for this, advanced by these same critics, is also plausible enough: namely, that the attempt to manage capitalism instead of supplanting it has made social democracy subservient to global political and economic interests that are not noted for their warmth towards egalitarian doctrines. Even social democracy in one country appears unattainable in a world system in which international, and above all American, capital imposes its own implacable logic.

However, the reason why social democratic governments have more or less willingly accepted the restrictive framework of international capitalism is due less to the innate perfidy of working-class

leaders, always detectable through Marxists lenses, than to the mani-
chean division of the industrialized world already alluded to. The first
and overriding question for social democratic parties and governments in the post-war era has been that of defining their stance in
relation to the great schism between bourgeois parliamentary democracy and Soviet totalitarianism. The issue was never perceived in
terms of Marxist categories of capitalism versus socialism, but in
terms of bourgeois categories of liberal democracy versus communist
dictatorship. Faced with that narrow ideological choice social democracy did not feel itself placed in much of a dilemma. Moreover, to opt
for liberal democracy implied at the same time endorsement of the
western alliance as a safeguard against the possibility that the Red
Army might be mobilized for other than purely defensive purposes.
Thus, what Marxists see as social democracy's prostration before
American monopoly capitalism is perceived by social democracy as a
necessary political strategy for defending the open society against its
powerful external enemies.

This perception of the matter would not come easily to western
Marxists, given their systematic disregard for those collective sentiments associated with the nation and the preservation of its boundaries. The Marxist concept of the state focusses almost exclusively
upon its internal functions as a repressive class agency and not at all
upon its equally important and *popularly supported* role of national
defence. Marx's proletariat without a homeland was historically pro-
grammed to defend the revolution, not the mere territory on which
the revolution happened to be made. The moral identification of the
real proletariat with a particular nation thus introduces a set of factors
into the political calculus that Marxism has always found awkward to
handle other than as delusionary manifestations. Social democracy,
operating as it does with the concept of the nation-state, has understandably attached far greater priority to the maintenance of national
independence through political alliances. If the nature of these political alliances is such as to put serious difficulties in the way of internal
social reforms and egalitarian programmes, so be it; the injustices and
the rage engendered by class divisions are deemed infinitely preferable to a westward extension of the Gulag archipelago. Interestingly
enough, however profound their distaste for Stalinism and all its
works, western Marxists have been prone to dismiss all doubts about
the pacific nature of the Soviet state as mythologies spun by the
beneficiaries of a 'permanent arms economy'.[38] It seems to be outside
the conceptual capacity of Marxism to comprehend that a working
class that defined itself as part of a linguistic and cultural community,
and which was emotionally attached to the symbols of homeland,
could be as much or even more concerned about the need to prevent

the forcible intrusion into that community by an external power as about the need for internal social change.

Early social democracy was itself imbued with a residual Marxism that led it to misrepresent itself as a movement of proletarian internationalism. So much so, that the *volte face* of 1914 came as almost as much of a shock to the fraternal parties themselves as it did to Lenin and his followers. But from that point on, social democracy ceased to portray itself as a party that placed the interests of class above those of nation. Modern social democracy, in its role as a governing party in the cold war era, has thus acted quite consistently in giving first priority to the task of defending national boundaries by seeking the umbrella protection of the leading capitalist power. Although this arrangement has given rise to severe tensions within the ranks of social democracy, aggravating the permanent strains between left and right, it has nevertheless been made palatable because of the long-standing enmity between social democracy and Soviet socialism. The feud between Lenin and Kautsky was merely a foretaste of what was to come, continuing with Stalin's denunciation of social democracy as the 'twin of fascism', and culminating in the incarceration and murder of social democratic leaders in Sovietized eastern Europe. In the light of this historic legacy social democratic parties and governments did not really need exposure to the persuasive charms of bourgeois ideology to reach the conclusion that the military and political power of Stalinist Russia and its dependencies might not be employed exclusively in a comradely spirit. It could be said, then, that modern social democracy has had to manoeuvre within a set of global constraints and imperatives, in the setting up of which Marxism itself has not been wholly innocent.

This is not of course to say that the slenderness of social democracy's achievements in the post-war period is wholly attributable to the uncongenial international climate; infirmity of political will within the movement itself has certainly taken its toll – though again it should be acknowledged that the record is not one of complete uniformity.[39] In addition, the fact that the majority of the west European working class continue to give their political allegiance to social democracy is no doubt a judgement of sorts upon its overall performance. At any rate, however sluggish this performance is bound to seem, the persistence of working-class loyalty suggests that the alternatives on offer are felt to have even fewer attractions, the revolutionary Marxist alternatives included. It might well be that western workers would find much to agree with in the Marxist critique of social democracy; but with the passage of more than half a century since the first of several experiments in proletarian dictatorship these same workers are now well placed to weigh up the evergreen Marxist claim to be able to offer something in advance of mere social democracy 'next time'.

## Notes

1 Lenin 1950:Vol. II, part II 54–5.
2 Miliband 1970:309.
3 Lenin decreed that professional groups 'must be given the opportunity of working in better conditions than they did under capitalism, since this stratum, which has been trained by the bourgeoisie, will not work otherwise. . . In this transition period we must accord them the best possible conditions of life'. Lenin 1950:Vol. II, part II 164–5.
4 The business of running the state could be 'reduced to the extraordinarily simple operations – which any literate person can perform – of supervising and recording, knowledge of the four rules of arithmetic, and issuing appropriate receipts'. Lenin 1950:Vol. II, part I 304–5.
5 Luxemburg (ed. Looker) 1972:108–9.
6 Lukacs 1971:270; Lenin 1950:Vol. II, part II 41.
7 Lenin 1950:Vol. II, part II 83.
8 Trotsky 1974:13.
9 Lenin, commenting upon the 'latest tactical devices of the enemies of Soviet power', explained that these enemies, 'having realized the hopelessness of counterrevolution under an openly Whiteguard flag, are now doing their utmost to utilize the disagreements within the Russian Communist Party and to further the counterrevolution in one way or another by transferring power to the political groupings which outwardly are closest to the recognition of Soviet power'. Lenin 1950:Vol. II, part II 498–9.
10 Trotsky 1935:127–39.
11 Trotsky 1935:103.
12 Lenin 1950:Vol. II, part II 623.
13 Trotsky 1935:159.
14 Thus, Lenin held that the moral commandments to 'Keep regular and honest accounts of money, manage economically, do not be lazy, observe the strictest labour discipline . . .' could properly be ignored by the proletariat under bourgeois rule. However, the 'practical application of these slogans by the *Soviet* state, by *its* methods, on the basis of *its* laws, is a necessary and *sufficient* condition for the final victory of Socialism'. Lenin 1950:Vol. II, part I 453–4.
15 Trotsky 1935:133.
16 Lenin 1950:Vol. II, part II 56.
17 Rawls 1971.
18 Balibar 1977:78.
19 More correctly, civil society was maintained by the fruitful *tension* between the state and autonomous intermediate groups; it is 'out of this conflict of social forces that individual liberties are born'. Durkheim 1957:63.
20 Luxemburg 1961:71.
21 Lock 1977:28–9.
22 Althusser 1969:197.

23  Carrillo 1977:103–4.
24  Carrillo 1977:90.
25  Carrillo 1977:105.
26  Carrillo suggests that certain of Kautsky's arguments are in fact more pertinent to present-day political circumstances than to the revolutionary period in which Kautsky sought to apply them. Carrillo 1977:151.
27  Carrillo 1977:149.
28  Bernstein 1909:163.
29  Trotsky 1970:144.
30  Lenin 1950:Vol. I, part II 573.
31  Kautsky 1902:13.
32  Kautsky 1909:64–5.
33  Engels 1969:196.
34  Engels 1969:195.
35  Engels 1969:201.
36  Engels 1969:199.
37  Engels 1969:201.
38  This benign view of Soviet power is not of course shared by those Marxists whose countries actually border on the USSR.
29  See, for example, Castles' recent work comparing the achievements of social democracy in societies with a powerful party of the Right and those in which the Right is politically fragmented. In the latter, social democracy is able to fashion the dominant value system pretty much to its own design; in the former, it manoeuvres within the framework of a predominantly bourgeois system of beliefs. Castles 1978.

# Bibliography

Adam, H. (1971) *Modernizing Racial Domination*. Berkeley: University of California Press.

Althusser, L. (1969) *For Marx*. Harmondsworth: Penguin Books.

— (1971) *Lenin and Philosophy and Other Essays*. London: New Left Books.

Anderson, P. (1967) The Limits and Possibilities of Trade Union Action. In, Blackburn, R. and Cockburn, A. (eds) *The Incompatibles: Trade Union Militancy and the Consensus*. Harmondsworth: Penguin Books.

— (1974) *Lineages of the Absolutist State*. London: New Left Books.

Avineri, S. (1968) *The Social and Political Thought of Karl Marx*. Cambridge University Press.

Bain, G. S. (1970) *The Growth of White Collar Unionism*. Oxford: Clarendon Press.

Balibar, E. (1977) *On the Dictatorship of the Proletariat*. London: New Left Books.

Baran, P. A. (1957) *The Political Economy of Growth*. London: Calder.

Bauman, Z. (1972) *Between Class and Elite*. Manchester University Press.

Becker, J. F. (1973) Class Structure and Conflict in the Managerial Phase. *Science and Society* **37** (3 and 4).

Beetham, D. (1974) *Max Weber and the Theory of Modern Politics*. London: Allen and Unwin.

Bell, D. (1975) Ethnicity and Social Change. In, Glazer, N. and

Moynihan, D. P. (eds) *Ethnicity*. Cambridge, Mass. Harvard University Press.

Berg, I. (1973) *Education and Jobs: The Great Training Robbery*. Harmondsworth: Penguin Books.

Berghe, P. van den (1967) *Race and Racism*. New York: Wiley.

Bernstein, E. (1909) *Evolutionary Socialism*. London: ILP Press.

Blackburn, R. (1965) The New Capitalism. *Towards Socialism*. London: Fontana.

Blauner, R. (1972) *Racial Oppression in America*. New York: Harper and Row.

Boggs, J. (1970) *Racism and the Class Struggle*. New York: Monthly Review Press.

Bosanquet, B. (1920) *The Philosophical Theory of the State*. London: Macmillan.

Boserup, A. (1972) Contradictions and Struggles in Northern Ireland. *Socialist Register*. London: Merlin Press.

Braverman, H. (1974) *Labor and Monopoly Capital*. New York: Monthly Review Press.

Carchedi, G. (1975) On the Economic Identification of the New Middle Class. *Economy and Society* **4** (1).

Carmichael, S. and Hamilton, C. V. (1967) *Black Power*. New York: Random House.

Carr, E. H. (1966) *The Bolshevik Revolution, 1917–1923*, Vol. III. Harmondsworth: Penguin Books.

Carrillo, S. (1977) *Eurocommunism and the State*. London: Lawrence and Wishart.

Castles, F. G. (1978) *The Social Democratic Image of Society*. London: Routledge.

Castles, S. and Kosack, G. (1973) *Immigrant Workers and Class Structure in Western Europe*. London: Oxford University Press.

Crompton, R. and Gubbay, J. (1977) *Economy and Class Structure*. London: Macmillan.

Dahrendorf, R. (1959) *Class and Class Conflict in Industrial Society*. London: Routledge.

Davies, R. (1973) The White Working Class in South Africa. *New Left Review* **82**.

Davis, K. and Moore, W. E. (1945) Some Principles of Stratification. *American Sociological Review* **X** (2).

Deutscher, I. (1954) *The Prophet Armed*. Oxford University Press.

Dickens, L. (1972) UKAPE: A Study of a Professional Union. *Industrial Relations Journal* **3** (3).

Dore, R. (1976) *The Diploma Disease*. London: Allen and Unwin.

Durkheim, E. (1957) *Professional Ethics and Civic Morals*. London: Routledge.

— (1964a) *The Division of Labour in Society*. New York: Free Press.
— (1964b) *The Elementary Forms of the Religious Life*. London: Allen and Unwin.
Easton, D. (1953) *The Political System*. New York: Alfred Knopf.
Elliott, P. (1972) *The Sociology of the Professions*. London: Macmillan.
Engels, F. (1969) Introduction to Karl Marx. The Class Struggles in France 1840–1950. In Karl Marx and Frederick Engels, *Selected Works I*. Moscow: Foreign Languages Publishing House.
— (1972) *The Origin of the Family, Private Property, and the State*. New York: Pathfinder Press.
Etzioni, A. (ed.) (1969) *The Semi-Professions and their Organization*. New York: Free Press.
Finer, S. E. (1975) The Unions and Power. *New Society*, 6 February.
Freidson, E. (ed.) (1973) *The Professions and their Prospects*. Beverley Hills, Calif. Sage.
Geras, N. (1976) *The Legacy of Rosa Luxemburg*. London: New Left Books.
Glazer, N. and Moynihan, D. P. (eds) (1975) *Ethnicity*. Cambridge, Mass.: Harvard University Press.
Giddens, A. (1973) *The Class Structure of the Advanced Societies*. London: Hutchinson.
Glyn, A. and Sutcliffe, B. (1972) *British Capitalism, Workers and The Profits Squeeze*. Harmondsworth: Penguin Books.
Goldthorpe, J. H. and Lockwood, D. (1963) Affluence and the British Class Structure. *Sociological Review* 11 (2).
Goldthorpe, J. H. and Llewellyn, C. (1977) Class Mobility in Modern Britain: Three Theses Examined. *Sociology* 11 (2).
Goldthorpe, J. H. (1978) The Current Inflation: Towards a Sociological Account. In, Hirsch, F. and Goldthorpe, J. H. (eds) *The Political Economy of Inflation*. London: Martin Robertson.
Goode, W. J. (1969) The Theoretical Limits of Professionalization. In, Etzioni, A. (ed.) *The Semi Professions and their Organization*. New York: Free Press.
Grunfeld, C (1978) Discussion. *Trade Unions: Public Goods or Public 'Bads'?* London: The Institute of Economic Affairs.
Harding, N. (1977) *Lenin's Political Thought*. London: Macmillan.
Hechter, M. (1975) *Internal Colonialism*. London: Routledge.
Hindess, B. and Hirst, P. Q. (1975) *Pre-Capitalist Modes of Production*. London: Routledge.
Hörning, K. H. (ed.) (1971) *Der 'neue' Arbeiter: zum Wandel sozialer Schichtstrukturen*. Frankfurt: Fischer.
Hutt, W. H. (1973) *The Strike-Threat System: The Economic*

*Consequences of Collective Bargaining*. New York: Arlington House.

Jencks, C. (1972) *Inequality*. New York: Basic Books.

Johnson, N. (1977) *In Search of the Constitution*. Oxford: Pergamon Press.

Kautsky, K. (1902) *The Social Revolution*. London: Twentieth Century Press.

— (1903) *On the Morrow of the Social Revolution*. London: Twentieth Century Press.

— (1909) *Der Weg zur Macht*. Hamburg: Erdmann Dubber.

— (1922) *Die proletarische Revolution und ihr Programm*. Berlin: Dietz.

— (1946) *Social Democracy versus Communism*. New York: Rand School Press.

Lansbury, R. (1974) Professionalism and Unionisation among Management Service Specialists. *British Journal of Industrial Relations* **12** (2).

Lenin, V. I. (1950) *Selected Works*. Moscow: Foreign Languages Publishing House.

— (1972) Letter to the Central Committee of the RSDLP(B). In, Marx, K., Engels, F., and Lenin, V. I. *On Historical Materialism*. Moscow: Foreign Languages Publishing House.

Lock, G. (1977) Introduction. In, Balibar, E. *On the Dictatorship of the Proletariat*. London: New Left Books.

Lockwood, D. (1958) *The Blackcoated Worker*. London: Allen and Unwin.

— (1970) Race, Conflict and Plural Society. In, Zubaida, S. (ed.) *Race and Racialism*. London: Tavistock.

Lukacs, G. (1971) *History and Class Consciousness*. London: Merlin Press.

Luxemburg, R. (1951) *The Accumulation of Capital*. London: Routledge.

— (1961) *The Russian Revolution and Leninism or Marxism?* Ann Arbor: University of Michigan.

— (1972) *Selected Political Writings*. Looker, R. (ed.) London: Cape.

— (1976) *The National Question: Selected Writings*. In, Davis, H. B. (ed.) New York: Monthly Review Press.

Macpherson, C. B. (1973) A Political Theory of Property. In, *Democratic Theory: Essays in Retrieval*. Oxford University Press.

Mackenzie, G. (1973) *The Aristocracy of Labour: The Position of Skilled Craftsmen in the American Class Structure*. Cambridge University Press.

Mandel, E. (1975) Introduction. In, Trotsky, L., *The Struggle Against Fascism in Germany*. Harmondsworth: Penguin Books.

Marceau, J. (1974) Education and Social Mobility in France. In, Parkin, F. (ed.) *The Social Analysis of Class Structure*. London: Tavistock.

Marcus, P. N. (1973) Schoolteachers and Militant Conservatism. In, Freidson, E. (ed.) *The Professions and their Prospects*. Beverley Hills, Calif.: Sage.

Marx, K. (1926) *The Eighteenth Brumaire of Louis Bonaparte*. London: Allen and Unwin.

— (1959) *Capital*, Vol. III. Moscow: Foreign Languages Publishing House.

— (1965) *The German Ideology*. London: Lawrence and Wishart.

Marx, K. and Engels, F. (1969) Manifesto of the Communist Party. *Selected Works I*. Moscow: Foreign Languages Publishing House.

Marx, K., Engels, F., and Lenin, V. I. (1972) *On Historical Materialism*. Moscow: Foreign Languages Publishing House.

Miliband, R. (1969) *The State in Capitalist Society*. London: Weidenfeld and Nicolson.

— (1970) Lenin's The State and Revolution. *Socialist Register*. London: Merlin Press.

— (1973) Poulantzas and the Capitalist State. *New Left Review* **82**.

— (1975) Political Forms and Historical Materialism. *Socialist Register*. London: Merlin Press.

— (1977) *Marxism and Politics*. Oxford University Press.

Miller, S. M. (1960) Comparative Social Mobility. *Current Sociology* **9** (1).

Mills, C. W. (1956) *White Collar*. New York: Oxford University Press.

Nairn, T. (1977) The Twilight of the British State. *New Left Review* **101–2**.

Nettl, P. (1969) *Rosa Luxemburg*. Oxford University Press.

Neuwirth, G. (1969) A Weberian Outline of a Theory of Community: Its Application to the 'Dark Ghetto'. *British Journal of Sociology* **20** (2).

O'Connor, J. (1973) *The Fiscal Crisis of the State*. New York: St Martin's Press.

Oppenheimer, M. (1973) The Proletarianisation of the Professional. In, Halmos, P. (ed.) *Professionalisation and Social Change*. Sociological Review Monograph No. 20.

Orwell, G. (1949) *Nineteen Eighty-Four*. London: Secker and Warburg.

Palfreeman, A. C. (1971) The White Australia Policy. In, Stevens, F. S. (ed.) *Racism: The Australian Experience*. Sydney: Australia and New Zealand Book Co.

## Bibliography

Parkin, F. (1971) *Class Inequality and Political Order*. London: Macgibbon and Kee.
— (ed.) (1974) *The Social Analysis of Class Structure*. London: Tavistock.
Parsons, T. (1951) *The Social System*. London: Routledge.
— (1969) Full Citizenship for the Negro American? In, *Politics and Social Structure*. New York: Free Press.
— (1970) Equality and Inequality in Modern Society, or Social Stratification Revisited. *Sociological Inquiry* **40** (2).
Parry, N. and Parry, J. (1976) *The Rise of the Medical Profession: A Study of Collective Social Mobility*. London: Croom Helm.
Perrucci, R. (1973) Engineering: Professional Servant of Power. In, Freidson, E. (ed.) *The Professions and their Prospects*. Beverley Hills, Calif.: Sage.
Plamenatz, J. (1963) *Man and Society*, Vol. II. London: Longman.
— (1975) *Karl Marx's Philosophy of Man*. Oxford: Clarendon Press.
Poulantzas, N. (1969) The Problem of the Capitalist State. *New Left Review* **58**.
— (1973) *Political Power and Social Classes*. London: New Left Books.
— (1974) *Fascism and Dictatorship*. London: New Left Books.
— (1975) *Classes in Contemporary Capitalism*. London: New Left Books.
— (1976) The Capitalist State: A Reply to Miliband and Leclau. *New Left Review* **95**.
— (1977) The New Petty Bourgeoisie. In, Hunt, A. (ed.) *Class and Class Structure*. London: Lawrence and Wishart.
Prandy, K. (1965) *Professional Employees*. London: Faber.
Price, C. A. (1974) *The Great White Walls are Built: Restrictive Immigration to North America and Australia 1836–1888*. Canberra: Australian National University Press.
Rawls, J. (1971) *A Theory of Justice*. Cambridge, Mass.: Harvard University Press.
Richta, R. *et al.* (1967) *Civilization at the Crossroads*. Prague.
Roberts, B. C. (1972) Affluence and Disruption. In, Robson, W. A. (ed.) *Man and the Social Sciences*. London: Allen and Unwin.
Roberts, B. C., Loveridge, R. and Gennard, J. (1972) *Reluctant Militants*. London: Heinemann.
Rose, D., Saunders, P., Newby, H., and Bell, C. (1976) Ideologies of Property: A Case Study. *Sociological Review* **24** (4).
Rowley, C. K. (1978) The Economics and Politics of Extortion. In, *Trade Unions: Public Goods or Public 'Bads'?* London: The Institute of Economic Affairs.

Scheidemann, P. (1929) *Memoirs of a Social Democrat*. London: Hodder and Stoughton.

Simons, H. J. and R. E. (1969) *Class and Colour in South Africa 1850–1950*. Harmondsworth: Penguin Books.

Simpson, R. L. and I. H. (1969) Women and Bureaucracy in the Semi-Professions. In, Etzioni, A. (ed.) *The Semi-Professions and their Organization*. New York: Free Press.

Sivanandan, A. (1976) Race, Class and the State: The Black Experience in Britain. *Race and Class* **XVII** (4).

Sturmthal, A. (1944) *The Tragedy of European Labour*. London: Gollancz.

Sweezy, P. M. (1946) *The Theory of Capitalist Development*. London: Dobson.

Trotsky, L. (1935) *Terrorism and Communism*. London: Allen and Unwin.

— (1937) *The Revolution Betrayed*. London: Faber.

— (1962) *The Permanent Revolution*. London: New Park Publications.

— (1970) *The Third International After Lenin*. New York: Pathfinder Press.

— (1971) *Lessons of October*. London: New Park Publications.

— (1972) *Problems of the British Revolution*. London: New Park Publications.

— (1974) *Stalinism and Bolshevism*. London: New Park Publications.

— (1975) *The Struggle Against Fascism in Germany*. Harmondsworth: Penguin Books.

— (1976) *Diary in Exile*. Harvard University Press.

Weber, M. (1945) *From Max Weber*, Gerth, H. H. and Mills, C. W. (eds) London: Routledge.

— (1964) *The Theory of Social and Economic Organization*. Parsons, T. (ed.) Glencoe: Free Press.

— (1968) *Economy and Society*. Roth, G. and Wittich, C. (eds) New York: Bedminster Press.

Westergaard J. and Resler, H. (1975) *Class in a Capitalist Society*. London: Heinemann.

Wolpe, H. (1975) The Theory of Internal Colonialism: The South African Case. In, Oxaal, I. *et al. Beyond the Sociology of Development*. London: Routledge.

— (1976) The White Working Class in South Africa. *Economy and Society* **5** (2).

Wright, E. O. (1976) Class Boundaries in Advanced Capitalist Societies. *New Left Review* **93**.

Yarwood, A. T. (1964) *Asian Migration to Australia: The Background to Exclusion 1896–1923*. Melbourne University Press.

# Index

# Index

labour aristocracy, 92, 158
Labour government, and trade union legislation, 99–101
Labour party (*see* Social Democracy)
Lansbury, R., 108
'law of uneven development', 169
'left opposition', 182
legalism and social closure, 98–101
Lenin, V. I.
  on armed insurrection, 196
  on domino theory, 157–64
  on Kautsky's Marxism, 162–64
  on liberty, 176–77
  on proletarian dictatorship, 176ff.
  on social democracy, 158–62
  on socialist transformation, 147ff.
  on stages of development, 155–57, 174
  on the state, 119
  on trade unions, 182–84
  on vanguard party, 154
liberal theory of distinctive justice, 186
liberty and equality, 176–79
Llewellyn, C., 62
Lloyd-George, D., 160
Lock, G., 193
Lockwood, D., 32, 39, 116
legal opposition under socialism, 180–82
lower professions, 101–10
Lukacs, G.
  on 'socialism or barbarism', 168–169
  on bourgeois legality, 180
  on bourgeois revolution, 149–51
  on class consciousness, 151–55
  on proletarian revolution, 149ff.
  on vanguard party, 153–55
Luxemburg, R., 39, 150, 163, 165, 168, 173, 179, 192

Mackenzie, G., 92
Mandel, E., 132
manual/non-manual model of class, 11–15
Marceau, J., 61
Marcus, P. M., 105
Marx, K.
  Amsterdam address, 197, 198
  on bourgeois democracy, 180
  on bourgeois ideology, 86, 88
  on nationalism, 31

on organic theory of social change, 145–47
on professions, 21
on the state, 121–22
'maximal' definition of class, 19–21
mental and manual labour, 18–19
migrant workers, exclusion of, 90–2
Miliband, R., 119, 123, 125, 126, 132, 142, 178
Miller, S. M. 62
Mills, C. W., 69
'minimal' definition of class, 17–19
militarization of labour, 183–84
mode of production, concept of, 5–9
Moore, W. E., 4, 48
Moynihan, D. P., 33, 41

Nairn, T., 40
nationalism and Marxism, 31–3
Nazism, 37
  (*see also* fascism)
Nettl, P., 164
Neuwirth, G., 45
new middle class, 15–27
new petty bourgeoisie (*see* new middle class)
*nomenklatura*, 67
Northern Ireland
  Catholics, exclusion of, 94–5
  communal conflict in, 37–8
  Orange state, 139
  Protestant workers, 4, 99

Oppenheimer, M., 105
Orange state, 139
organic theory of social change, 145–47
organized labour (*see* trade unions)
Orwell, G., 63

Parry, N. and J., 116
Parsons, T., 38, 49, 50, 51, 70, 82, 178
Perrucci, R., 116
Peterloo, 184
picketing, 74, 111
Plamenatz, J., 49, 127
power and social closure, 45–6
Poulantzas, N.
  on fascism, 171–72
  on ideology and class, 25–7
  on mental and manual labour, 18–19
  on mode of production, 7

# Index